OCCASIONAL PAPER 241

The Design of IMF-Supported Programs

Atish Ghosh, Charis Christofides, Jun Kim, Laura Papi, Uma Ramakrishnan, Alun Thomas, and Juan Zalduendo

INTERNATIONAL MONETARY FUND
Washington DC
2005

Production: IMF Multimedia Services Division
Typesetting: Alicia Etchebarne-Bourdin

Cataloging-in-Publication Data

The design of IMF-supported programs/Atish Ghosh . . . [et al.]—Washington, D.C.: International Monetary Fund, 2005.

p. cm.—(Occasional paper, 0251-6363; no. 241)

Includes bibliographical references.
ISBN 1-58906-193-4

1. International Monetary Fund. 2. Economic policy. I. Ghosh, Atish R. II. Occasional paper (International Monetary Fund); no. 241.

HG3881.5.I58D37 2005

Price: US$25.00
(US$22.00 to full-time faculty members and
students at universities and colleges)

Please send orders to:
International Monetary Fund, Publication Services
700 19th Street, N.W., Washington, DC 20431, U.S.A.
Tel.: (202) 623-7430 Telefax: (202) 623-7201
E-mail: publications@imf.org
Internet: http://www.imf.org

recycled paper

Contents

The following symbols have been used throughout this paper:

. . . to indicate that data are not available;

— to indicate that the figure is zero or less than half the final digit shown, or that the item does not exist;

– between years or months (e.g., 2003–04 or January–June) to indicate the years or months covered, including the beginning and ending years or months;

/ between years (e.g., 2003/04) to indicate a fiscal (financial) year.

"n.a." means not applicable.

"Billion" means a thousand million.

Minor discrepancies between constituent figures and totals are due to rounding.

The term "country," as used in this paper, does not in all cases refer to a territorial entity that is a state as understood by international law and practice; the term also covers some territorial entities that are not states, but for which statistical data are maintained and provided internationally on a separate and independent basis.

Preface

The past 15 years have seen important developments in the challenges facing IMF member countries, and therefore in the objectives of the economic programs for which national authorities have sought the IMF's support. Yet the very responsiveness of the IMF to these evolving needs has inevitably complicated program design and the evaluation of program success. In this occasional paper, IMF staff take a detailed look at the experience with IMF-supported programs during 1995–2000.

The Design of IMF-Supported Programs was prepared by a staff team headed by Atish Ghosh and comprising Charis Christofides, Jun Kim, Laura Papi, Uma Ramakrishnan, Alun Thomas, and Juan Zalduendo, assisted by Barbara Dabrowska, Siba Das, Olivia Carolin, and Neri Gomes, under the overall supervision of G. Russell Kincaid and Mark Allen. Esha Ray of the External Relations Department edited and coordinated production of the publication.

An earlier draft of this occasional paper was discussed by the IMF's Executive Board. The opinions expressed in the paper are those of the authors, however, and do not necessarily reflect the views of national authorities, the IMF, or IMF Executive Directors.

Abbreviations

AREAER	*Annual Report on Exchange Arrangements and Exchange Restrictions*
CAC	Capital account crisis
CIS	Commonwealth of Independent States
EFF	Extended Fund Facility
EMBI	Emerging Market Bond Index
ERBS	Exchange-rate-based stabilization
ESAF	Enhanced Structural Adjustment Facility
EU	European Union
FDI	Foreign direct investment
G-7	Group of Seven countries
GDP	Gross domestic product
GIR	Gross international reserves
GRA	General Resources Account
HIPC	Heavily Indebted Poor Countries
ICOR	Incremental capital output ratio
IEO	Independent Evaluation Office
IFS	*International Financial Statistics*
MBS	Money-based stabilization
MONA	Monitoring of Fund Arrangements database
NDA	Net domestic assets
NIR	Net international reserves
NPV	Net present value
PPP	Purchasing power parity
PRSP	Poverty Reduction Strategy Paper
RMSE	Root mean squared error
SAF	Structural Adjustment Facility
SBA	Stand-By Arrangement
UIP	Uncovered interest rate parity
WEO	*World Economic Outlook*

Part I

Overview

Overview

According to its Articles of Agreement, one of the fundamental purposes of the IMF is to make its resources temporarily available to members to help correct balance of payments problems without resorting to measures "destructive of national or international prosperity." But that still leaves open many questions regarding the economic programs for which national authorities seek the IMF's financial support. What are the specific goals of such programs, and what challenges do they face? How are programs formulated? What do they consist of? And are they successful? This collection of papers on the design of IMF-supported programs—"Objectives and Outcomes," "Policy Formulation, Analytical Frameworks, and Program Design," and "Macroeconomic and Structural Policies: Review of Experience"—seeks to answer these questions.

This project, mandated by the IMF's Executive Board as part of the 2004/05 Conditionality Review and complemented by the review of the application of the conditionality guidelines,[1] examines the design of IMF-supported programs over the period 1995–2000. In order to seek insights from a comparison across different types of programs—and in contrast to earlier studies[2]—the present collection of papers covers IMF financial arrangements in both middle-income countries (supported by the General Resources Account (GRA) and consisting of Stand-By Arrangements (SBAs) and Extended Fund Facility (EFF) arrangements) and in low-income countries (supported by the Enhanced Structural Adjustment Facility (ESAF), which was replaced by the Poverty Reduction and Growth Facility (PRGF) in 1999).

Objectives and Outcomes

The starting point of the analysis—and indeed of the design of any IMF-supported program—is the program's objectives. The past fifteen years have seen important changes in this regard, reflecting the diversity of challenges facing IMF members, including helping countries transform from centrally planned to market economies, promoting growth and poverty reduction, and dealing with capital account crises where massive capital outflows have pervasive macroeconomic consequences. Yet the very responsiveness of the IMF to the evolving needs of its members has inevitably complicated program design, making it difficult to judge program success. Indeed, it is not uncommon to find IMF-supported programs criticized for failing to achieve objectives that were never, in fact, part of the program's goals.

The first paper—"Objectives and Outcomes" (Part II of this occasional paper)—therefore seeks to classify programs by their main purposes and to propose some metrics for judging their success. It finds that, while individual programs naturally vary in myriad details, most can be placed into one of three or four broad categories. IMF-supported programs in middle-income countries ("GRA-supported programs") conform—perhaps to a surprising degree—to the classic external adjustment paradigm. In these programs, the country is typically facing difficulties in financing its current account deficit (either because the economy has overheated and has lost competitiveness or because of an external shock). Program policies are intended to reduce the current account deficit to a sustainable level, while the IMF provides financing over a timeframe that enables the country to reconstitute its gross international reserves. Since the purpose of the program is to cool the economy and reduce the current account deficit, it is not surprising that the rate of output growth generally dips during the

[1]The Review of the 2002 Conditionality Guidelines was discussed by the Executive Board in March 2005. The public information notice and related papers have been placed on the IMF's external website (http://www.imf.org/external/np/sec/pn/2005/pn0552.htm).

[2]Susan Schadler and others, *IMF Conditionality: Experience Under Stand-By and Extended Arrangements*, IMF Occasional Paper No. 128 (Washington: International Monetary Fund, 1995); International Monetary Fund, *The ESAF at Ten Years*, IMF Occasional Paper No. 156 (Washington: International Monetary Fund, 1997); and Hugh Bredenkamp and Susan Schadler, eds., *Economic Adjustment and Reform in Low-Income Countries: Studies by the Staff of the International Monetary Fund* (Washington: International Monetary Fund, 1999).

program period, recovering to its previous level thereafter.

Although this classic adjustment paradigm applies to the bulk of middle-income country programs, there is an important subset where the magnitude of the capital outflows—as maturity and foreign exchange mismatches on domestic balance sheets unwind—forces an abrupt external adjustment and, typically, a collapse of the exchange rate and of economic activity. The time pattern of key macroeconomic variables in these capital account crises is similar—albeit more pronounced—to the classical case, with the notable difference that monetary and fiscal policies are geared more toward restoring confidence and mitigating the adverse impact on activity than to promoting external adjustment because adjustment is anyway forced on the country through the withdrawal of private financing.

The third group consists of transition economies and low-income countries—while these obviously differ in many respects, their IMF-supported programs share a common emphasis on macroeconomic stabilization and structural transformation to enhance economic efficiency and promote sustained growth—subject to maintaining external viability.

Finally, in a few cases the external accounts have largely been in balance and the IMF-supported program was intended primarily to enhance policy credibility, lowering interest rates and spreads and helping to put public debt dynamics on a more sustainable footing.

How, then, should program success be judged? Although the taxonomy suggests that the differing program types should be judged differently, all members should emerge from their IMF-supported programs with viable external positions. This is to ensure that the member is better able to cope with new shocks and to repay the IMF, safeguarding the revolving nature of its resources and allowing it to lend to others in need. One criterion for judging program success is therefore the record on external adjustment. But external adjustment involves an intertemporal trade-off: at one extreme, the country may have little recourse to financing, leading to a rapid reduction in its external indebtedness, but at the cost of a wrenching adjustment in the short run including of the exchange rate that is likely to take a significant toll on activity. More traditionally, the country attenuates its adjustment by receiving additional financing, including from the IMF, allowing time for some positive supply response. The challenge is of course to strike the proper balance between adjustment and financing.

Judging whether external adjustment was appropriate under the IMF-supported program therefore requires a metric against which the record can be judged. One such metric is simply a comparison between programmed and actual current account balances, on grounds that individual program design would have targeted the appropriate adjustment. This is subject to the obvious criticism, however, that program design may have anticipated a lack of sufficient (private plus public) financing, so that both the programmed and actual current account adjustment would be greater than what was considered optimal. A second metric, therefore, is medium-term debt sustainability: that is, a country should undertake sufficient—but no more—adjustment to ensure that its external debt position is stabilized at a moderate level. The IMF's financial role is to provide sufficient financing—both directly and through catalytic effects on markets and donors—to enable the member country to adjust at the appropriate pace, while its policy advice role is to help design a program that minimizes the economic and social disruption of the requisite adjustment (avoiding "measures destructive of national prosperity" in the parlance of the IMF's Articles of Agreement).

How has external adjustment fared by these criteria? The findings in "Objectives and Outcomes" suggest a sharp demarcation between the experience of middle-income (GRA-supported) countries and that of low-income (ESAF/PRGF-supported programs). GRA-supported programs have generally targeted current account adjustments in line with debt sustainability considerations. A positive relationship exists between the initial level of external debt and the external adjustment targeted and achieved. As such, external adjustment was largely consistent with that required by medium-term debt sustainability. But in some cases—especially, but not exclusively, in capital account crises—external adjustment was greater than would be indicated by debt sustainability considerations. This pace of external adjustment did not reflect tight macroeconomic policies—on the contrary, fiscal consolidation generally fell short of program targets—but rather a lack of financing and corresponded to lower investment. At the same time, there is evidence that IMF-supported programs helped achieve a *given* improvement in the current account at lower cost in terms of lost output growth, perhaps because of more efficient policy choices.

The adjustment story in low-income countries is almost diametrically opposite: IMF-supported programs generally did not target sufficient external adjustment to ensure debt sustainability, and the actual improvement in the current account balance was *less* than programmed. As such, programs in these countries did not aim at (a fortiori did not achieve) external viability through external adjustment, but instead implicitly relied on future debt relief. The Heavily Indebted Poor Countries

(HIPC) and enhanced HIPC initiatives were instituted during this period, but it is noteworthy that programmed and actual current account balances would also have been insufficient to stabilize debt ratios at the lower debt levels achieved following this debt relief.

External viability, of course, is just one program objective—albeit an important one; as discussed above, depending upon country circumstances, programs may also seek to stabilize the economy, raise output growth, and reduce poverty. In contrast to experience in the 1980s, middle-income countries with IMF-supported programs saw durable reductions in inflation over the program period. Consistent with the classic adjustment paradigm, these programs saw a dip in real GDP growth during the program followed by a recovery of growth rates to their preprogram performance but not faster growth. Again, the experience of low-income countries is rather different. Consistent with the purposes of the ESAF and PRGF—and in contrast to experience in the 1980s—programs in these countries saw sustained improvements in growth performance during and following the program, driven by a combination of better macroeconomic policies (lower inflation and smaller after-grants fiscal deficits) and a more benign external environment (faster growth in industrial countries, smaller terms of trade shocks).

Overall, the findings of "Objectives and Outcomes" leave two important sets of questions. For programs dealing with capital account crises, the key question is how to better attenuate the improvement in the current account balance, avoiding disruptive adjustment, and bringing it better into line with debt sustainability considerations. Would this require greater IMF financing? Use of capital controls? A stronger policy response? Or is it an unavoidable consequence of a crisis, with prevention the only cure? For programs in low-income countries, the key challenge will be to sustain the improved growth performance—through lower inflation and smaller after-grants fiscal deficits—while moving toward external viability without depending on future debt-relief, avoiding a new cycle of lend and forgive. Will this require a larger proportion of financing in the form of grants rather than loans? Or a fundamental rethinking of program design in these countries?

Policy Formulation, Analytical Frameworks, and Program Design

If programs are to achieve their objectives, their design requires an analytic basis for linking program policies to program goals. In fact, one can think of a program as being defined by a set of intended policies—for instance, monetary and fiscal policy—that simultaneously determine, and are determined by, key macroeconomic targets, including growth, inflation, and the current account; together, these constitute the macroeconomic framework. But how are these projections for policies and targets undertaken? Using what analytical models? And how well does this process work in practice? "Policy Formulation, Analytical Frameworks, and Program Design" (Part III of this occasional paper) takes up these issues, examining the process of program design, the analytical tools employed, and the performance of the program design process.

Studying how programs are put together in practice suggests that there is no single "IMF model" employed by country teams in advising national authorities on program design. Rather, a wide variety of analytical methods—small econometric models, single equation estimates, cross-country parameters, and economic judgment—are used to model the program's short-run macroeconomic framework. *Financial programming* is typically *not* used in the manner described in textbooks to pin down the permissible fiscal deficit given a foreign exchange reserves target and assumptions about the behavior of money demand. Rather, financial programming is used to check and ensure consistency across the various elements of the macroeconomic framework, each of which may have been modeled using a variety of techniques. This eclectic approach allows for program design to be tailored to country circumstances, including the availability of data and the stability of key time series. It also allows for policies to be adapted rapidly—typically at quarterly or semiannual reviews—in light of initial outcomes relative to program targets. Such adaptability is particularly important in capital account crises, where balance sheet exposures and capital outflows can alter the magnitude, and possibly even the sign, of traditional policy multipliers—such as the effect on the exchange rate of tightening monetary policy. In this regard, a recently developed tool—the *balance sheet approach*—can offer important insights into the implications of maturity and currency exposures on domestic balance sheets, though the data and analytical challenges in its use remain formidable.

Beyond the short-run macroeconomic framework, program design requires longer-term projections, especially for output growth. Here, again, country teams use a variety of methods—univariate approaches, production functions, aggregate demand decompositions, cross-country growth models—though formal modeling is relatively uncommon. These growth projections feed into debt sustainability assessments, which are usually undertaken in the format of the IMF's *debt sustainability templates* that help discipline projections, lay bare the underlying assumptions, and apply systematic stress testing to the baseline scenario for debt dynamics.

How well does this approach work? Since program documents do not lay out an explicit model, the only way to test performance is by a comparison of program projections to outcomes. For the short-run macroeconomic framework (a one-year horizon), the record is perhaps surprisingly good: with the exception of capital account crises (where capital outflows triggered a sudden collapse of output and the exchange rate), neither inflation nor growth projections exhibit systematic biases. The current account deficit is overestimated in GRA-supported programs and underestimated in ESAF/PRGF-supported programs. At longer horizons, however, projections do not fare as well: beyond the first year of the program (and for three-year averages), growth projections have optimistic biases, especially in low-income countries.

Medium-term debt projections also tend to be too rosy, although the reasons are complex. For low-income countries, in the absence of debt relief, the external debt-to-GDP ratio would be significantly higher than programmed because real GDP growth is lower than projected, real exchange rates tend to be weaker, and, as noted above, external adjustment is smaller than expected. In capital account crises, output growth, the real exchange rate, and the banking systems usually collapse, leading to sharply higher external debt ratios, but this is partly offset by the much greater external adjustment than programmed. For other middle-income countries, external debt projections are relatively accurate.

Projection errors of course confound modeling mistakes—of interest here—with policy slippages and exogenous shocks. Although individual program documents do not lay out the model underlying the design of the program, by looking *across* programs, it is possible to infer the relationships between policies and targets—for instance, between money growth and inflation or between fiscal expenditure and output growth—implicitly assumed by country teams. The relationships implicit in programs generally do not differ systematically from the actual relationships—with the exception of the effect of fiscal consolidation, where programs underestimate the positive impact on output growth and the improvement in the current account balance.

Overall, the findings suggest that the program design process works relatively well, particularly given the difficulties of modeling economies that are likely to be going through a period of disruption or structural transformation. At the same time, there are important challenges: predicting and understanding the implications of large capital flows in capital account crises, better modeling of medium-term growth, and improving debt sustainability assessments, especially the impact of exchange rates and financial crises.

Macroeconomic and Structural Policies: Review of Experience

Given program goals, and an analytical link between program objectives and policies, the third element of course is the policy content of the program—the exchange rate regime, monetary and exchange rate policies, fiscal policy, and structural reforms. To make this potentially enormous topic tractable, the discussion in "Macroeconomic and Structural Policies: Review of Experience" (Part IV of this occasional paper) centers around three questions: Was use of the policy geared toward achieving program objectives? Were the intended policies carried out? And what was the outcome?

Given that external adjustment is usually a cornerstone of IMF-supported programs, it is perhaps surprising that the exchange rate regime is no more likely to be altered at the outset of a program than at other times, and that up-front devaluations as part of an IMF-supported program are extremely rare. Nevertheless, middle-income countries embarking on disinflation efforts tend to adopt an exchange rate peg, especially the transition economies seeking to reestablish price stability following initial liberalizations. By contrast, low-income countries generally attempted disinflations under floating regimes. Was one strategy more successful than the other? No. Success rates at disinflation were almost identical under pegged and floating regimes. What appears to have differentiated successes from failures is whether the programmed fiscal consolidation was achieved. External adjustment was easier under floating exchange rate regimes, in the sense that a given improvement in the current account balance was associated with a smaller reduction in output growth, though the effect is not quantitatively large. Finally, countries with pegged exchange rate regimes were hypothesized to be more prone to excessive foreign currency borrowing and therefore suffered sharper external adjustment when pegs collapsed and capital outflows forced larger current account surpluses. While this may have happened in some capital account crises, the association between exchange rate pegs and sharper subsequent adjustment does not hold in the sample more generally.

Turning to monetary policies, across programs broad money growth rates are targeted to decline, as are inflation rates—though generally less so in low-income countries than in middle-income countries. The targeted monetary tightening is closely related to the programmed reduction in inflation and improvement in the current account balance, and negatively related to the output gap or to floating regimes. It is notable that disinflations undertaken in the context of IMF-supported programs are associated with faster growth in money demand—perhaps reflecting greater credibility of the authorities' policies—than disinflations undertaken in the absence of a program, leading to lower inflation for a given broad money growth. Programs do succeed in lowering inflation, though not always by as much as was targeted, in part because of broad money overruns. Importantly, the source of the monetary overruns—whether reflecting balance of payments inflows or domestic credit creation—does not seem to matter for their inflationary impact, raising concerns about the need to sterilize large donor inflows or capital inflows if inflation targets are to be achieved. While the monetary stance is typically tightened in programs, there is no evidence that this tightening resulted in slower output growth.

Depending upon initial levels of government expenditure, the fiscal deficit, and the programmed improvement in the current account balance, programs on average envisage a fiscal tightening of around 1 to 2 percentage points of GDP over a two-year period; controlling for these initial conditions, programs in low-income countries target about 1 percent of GDP less fiscal adjustment than middle-income country programs. While the fiscal tightening in the initial program year is generally achieved, important slippages occurred by the following year, particularly when growth turned out to be weaker than expected or the envisaged adjustment was particularly large or based primarily on revenue effort. In turn, fiscal slippages contribute to failures at disinflation and to worse public debt dynamics—though the largest source of errors in projections of public debt dynamics comes from valuation changes on foreign-currency-denominated debt and from the fiscal costs of banking crises.

An often controversial aspect of IMF-supported programs is the possibly contractionary impact of fiscal tightening on economic activity and output growth. Yet the empirical evidence does not suggest that fiscal consolidation in programs resulted in slower output growth; on the contrary, smaller budget deficits were associated with faster output growth—even controlling for the obvious endogeneity of the fiscal balance to growth—most likely because of confidence effects and crowding-in through lower interest rates and greater availability of banking system credit for the private sector.

Finally, IMF-supported programs incorporate structural measures to underpin macroeconomic adjustment, enhance economic efficiency, and reduce vulnerability to future crises. Returning to the taxonomy above, the evidence suggests some alignment between these types of structural measures and program goals. Thus programs in transition and low-income countries have a relatively larger proportion of economic efficiency enhancing reforms while programs in capital account crises have a relatively larger share of measures directed at reducing vulnerabilities, especially in the financial sector. Assessing the impact of individual measures on program goals is difficult, not least because structural measures are difficult to quantify. Nonetheless, there is a statistically significant association between fiscal adjustment being achieved and the number of structural fiscal measures in the program, and between higher output growth and the number of efficiency enhancing reforms.

Overall, the results suggest broad alignment between program goals and various macroeconomic policies and structural reforms. By the same token, this also means that policy slippages are reflected in program targets being missed.

* * *

While the papers in this volume cover a great deal of material, they are not, of course, intended to be the last word on program design. Indeed, there is a substantial agenda of analytical follow-up work already under way examining more closely the design of IMF-supported programs in low-income countries, including on how sound macroeconomic policies and sustained growth may be fostered while also tackling the sustainability of external debt dynamics. For programs in middle-income countries, analysis is focusing on how the catalytic response of financial markets may be enhanced—especially to help *prevent* crises by a sufficiently vigorous policy response coupled with IMF financing at times of heightened vulnerability.

Nevertheless, it is worth asking how program design might change as a result of the present study. Three aspects come to mind. First, program design is likely to be much more clearly defined by considerations of medium-term debt dynamics than it was in the past, when programs typically focused on reestablishing viability of the *flow* balance of payments—often at the cost of paying insufficient attention to worsening debt dynamics. Second, in part to improve assessments of public and external debt sustainability, programs will be underpinned by better analytical work to model medium-term output growth and, in emerging market countries, to better understand the nexus of the financial, public, and external sectors in driving capital flows and crisis dynamics. Third, the findings in these papers may influence the choice and use of specific policy instruments, including greater scrutiny of the consistency of the exchange rate regime with program objectives and other macroeconomic policies, the need to sterilize large donor or capital inflows in the monetary program, greater emphasis on sustaining fiscal adjustment efforts and the need to design the fiscal program accordingly, and sharper alignment of structural measures with program objectives.

These would not be revolutionary changes—indeed, the findings in these papers suggest that fundamental rethinking about program design is neither needed nor would be appropriate—rather, they represent shifts in emphasis. Still, if undertaken, they would contribute to better designed, better implemented, and ultimately more successful IMF-supported programs.

Part II

Objectives and Outcomes

Contents of Part II

Figures

Tables

Appendix Figures

Appendix Table

I Introduction

This paper reviews experience with programs supported by the General Resources Account (GRA)—Stand-By Arrangements (SBAs) and Extended Fund Facility (EFF) arrangements—as well as those supported by concessional facilities—the Enhanced Structural Adjustment Facility (ESAF) and the Poverty Reduction and Growth Facility (PRGF)—over the period 1995–2003.[1] It differs from earlier studies in three important respects.[2] First, it takes explicit account of the evolution of the design and purpose of IMF-supported programs over the past decade. Second, it seeks new insights by comparing programs supported by GRA resources and those supported by concessional facilities; as elaborated below, there are important differences, particularly as regards external adjustment and output growth. Third, it goes beyond traditional flow balance of payments measures of external adjustment to consider the impact of the adjustment effort on external debt dynamics.

Like previous studies, this paper has to grapple with unknowable counterfactuals—that is, how would the economy have performed (in terms of external adjustment and other macroeconomic objectives) in the absence of IMF support. As discussed below, it is difficult to solve the identification problem convincingly, particularly for low-income countries that may undertake successive IMF-supported programs. Accordingly, the approach taken in this paper is to examine performance under recent IMF-supported programs—and to try to understand the reasons behind it—rather than attempting the finer distinction of whether IMF support was responsible for the outcomes.

[1]To include both program and postprogram experience, the sample covers programs approved over the period 1995–2000; see Appendix I. During this period, the IMF's engagement with low-income countries underwent important changes with the shift from the ESAF to the PRGF. The findings for low-income countries in this paper pertain primarily to ESAF-supported programs.

[2]See Schadler and others (1995), which covered a sample of Stand-By and Extended Arrangements approved between 1988 and 1991.

This paper begins (Section II) by characterizing the nature and objectives of different types of IMF-supported programs. Individual differences aside, the paper finds that there are three main groups of programs. First, there is the traditional current account adjustment problem that gives rise to the "classical" IMF-supported program.[3] Second, and more recently, are the so-called capital account crisis programs, where the abruptness and magnitude of the reversal of capital flows have pervasive consequences for current account dynamics and for macroeconomic performance more generally. The third set comprises the early programs in transition economies and programs in low-income countries—the latter supported by PRGF arrangements since 2000 (and by ESAF arrangements before then). The transition and low-income countries obviously differ in many respects. Nevertheless, they share a common logic in that the structural transformation of the economy and the promotion of growth and of poverty reduction are key objectives, with the need to maintain external viability acting as an overarching constraint. Indeed, some measures adopted—for instance, liberalizing import restrictions—may themselves widen the current account deficit but also contribute to removing economic distortions and placing the economy on a more sustainable path for growth and the balance of payments.

The paper reveals a number of novel results, especially in relation to the differences in economic adjustment between GRA- and PRGF-supported programs. In particular, Section III casts the discussion of external adjustment in terms of medium-term debt sustainability rather than just the flow balance of payments. A useful metric in this regard is the external debt-stabilizing current account balance. In GRA-supported programs, consistent with considerations of debt sustainability, there is a positive relationship be-

[3]As discussed below, among GRA-supported programs there is a subset where the primary focus is on the endorsement of a policy package, since IMF financing is not envisaged. In some of these cases, the thrust of the program is to reduce domestic interest rates and retain access to external markets rather than external adjustment.

tween the external adjustment targeted (and achieved) and the initial level of external debt. At the same time, these programs are characterized by current account improvements that, on average, are sharper than anticipated for the program's first year; in about one-fourth of the cases, the current account balance exceeds the debt-stabilizing balance despite a relatively low initial level of external debt. Moreover, the sharp adjustment in the first year of the program is subsequently reversed, so that the cumulative difference between the actual and programmed current account position largely disappears over a three-year period. In addition to rapid adjustment in the current account balance, these economies experienced a V-shaped growth pattern. These patterns are particularly pronounced in capital account crises, where the external adjustment and output contraction were typically much more than envisaged under the program because of the larger capital outflows than expected.

IMF resources typically finance the replenishment and accumulation of gross reserves, which, on average, increase by more than the financing provided by the IMF. By adding to reserves and helping to restore confidence, such financing nevertheless contributes to limiting vulnerabilities. IMF financing is small in relation to the member's total financing requirement—typically about 10 percent—which is expected to be financed by flows from the private and official sectors. As noted above, however, in some cases, this projected financing does not materialize and a sharper programmed adjustment of the current account balance results. Nevertheless, perhaps because the IMF will only support the authorities' economic program if it considers the policies to be appropriate, countries undertaking external adjustment in the context of an IMF-supported program grow about 1 percentage point a year faster than countries making the same current account adjustment without an IMF-supported program; these results are subject to a number of econometric qualifications, including possible selection bias.

The typical low-income program displays a strikingly different pattern to the GRA-supported program, with relatively little current account adjustment but an increase in growth during the program, partly attributable to improved macroeconomic stability. In contrast to GRA-supported programs, in the low-income countries, current account deficits were, on average, larger than projected—a divergence that increases with the time horizon. The positive relationship between external adjustment and initial external debt ratios characteristic of the GRA sample is not apparent for the low-income countries and the actual and programmed current account deficits exceed those consistent with stabilizing the initial external debt ratios. The implied increases in external debt ratios, however, were largely offset by additional debt relief, moderating the debt buildup.

Beyond external viability, IMF-supported programs typically target a number of other macroeconomic objectives such as reducing inflation and raising growth, which are considered in Section IV. While the counterfactual is difficult to establish, the evidence suggests that, under their IMF-supported programs, member countries have been largely successful in lowering inflation and maintaining price stability thereafter. GRA-supported programs have generally succeeded in restoring real GDP growth to precrisis levels but, consistent with the classic adjustment paradigm, are not associated with higher long-run growth rates. By contrast, a majority of members with PRGF-supported programs in the 1990s have seen a marked improvement in their real GDP growth performance.

II Initial Conditions and the Setting of IMF-Supported Programs

Introduction

In the archetypical IMF-supported program, a member faces external financing difficulties and external and internal imbalances, requiring stabilization measures. Under a fixed exchange rate regime, balance of payments difficulties reflect either an overheating of the economy that could also be associated with a loss of competitiveness, or an external shock—such as a deterioration in terms of trade or reduced net capital inflows. Correspondingly, under a floating regime, the external financing difficulties are manifested in a persistent depreciation of the real exchange rate. Either way, the problems stemming from current account imbalances can be exacerbated by net capital outflows.

Facing external imbalances, the member must either adjust, obtain financing from official sources, or restructure its external obligations. In the textbook case of a purely temporary disequilibrium, financing would be appropriate, while a permanent shock requires adjustment. More generally, some external adjustment and financing is required. The key objective in traditional IMF-supported programs, therefore, is to reduce the current account deficit to a sustainable level and to reconstitute reserves over a timeframe that complements the financing that the IMF is providing. Over the longer run, as confidence returns, capital inflows resume and the country is again able to finance its now sustainable current account deficit and replenish its international reserves.

Thus economic policies are intended to bring about the required external adjustment, while IMF financial support is intended to ease this adjustment by spreading it out over time, and to help reconstitute international reserves. In principle, the requisite external adjustment can be achieved either by raising aggregate supply or by reducing domestic demand. In practice, given lags in the supply response, the brunt of the adjustment falls on demand management with IMF financing provided to ease the adjustment burden while the country implements expenditure-switching and expenditure-reducing policies. Since a given adjustment can be achieved through different combinations of macroeconomic policies, making good policy choices naturally involves picking those alternatives that raise the likelihood of restoring external viability in the least costly way—avoiding "measures destructive of national or international prosperity" in the parlance of the Articles of Agreement—taking account of economic relationships and social and political realities.

The last comprehensive review of IMF-supported programs found that most programs were characterized by a classic external adjustment paradigm in which a member requests support from the IMF to deal with a continuing loss of reserves associated with current account imbalances, often in the context of poor macroeconomic performance such as high inflation or low growth (Schadler and others, 1995). The 1995 study documented an improvement in the country's external position—its current account balance (new users) and its net international reserves, but the effects on inflation and growth were much less favorable.[4] In cases where the balance of payments problem was precipitated by overheating of the economy, the country may have had rapid growth (and high inflation) prior to the emergence of economic problems, but the subsequent slowdown of capital inflows and financing, together with tightened macroeconomic policies resulted in a temporary slowing in economic activity. In other cases, the country's growth performance in the runup to the authorities' adjustment program may have been weak, but their program was associated only with growth returning to its historical average rather than with a marked increase in the long-term growth rate. In either case, despite generally tighter monetary policy (relative to the preprogram period), a discrete devaluation gave an additional fillip to inflation. The results of a study on ESAF-supported programs approved between 1986 and 1995 are similar, except for slightly greater emphasis on growth outcomes—see Box 2.1 for a summary of the conclusions of these reports.

[4]As discussed below, this is less true of more recent programs.

Box 2.1. Conclusions from Previous Reviews of IMF-Supported Programs

Over the last decade, two studies have been undertaken to examine experiences in IMF-supported programs: a study of all stand-by and extended arrangements approved during the period 1988–91 (Schadler and others, 1995) and a review of the ESAF over the period 1986–96 (Bredenkamp and Schadler, 1999).

The study of experiences under Stand-By and Extended Arrangements notes an improvement in the external position of countries requesting IMF support but more mixed results in terms of other macroeconomic objectives (Table A). Specifically, the current account deficit fell during the program for all countries except for those with several previous arrangements. Moreover, about a third of the program countries benefited from large increases in capital flows and reserves rose from slightly over two months of imports in the year prior to a program to over three and a half months by the end of the program for all categories. In contrast, the record on inflation and growth was more mixed. Countries entering their arrangements with annual inflation rates above 10 percent saw significant reductions while other saw little change (or even small increases) in inflation rates. With regard to growth, countries with one previous arrangement bounced back rapidly during the program period, whereas for new users and for countries with several previous arrangements, the growth profile was comparable prior to and by the end of the program period, with a temporary dip at the beginning of the program.

The study of ESAF arrangements showed that the gap in per capita output growth between ESAF countries and other developing countries was eliminated by the mid-1990s, and that half of this improvement was associated with improved macroeconomic and structural policies (Table B). However, the study also documents a mixed record in attaining low inflation, even though the negative association between growth and inflation is robust.

A. Synopsis of Quantitative Findings for Stand-By and EFF Arrangements

	t–3	*t*–2	*t*–1	*t*[1]	*t*+1	*t*+2
Current account deficit (in percent of exports)						
New users			>50%	30–35%	30–35%	30–35%
Repeat users			35–40%	40–45%	40–45%	40–45%
Reserve cover (in months of imports)						
New users			2.0–2.5	2.5–3.0	3.0–3.5	3.5–4.0
Repeat users			2.0–2.5	2.0–2.5	2.5–3.0	4.0–4.5
Growth (in percent)						
New users	3.0	2.0	0.0	–2.0	3.0	4.0
More than one previous arrangement	2.0	3.0	2.0	2.5	3.0	2.5
One previous arrangement	–3.5	–2.0	4.5	4.0	4.5	
Inflation (annual; in percent)						
Countries with initial inflation between 10% and 50%			23	30[2]		17
Countries with initial inflation <10%			5	7[2]		7

[1]*t* refers to the first program year.
[2]Target of IMF-supported program.

B. Synopsis of Quantitative Findings for ESAF Arrangements

	1981–85	1985–90	1991–95	1995
Per capita growth				
ESAF excluding transition economies	–1.4	0.4	0.3	1.5
Non-ESAF developing countries	0.3	1.0	1.0	1.4

	t–3	*t*–2	*t*–1	*t*	*t*+1	*t*+2
Inflation						
Low initial inflation	11.0	9.0	6.2	10.2	8.0	7.2
Intermediate initial inflation	15.8	16.2	20.2	16.3	15.1	11.7
High initial inflation	80.0	126.0	170.0	75.0	26.0	25.0

Traditional IMF-Supported Adjustment Programs

The behavior of key macroeconomic variables in programs supported by the GRA—Stand-By Arrangements (SBAs) and Extended Fund Facility (EFF) arrangements excluding those with transition economies—show striking similarities to the predictions of the traditional model.[5] Figure 2.1 plots the key economic indicators.[6] In particular, growth is V-shaped, falling during the program period, but recovering by the third year after the program.[7] Inflation, which is usually on a downward trajectory prior to the program, increases slightly in the program year. The key characteristic, however, is the country's external financing difficulties, which are manifested in the switch from an inflow of capital averaging 2 percent of GDP over the three years preceding the program to a net outflow of over 1 percent of GDP in the program year (before recovering to an inflow of about 1 percent of GDP two years later). The current account deficit narrows from 3 percent of GDP on average over the three years preceding the program to about zero in the program year. Adjustment of the fiscal balance, which improves by about 1 percent of GDP over the same period, explains less than half of the external adjustment, the remainder coming from the private sector.[8] The current account improvement reflects both a decline in investment and a rise in domestic saving during the program period, but over a three-year horizon is driven entirely by a decline in investment with saving returning to its historical average.[9] Foreign exchange reserves improve steadily once program implementation begins and this improvement is maintained.

Of the 25 arrangements shown in Figure 2.1, 9 arrangements were treated as precautionary (36 percent). With the exception of real GDP growth—which rises during the program period—the behavior of other economic variables among members that had precautionary arrangements is similar to those for arrangements where the member made a purchase.[10] In particular, both are characterized by sharp improvements in the fiscal and current account balances during the program and a corresponding buildup in reserves (Figure 2.2). Over the longer term, the main difference between the two types of arrangements is that the savings ratio rises among precautionary programs but remains flat in all other GRA-supported programs. These similarities between precautionary and nonprecautionary arrangements indicate that a common standard has been applied, but also suggests that IMF financing had little direct impact on current account adjustment where the member drew on IMF's resources.

Among the GRA sample, there are also programs whose primary focus is enhancing the credibility of macroeconomic policies rather than undertaking external adjustment—a group that is not as clearly defined as, but partly overlaps, the sample of precautionary arrangements considered in Figure 2.2. Members may request such an arrangement because they have achieved macroeconomic stability but still have a large structural reform agenda (for instance, some of the later programs in Estonia or Latvia); to reassure markets during election cycles or periods of political uncertainty (Peru, in 1999); or because they are trying to tackle a problem of high inflation or public debt sustainability (though they do not face acute balance of payments difficulties). Turkey's 1999 Stand-By Arrangement is an example of the latter case: with the current account barely in deficit and readily financeable through private capital flows, the primary role of the IMF-supported program was to enhance the credibility of monetary and fiscal policies, which was essential to reduce inflation expectations and nominal and real interest rates. In Brazil's 2002 Stand-By Arrangement, the credibility of the authorities' commitment to generating the requisite primary surpluses was key to reducing spreads and to improving public debt dynamics.

Other Types of Programs

Capital Account Crises

The behavior of the main economic variables in capital account crisis programs mimics that in the

[5]As discussed below, the pattern for capital account crises is also similar in some respects, though it differs markedly for the behavior of fiscal policy.

[6]For Figures 2.1 through 2.5, only the most recent program is taken in cases of multiple arrangements. To minimize the effect of outliers, all variables are mapped to lie in the interval (–100,100) percent by the transformation $100(z/100+z)$ if $z>0$ and $100(z/100-z)$ if $z<0$, where z is the annual growth rate or percentage of GDP, as applicable.

[7]The average duration of Stand-By Arrangements, which constitute 75 percent of the sample of Stand-By and EFF programs, is 15 months.

[8]The Independent Evaluation Office (IEO) study of "Fiscal Adjustment in IMF-Supported Programs" (IEO, 2003b) finds that most of the fiscal adjustment takes place in the first year of the program.

[9]Movements in the real exchange rate are too small to have contributed significantly to the external adjustment; while depreciating by about 5 percent in the program period, it reappreciated by about 5 percent over the subsequent two years.

[10]A precautionary arrangement is one under which the authorities indicate that they do not intend to make a purchase. It is not legally different from a nonprecautionary arrangement, since the member retains the right to draw (provided that it has met the relevant conditionality).

Figure 2.1. Macroeconomic Performance Under GRA-Supported Programs (Excluding Transition Economies), 1995–2000[1]

Sources: IMF, WEO database; and IMF staff estimates.
[1]Standard error bands for real GDP growth, inflation, and government balances are given by the dotted lines.

Figure 2.2. Macroeconomic Performance Under GRA-Supported Programs with Precautionary Arrangements, 1995–2000[1]

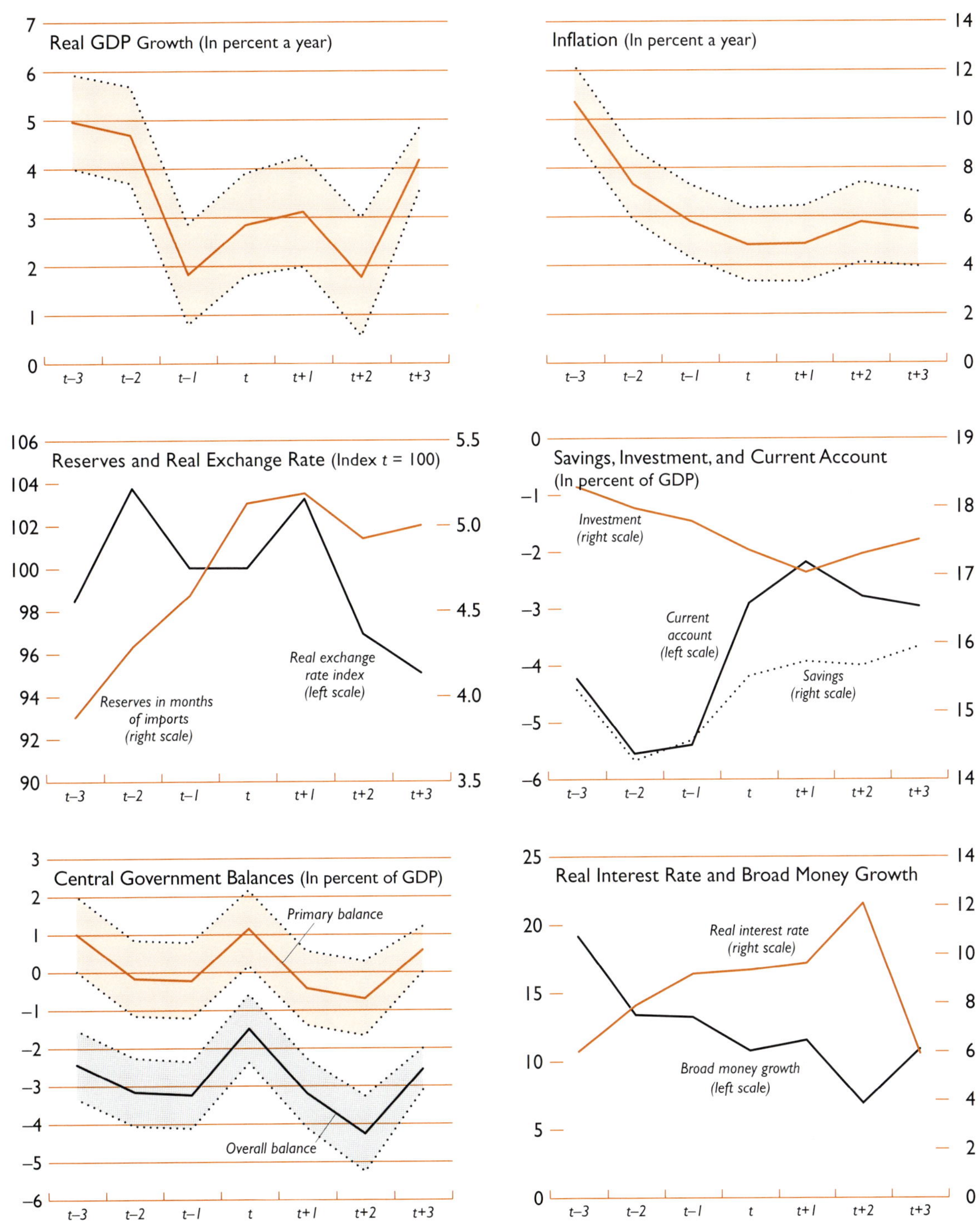

Sources: IMF, WEO database; and IMF staff estimates.

[1]Standard error bands for real GDP growth, inflation, and government balances are given by the dotted lines.

Figure 2.3. Macroeconomic Performance Under Capital Account Crisis Programs, 1995–2000[1]

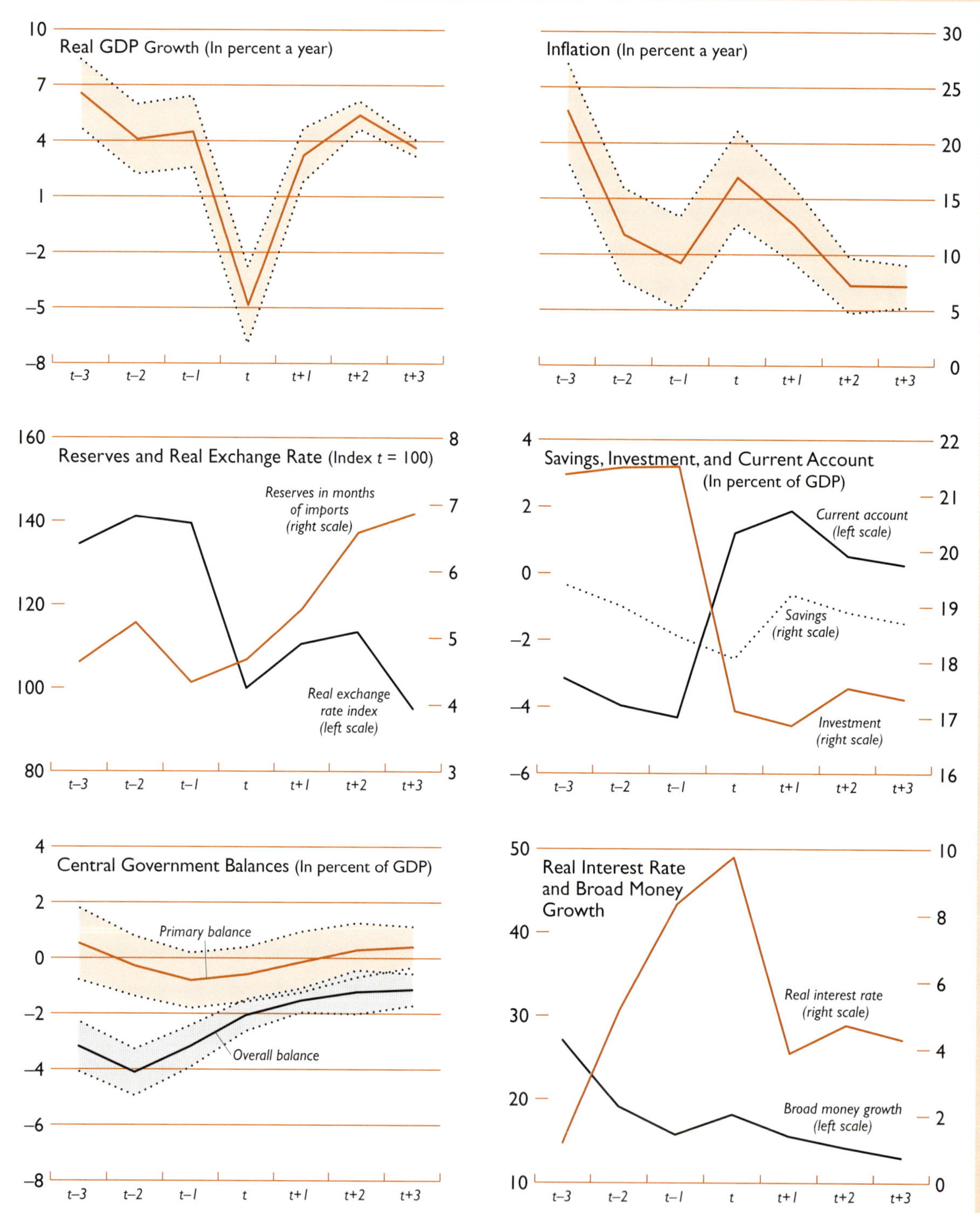

Sources: IMF, WEO database; and IMF staff estimates.

[1]Standard error bands for real GDP growth, inflation, and government balances are given by the dotted lines.

Box 2.2. Fiscal Adjustment in Capital Account Crises

Among the more controversial elements of program design in capital account crises is the stance of fiscal policy. In traditional adjustment programs, fiscal policy is typically tightened in order to reduce aggregate expenditure in relation to aggregate income and bring about the necessary external adjustment, especially when the public sector is seen as a major source of the external deficit.

Although the precrisis public sector deficits in the Asian crisis countries were not viewed as excessively large (with the possible exception of Thailand), the original program design in each of these countries called for at least some fiscal tightening. In particular, given capital outflows, there was a necessary improvement in the current account balance. Since the current account balance, in turn, equals the excess of public and private saving over investment, the greater the public sector's share of the adjustment, the smaller the private share will need be.

While this is arithmetically correct, whether it translates into a smaller *burden* of adjustment on the private sector—in the sense of a smaller decline in private consumption or investment—depends upon the nature of the shock. If the country has suffered a shock to aggregate supply, then output is exogenous with respect to government spending, and an improvement in public saving will imply a smaller required adjustment of private consumption. Conversely, if the country has suffered a shock to aggregate demand, then the higher public saving, while still implying a smaller required increase in private saving, will be associated with weaker activity and lower income and private consumption—that is, the smaller required increase in private saving will take place not through a smaller decline in private consumption, but through a decline in income and a decline in consumption (see Ghosh and others (2002) and IEO (2003b) for a fuller discussion).

In the event, the programmed fiscal tightening in the Asian crisis countries was quickly reversed as it became apparent that the private sector was (over) adjusting and activity was collapsing. Fiscal policy in capital account crises has continued to be controversial, however. In particular, in the run-up to Argentina's 2002 crisis, there were numerous slippages of the primary and overall deficit relative to program targets that were countenanced by subsequent waivers. Thus, the IMF-supported programs initially targeted too much fiscal adjustment in the Asian capital account crises but targeted (or at least achieved) too little adjustment in the case of Argentina.

Programmed and Actual Fiscal Balances in Selected Capital Account Crisis Programs
(In percent of GDP)

	Coverage	Previous Year	Original Program	First Review	Second Review	Third Review	Fourth Review	Outcome
Indonesia (FY1998/99)	Central	0.8	1.0	–3.2	–8.5	–8.5	–8.5	–2.1
Korea (1998)	Central	–0.5	1.0	–0.7	–0.9	–3.3	–4.2	–3.9
Thailand (FY1997/98)	Central	–1.1	1.1	1.0	–1.6	–2.4	–2.7	–2.6
Argentina (2001)	Central	–2.5	–1.4	–2.0	–3.1	–3.2	–3.3	–6.3

traditional case, though the patterns are more pronounced. Indeed, in these capital account crisis programs the abruptness and magnitude of the reversal of capital inflows had pervasive consequences for economic performance and policy formulation and implementation (Figure 2.3).[11] A sharper dip in growth and spike in inflation is observed when the crisis erupts (which typically precedes the arrangement's approval date).[12] Underlying these outcomes is the reversal from capital inflows to outflows. In the three years preceding the program, private capital inflows to these countries average over 5 percent of GDP, turning to a net outflow of more than 1 percent of GDP when the crisis erupts, before recovering to an inflow of 2 percent of GDP two years later.

[11]There is no definitive sample of "capital account crises"; Ghosh and others (2002) list Mexico (1995), Argentina (1995), Thailand (1997), Korea (1997), Indonesia (1997), and Brazil (1998). To this list may be added the 2000 augmentation of the 1999 Stand-By Arrangement for Turkey, and also the Stand-By Arrangements for Argentina (2000) and Brazil (2001 and 2002). In Figure 2.3, to illustrate the crisis dynamics more clearly, year "*t*" is aligned as follows: Argentina (1995), Brazil (1999), Indonesia (1998), Mexico (1995), Korea (1998), Thailand (1998), and Turkey (2001).

[12]In a few cases, for example, Turkey, the member had an IMF arrangement in place when the crisis broke.

Figure 2.4. Macroeconomic Performance Under Stand-By and Extended Fund Facility Programs in Transition Economies, 1995–2000[1]

Sources: IMF, WEO database; and IMF staff estimates.
[1]Standard error bands for real GDP growth, inflation, and government balances are given by the dotted lines.

These movements force large swings in the current account balance which, on average, switches from a deficit of 4 percent of GDP to a surplus of 2 percent (and considerably more in some cases).

The key difference between capital account crises and more traditional adjustment programs lies in the orientation of policies. In traditional adjustment programs, monetary and fiscal policies are intended to bring about external adjustment; in a capital account crisis the emphasis often shifts to mitigating the external adjustment that the member is forced to undertake in response to capital outflows. Whereas the fiscal balance improves by about 1 percent of GDP in traditional programs (Figure 2.1), in the capital account crisis programs the fiscal deficit widens by about 3 percent of GDP (Figure 2.3), though often this was not the orientation of policies in the original program (Box 2.2). Monetary policy is tightened, but the purpose of that tightening is less to dampen activity and promote adjustment than to attract capital flows through higher expected returns.

Transition and PRGF Programs

Another set of IMF-supported programs that differs from the traditional model consists of the GRA-supported programs with the transition economies and the PRGF-supported programs in low-income countries. As previously discussed, these countries form a diverse group, but examining these programs together is justified by their focus on structural reforms and efforts to promote growth and poverty reduction.

In the transition economies, although the need to maintain external viability acted as a constraint to some degree, the primary objective, at least initially, involved restoring macroeconomic stability following price liberalization and transforming centrally planned economies to those based on market principles. The growth picture differs considerably from the other GRA-supported programs mainly because of the abrupt transformation in the allocation of productive resources and of the disruption of existing trade linkages that the shift from central planning entailed (Figure 2.4). In terms of macroeconomic policies, on average, the fiscal deficit improved by 1 percentage point of GDP, while the current account deficit also improved. These policies and developments helped restrain money creation and lower inflation. Indeed, monetary policy was tightened, with a switch to positive real interest rates.

For programs supported by the PRGF, the primary objectives are its eponymous goals—raising growth and reducing poverty—rather than narrowing the current account deficit, though, again, the need to maintain external flow financing may act as a constraint.[13] Not surprisingly, the most important difference between PRGF and more traditional adjustment programs lies in the behavior of output growth (Figure 2.5). Instead of the sharp V-shaped path in growth characteristic of traditional Stand-By or capital account crisis programs, IMF-supported programs in low-income countries in the 1990s have been associated with an increase in the longer-term growth performance. Inflation is on a downward trajectory prior to the program and continues to decline over the program period. The fiscal deficit improves by 1 percentage point of GDP during the early stages of a program, but this improvement reverses over time. In contrast, the current account deteriorates by about 1 percentage point of GDP in the first program year only to bounce back to its preprogram level (a deficit of 8 percent of GDP) by the third year of the program. While there is no secular improvement in the current account deficit over time, both domestic saving and investment rise by 1 percentage point of GDP, thereby enhancing future growth prospects. Indeed, the composition of inflows changes during IMF-supported programs with increased foreign direct investment. Moreover, a number of programs have included measures on liberalizing imports to foster future growth and put the balance of payments on a sustainable path, although these measures may adversely affect the current account balance in the short term.[14] Real interest rates rise and money growth decelerates throughout the duration of these programs.

[13]As noted above, the sample period covers primarily ESAF arrangements and preliminary experience with PRGF arrangements.

[14]More than half of ESAF/PRGF-supported programs over the period 1995–2000 introduced trade liberalization measures.

Figure 2.5. Macroeconomic Performance Under ESAF- and PRGF-Supported Programs, 1995–2000[1]

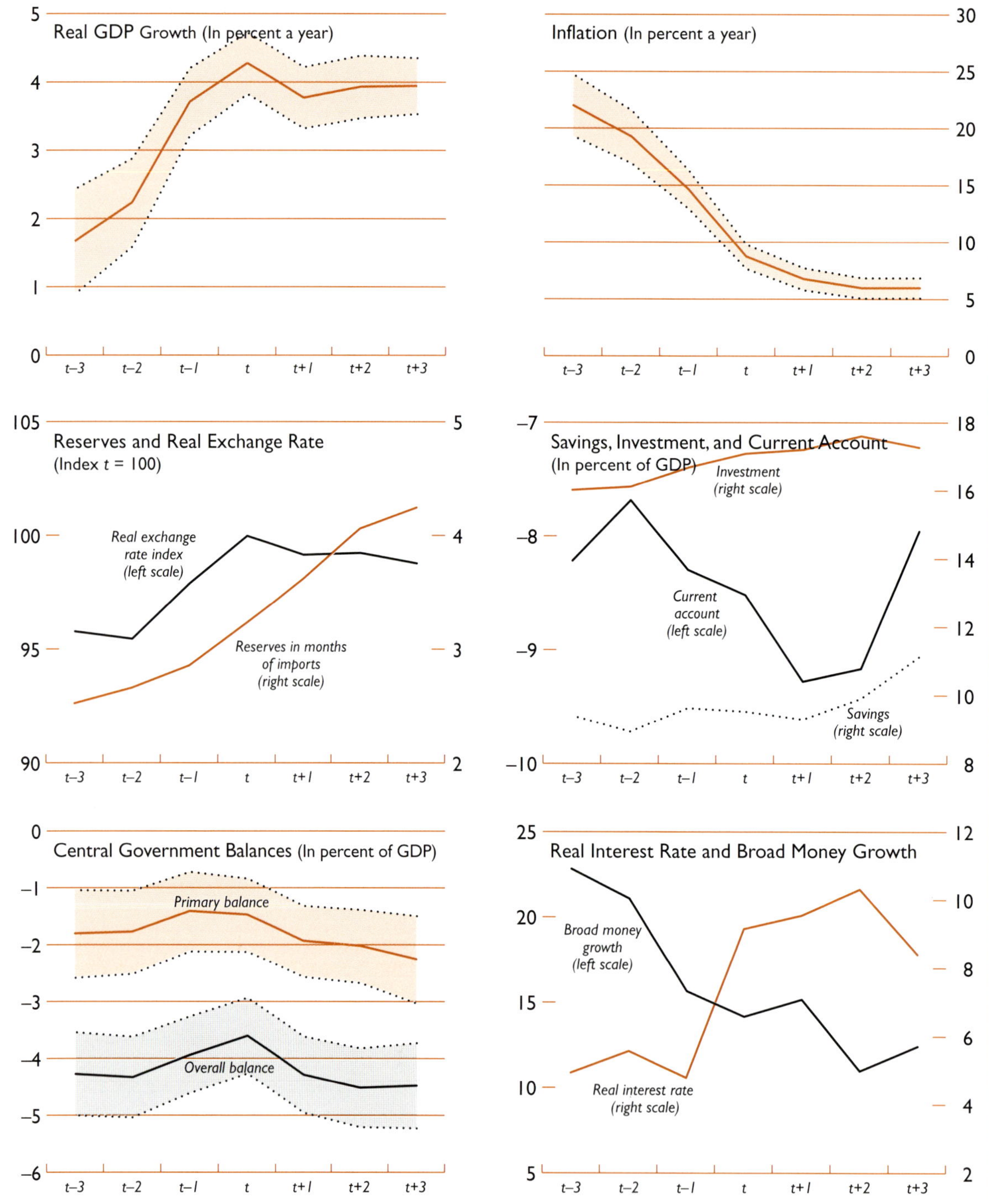

Sources: IMF, WEO database; and IMF staff estimates.
[1]Standard error bands for real GDP growth, inflation, and government balances are given by the dotted lines.

III External Viability

IMF resources are made available to member countries to correct balance of payments imbalances while easing the burden of adjustment (Box 2.3). An obvious starting point for judging program success is therefore the record on external adjustment—in particular, whether programs have achieved an appropriate mix between adjustment and financing. This naturally raises the question of the best metric for assessing external adjustment. A first measure is given by a comparison between program projections and outcomes, on grounds that in designing economic programs, the authorities would have targeted a current account balance that was appropriate to the country's circumstances. Going beyond this comparison, this section first discusses some of the shortcomings of traditional flow financing measures of adjustment and proposes medium-term debt sustainability as an alternative metric for assessing external adjustment. Next, it examines external adjustment in GRA-supported programs: how outcomes compared to projections, whether planned and actual adjustment was in line with considerations of medium-term debt sustainability, and did IMF support make a difference to the economic impact of the adjustment. Finally, it turns to the low-income countries where, especially for HIPCs the record is in marked contrast to the experience of GRA-supported countries.

Adjustment Versus Financing

Since the use of IMF resources adds to the country's external obligations as well as to its assets, the IMF's financial support alters the time profile of the country's adjustment—defined as the change in the current account balance and net international reserves (NIR)—with little direct effect on the extent of the external adjustment ultimately required. Nevertheless, by providing the country with more time to adjust and enhancing the credibility of policies, IMF support can ease the burden of adjustment because sharp reductions of absorption are likely to be more economically and socially costly and additional time is needed for a positive supply response. This also implies, however, that there is an intertemporal trade-off: to the extent that short-run adjustment is limited and financing is sufficient, the country has more external debt and hence will require greater future adjustment—especially when it starts from a high level of external indebtedness.

The two extremes of this spectrum are best illustrated by the examples of Argentina (1995) and Korea (1997). Argentina in early 1995 faced massive outflows of bank deposits in the aftermath of the Tequila crisis, but was nevertheless able to avoid a devaluation, stabilize capital outflows, and, by the end of the year, was even tapping the international capital markets. As a result, both the external adjustment and the decline in growth, while sizable, were significantly smaller than in many other capital account crises (e.g., Mexico or the Asian crisis countries). By all accounts, therefore, the IMF-supported program was highly successful in dealing with the immediate balance of payments problem. Yet, in retrospect, it is also clear that Argentina failed to tackle the underlying weaknesses of its public finances—and their inconsistency with the currency board arrangement—setting the stage for the growing public and external debt that culminated in late 2001 with an economic and political crisis.[15] By contrast, Korea's (1997) Stand-By Arrangement met with very little initial success in stemming capital outflows or preventing a collapse of the exchange rate and of economic activity, and the economy only began to recover after macroeconomic policies were strengthened, coupled with a rollover agreement with creditors.[16] Over the somewhat longer term, however, by enhancing the credibility of macroeconomic policies and instituting structural reforms, the IMF-supported program succeeded in restoring confidence and a return of private capital together with a replenishment of foreign exchange reserves. The experience of

[15]For a fuller discussion see Daseking and others (2004) and IEO (2004).

[16] For instance, during the last quarter of 1997, the real exchange rate depreciated by 35 percent, private capital outflows amounted to almost 25 percent of GDP, and the current account balance improved by some 12 percent of GDP; as a result of the severe economic disruption, output growth fell by 12 percentage points.

Box 2.3. Use of IMF Resources: Balance of Payments and Budget Gaps

A common question raised in the context of both GRA- and PRGF-supported programs concerns the relationship between the use of IMF resources and the balance of payments and budget financing gap.[1] To get a handle on this question, the terms "balance of payments gap" and "budget financing gap" need to be defined.[2] Starting from the balance of payments identity: $CA + KA = \dot{R}$ or, since the capital account is simply net borrowing by the government (excluding the central bank) or the private sector: $CA + \dot{B}^{*p} + \dot{B}^{*g} = \dot{R}$, where $\dot{B}^{*p}$ is net external borrowing by the private sector, including the publicly owned financial sector, $\dot{B}^{*g}$ is external borrowing by the nonfinancial public sector, and $\dot{R}$ is the net change in central bank reserves. Under a fixed exchange rate, a balance of payments gap exists if the country is losing reserves. The corresponding condition under a floating exchange rate is that the country *would* lose reserves if the exchange rate and output were to remain constant: $CA(\bar{y}, \bar{e}) + \dot{B}^{*p} + \dot{B}^{*g} = \dot{R} < 0$.

Defining a "budget gap" is more tricky: clearly, it is more than just an overall budget deficit. The consolidated nonfinancial public sector can finance itself by borrowing domestically or borrowing from abroad: $\dot{B}^g + \dot{B}^{*g} = Def$. One definition of a budget financing gap, therefore, is that, at a reasonable interest rate, the domestic private sector's desired level of saving is insufficient to meet the budget financing gap. Monetary policy is assumed geared toward its objectives for inflation and growth.

With these definitions, suppose that the public sector deficit increases by an amount ΔDef: $(\dot{B}^g + \Delta\dot{B}^g) + (\dot{B}^{*g} + \Delta\dot{B}^{*g}) = Def + \Delta Def$. Under the definition of a budget financing gap, $\Delta\dot{B}^g = 0$ so that the public sector can only finance itself through external borrowing: $\Delta\dot{B}^{*g} = \Delta Def$. If, coincidentally, initially the country happens to have precisely the same balance of payments gap: $CA(\bar{y}, \bar{e}) + \dot{B}^{*p} + \dot{B}^{*g} = \dot{R} = -\Delta Def$, then closing the budget financing gap through additional external borrowing is entirely consistent with closing the balance of payments gap. Next consider a case in which the country does *not* have an ex ante balance of payments gap: $CA(\bar{y}, \bar{e}) + \dot{B}^{*p} + \dot{B}^{*g} = \dot{R} = 0$.

Now additional external borrowing by the public sector will either add to reserves (so that net borrowing by the public sector is zero), or there must be a corresponding decrease in external borrowing by the private sector $\Delta\dot{B}^{*p} = -\Delta def$ (or an increase in the current account deficit, though this is ruled out by the assumption that the exchange rate and macroeconomic policies remain constant). But if the private sector is decreasing its external borrowing, then it is increasing its savings by precisely the amount of the enlarged deficit. In other words, the domestic private sector *could*, with this increased saving, have financed the budget deficit, but the private sector may choose to hold this additional saving in a foreign asset (rather than using it to finance the government). This may occur when the expected rate of return on foreign assets exceeds the interest rate on public sector debt. In this case the inflow of IMF resources would be offset by capital flight—leaving the country's *net* external borrowing unchanged. *It follows that external financing can be used (in the sense of effecting a real resource transfer) to close a budget gap only to the extent that there is a corresponding balance of payments gap.*

[1]This is the counterpart to the "international transfer problem" studied by Keynes in the context of reparations by Germany following World War I. As Keynes (1929, pp. 1–7) notes, there are two distinct problems: the *budgetary* problem and the *transfer* problem and it is only under very restrictive assumptions that the two become identical.

[2]The central bank acts as the fiscal agent of the government and receives the IMF's disbursements. By allowing a corresponding increase in central bank credit to the government, however, IMF resources can, in effect, be loaned to the government. The equivalence is not exact because, inter alia, there are different implications for exchange rate and credit risk associated with the IMF purchase.

these countries suggests that neither extreme is optimal. Korea achieved rapid reduction in its external debt, but at the cost of a wrenching external adjustment and sharp contraction of output. In Argentina, although some of the short-run costs of adjustment were avoided, the insufficient adjustment was extremely disruptive to the economy in the long run.

This suggests that, beyond the flow financing constraint (i.e., whether the country stops losing reserves, and begins replenishing them), considerations of medium-term external debt sustainability may provide a useful benchmark for judging the appropriate current account adjustment. The basic principle is that, to the extent that a country is solvent, it should be able to obtain financing rather than having to adjust its current account balance in response to a temporary shock.[17] Therefore, unless the

[17]IMF financing cannot resolve a "solvency" problem (whereby the country is unable to generate the required surpluses to satisfy the intertemporal budget constraint), since it effectively replaces one source of financing (the private sector) with another (the official sector). There are two possible exceptions. First, to the extent that IMF resources are made available at a cost below the marginal cost of market borrowing, the present value of the debt is correspondingly lower; for plausible amounts of IMF financing, however, this effect is likely to be negligible. Second, the IMF's support of a member's adjustment program could, via confidence effects, lower the market cost of its borrowing and help spur growth, making an otherwise unmanageable level of debt more sustainable.

country is constrained in the financing it is able to obtain, the current account balance should adjust by as much as is required to maintain solvency—with two provisos. First, if the country has already a high level of external debt, it would be appropriate to run a smaller current account deficit in order to reduce vulnerability to future balance of payments problems. Second, relatedly, even if the external debt ratio is low, the authorities may wish to run a current account balance that permits foreign exchange reserves to be replenished and reduces vulnerability to liquidity crises.

Of course the mix between financing and adjustment is not always under the direct control of the authorities, depending, inter alia, on the nature of external capital flows on which the country relies. For low-income, PRGF-supported countries, which rely mainly on official financing, a challenge in determining the appropriate path of adjustment is to deal with the uncertainty regarding the magnitude and timing of official aid.[18] For countries that rely on private capital flows but that, in stock terms, have relatively small exposure, there may be uncertainty about when capital inflows will resume but only limited risk of massive outflows (though the challenge of tailoring specific macroeconomic policies to induce the desired degree of adjustment remains).

If a capital account crisis erupts, the authorities may have little control over the pace of external adjustment undertaken because of liquidity constraints on external financing. Not only is the availability of official financing (and use of gross international reserves) likely to fall well short of potential capital outflows, official financing could simply facilitate the faster exit of private capital, especially if a sufficient policy response is lacking. Another possibility is to use capital controls or debt standstills to limit the outflows. However, the use of direct controls on capital outflows is highly controversial, may be technically difficult to implement and enforce, and is potentially counterproductive—spurring further outflows as well as delaying the country's return to the capital markets (Box 2.4).[19] In these circumstances, the authorities must rely on trying to restore confidence through the macroeconomic and structural policies they adopt. For the purposes of program design, the usual—if unsatisfactory—practice is that the magnitude of adjustment becomes the residual, given available official financing and expected capital outflows.

[18]See "Debt Sustainability in Low-Income Countries" (IMF, 2004) and Bulíř and Hamann (2003) and Bulíř and Lane (2002).

[19]A useful summary of the issues and work in this area may be found in "Private Sector Involvement in the Prevention and Resolution of Financial Crises—Report of the Managing Director to the International Monetary and Financial Committee" (IMF, 2001).

External Adjustment in GRA-Supported Programs

The foregoing discussion points to three ways in which IMF support may help ease external adjustment. First, for a given net flow of private capital, an arithmetical correspondence exists between external adjustment (or the gross financing requirement) and disbursements of IMF resources. Second, in combination with the policy commitments of the authorities, IMF support may induce a positive response, or "catalytic effect," such that private capital inflows resume or at least further outflows are stemmed. Third, by inducing better policy choices, a program may help achieve a given external adjustment—that is, improvement in the current account—at lower cost in terms of output contraction or real exchange rate depreciation.

Use of IMF Resources

Conceptually, it is useful to consider first the effects of IMF disbursements on external adjustment abstracting from any induced effects on other resource flows, and then take up the question of catalytic effects on flows separately. In this connection, it is noteworthy that, on average, IMF disbursements cover about 12 percent of the gross external financing gap in GRA-supported programs (Table 2.1). A key question in designing an adjustment strategy is the targeted level of gross (net) international reserves coupled with the envisaged change in the current account balance. IMF-supported programs set targets for gross international reserves (GIR), which are back-stopped by floors for NIR.[20] Expected net capital flows need to be allocated between these two objectives. However, the magnitude of flows may themselves be affected by these targets. But judging the effect on other flows is extremely difficult. On the one hand, replenishing reserves may give confidence so that (once the exchange rate has been allowed to adjust) capital outflows are stemmed, while allowing IMF resources to be spent may simply encourage the private sector—domestic or foreign—to exit faster. Higher reserve levels also give the authorities additional breathing space should the economy or external flows respond more slowly than expected. On the other hand, from the balance of payments identity, for a given level of other flows, disbursements of IMF resources that are added to reserves are also not available to moderate the cur-

[20]These floors are intended as safeguards or "tripwires" that indicate a possible need to reconsider program policies: they are not intended to delineate the baseline adjustment path.

Box 2.4. Capital Controls on Outflows in Crises

Capital controls have been used as a tool to address capital outflows during financial crises.[1] The controls have taken a variety of forms, ranging from administrative or direct controls (outright prohibitions, or quantitative limits on, or approval procedures for cross-border flows for residents or nonresidents) to more market-based controls that attempt to discourage particular capital movements by making them more costly (including explicit or implicit taxation of cross-border financial flows or dual or multiple exchange rates applicable to different types of international transactions). In many cases, controls on capital outflows have been applied in tandem with other policy measures, rather than in isolation, and in several cases were accompanied by other administrative measures, including exchange controls on transactions in domestic or foreign currency, controls on current international transactions, default on public and/or private external debt, or freezing of bank deposits.

Capital controls have been viewed as a tool to reconcile conflicting policy objectives and direct monetary policy toward domestic objectives while limiting pressure on the exchange rate. In crises, countries have typically imposed these controls to counter volatile speculative flows that undermine the stability of the exchange rate and deplete foreign exchange reserves, and help the authorities to buy time to implement adjustment measures and structural reforms. Controls have been imposed against the background of significant downward pressure on the exchange rate, sharply declining foreign exchange reserves, a sharp loss of access to international capital markets, and limited room to use interest rates to defend the currency reflecting concerns about their adverse impact on economic activity and balance sheets of the public and private sectors. Examples of countries that imposed such controls include Argentina (2001), Indonesia (2001), Malaysia (1998), Pakistan (1998), Russia (1998), Spain (1992), Thailand (1997), and República Bolivariana de Venezuela (1994). In several of them (Argentina, Pakistan, and Russia), the controls were accompanied by more extensive measures, including restrictions on current account transactions, default on debt-service obligations, and restrictions on deposit withdrawals.

The effectiveness of capital controls during crises has been a subject of controversy. There is as yet no firm conclusion on their effectiveness, reflecting a number of factors, not least the challenge of constructing an appropriate counterfactual against which the controls can be evaluated and the difficulty of disentangling the impact of the controls from that of other factors (e.g., the accompanying measures or favorable external factors). Nevertheless, it is possible to make a number of observations on the basis of country experiences:

- Temporary controls may provide a temporary breathing space, but not a lasting protection if there are incentives for circumvention (e.g., attractive return differentials in the offshore markets and strong market expectations of exchange rate depreciation) and these are large relative to the expected costs of circumvention.
- The use of capital controls must be weighed against the possibility that their imposition may itself undermine confidence and engender capital outflows. If they are used, they must be comprehensive (so as to limit circumvention), implemented by authorities with strong enforcement capacity (to detect and close loopholes), and accompanied by policy adjustments and reforms to restore macroeconomic stability. Over time, the authorities should do their utmost to reduce the need for these controls, and hence, reduce incentives to circumvent them.
- However, comprehensive controls are more distortionary, interfering with desirable transactions (such as foreign direct investment, long-term portfolio flows, and trade-related financial transactions), and strong enforcement capacity entails nontrivial administrative costs, particularly when measures have to be broadened to close potential loopholes for circumvention.
- Controls may give rise to negative market perceptions and damage countries' creditworthiness, thereby making it more difficult and costly to reaccess international markets.

[1]The box draws on Ariyoshi and others (2000).

rent account adjustment. In any event, the IMF's financing contribution is not large.[21]

Most IMF-supported programs targeted an increase in NIR.[22] Indeed, over the sample period, only in 12 percent of GRA-supported programs in nontransition countries was NIR programmed to decline during the first program year (Table 2.1), with

[21]Of course, IMF disbursements add to the country's foreign exchange liabilities and therefore require it to adjust eventually. These disbursements, however, help the country to avoid abrupt adjustment that would be disruptive to economic activity.

[22]While IMF disbursements raise GIR, there is no change in NIR since assets and liabilities increase by the same amount. For the median program country, the IMF disburses about 1 percent of GDP (20 percent of the current account balance for the previous year) during the first year of a program, varying narrowly between 1 percent of GDP for "traditional" SBAs and EFFs (40 percent of the current account for the previous year) and 1.2 percent of GDP (47 percent of the current account for the previous year) for capital account crisis countries.

Table 2.1. Share of IMF Financing and NIR in IMF-Supported Programs

	Total	Share of IMF Financing (In percent)[1]	Programmed Change in NIR (In percent of GDP)		Number of Cases with Programmed Decrease in NIR	Proportion of Cases with Programmed Decrease in NIR
			Median	Mean		
GRA-supported programs	73	12.0	0.98	1.44	15	20.5
Nontransition economies	43	10.4	0.98	1.85	5	11.6
Nonprecautionary	25	12.0	1.05	1.76	3	12.0
Precautionary	18	8.1	0.98	1.97	2	11.1
Transition economies	30	14.2	0.81	0.86	10	33.3
Nonprecautionary	20	18.7	1.20	1.03	5	25.0
Precautionary	10	5.2	−0.02	0.52	5	50.0
PRGF-supported programs[2]	44	7.9	1.29	1.13	8	18.2
Nontransition economies	36	7.3	1.12	1.18	6	16.7
Transition economies	8	11.0	1.48	0.89	2	25.0

Sources: IMF, WEO and MONA databases; and IMF staff estimates.

[1]In relation to the gross financing requirement.

[2]Excluding countries using the CFA franc for the cases of programmed decrease in NIR because no NIR target was set.

a slightly smaller proportion for precautionary programs and a rather larger proportion for programs in transition economies.[23] For the median program country, the floor set on net international reserves required the central bank to accumulate NIR of about 1 percent of GDP during the first program year. This substantial planned accumulation of NIR indicates the importance that the authorities attach to reducing vulnerabilities through increasing reserves.[24]

Establishing whether IMF support has a catalytic effect on capital flows—or, indeed, simply finances larger outflows—is difficult because the counterfactual is unknown. Indeed, the existing empirical literature shows mixed results on the extent to which IMF endorsement of a country's macroeconomic strategy helps to mobilize private external financing.[25] In this study, we do not attempt to tackle this issue directly. Rather, a related but slightly different issue is explored—to what extent do IMF-supported programs accurately project capital flows? Program projections for the current account (or capital flows) are compared against outcomes. To the extent that outcomes are worse than projected—capital flows are smaller and the improvement in the current account balance is larger—the catalytic effect may not be as large as projected—though it is also possible that other developments—such as favorable terms of trade—are the source of the projection error in the current account balance. The difference between actual outcomes and projections of the current account balance are substantial in the first program year. In some cases, the authorities created an additional buffer against vulnerabilities through sizable increases in international reserves (see below).

A scatter plot of projections versus outcomes of the current account balance in the first program year for GRA-supported programs (Figure 2.6, top panel) shows that almost 60 percent of observations lie above the 45 degree line. On average, the current account deficit narrowed by (a statistically significant) 1.3 percent of GDP more than originally projected (though the median difference is only 0.3 percent of GDP). Private capital flows fell short of expectations by a comparable amount (but by as much as 5 to 15 percentage points of GDP in some capital account

[23]This may explain why, in Figure 2.2, the current account adjustment is so similar in precautionary and nonprecautionary arrangements.

[24]In some cases the IMF has helped a country avoid a potentially costly default (Mexico, 1995).

[25]See Cottarelli and Curzio (2002) for a discussion. Killick, Malik, and Manuel (1992) and Bird and Rowlands (1997) find no empirical evidence for a catalytic effect of IMF support. In contrast, Marchesi (2003) shows that such support helps a country to reschedule its private debt obligations, while Mody and Saravia (2003) note that it raises the likelihood that a debtor country may issue a bond and reduce its spreads at the time of issuance. Bordo, Mody, and Oomes (2004) show that IMF-supported programs are effective in reducing bond spreads when the debt-to-GDP ratios are between 30 percent and 70 percent. They also highlight that, while precautionary programs have no independent effect on the probability of bond issuance, they are associated with significantly reduced spreads. Further, they stress that IMF-supported programs raise capital flows after one year in countries with poor initial conditions.

Figure 2.6. Current Account Balance in GRA-Supported Programs: Projections and Outcomes[1]
(In percent of GDP)

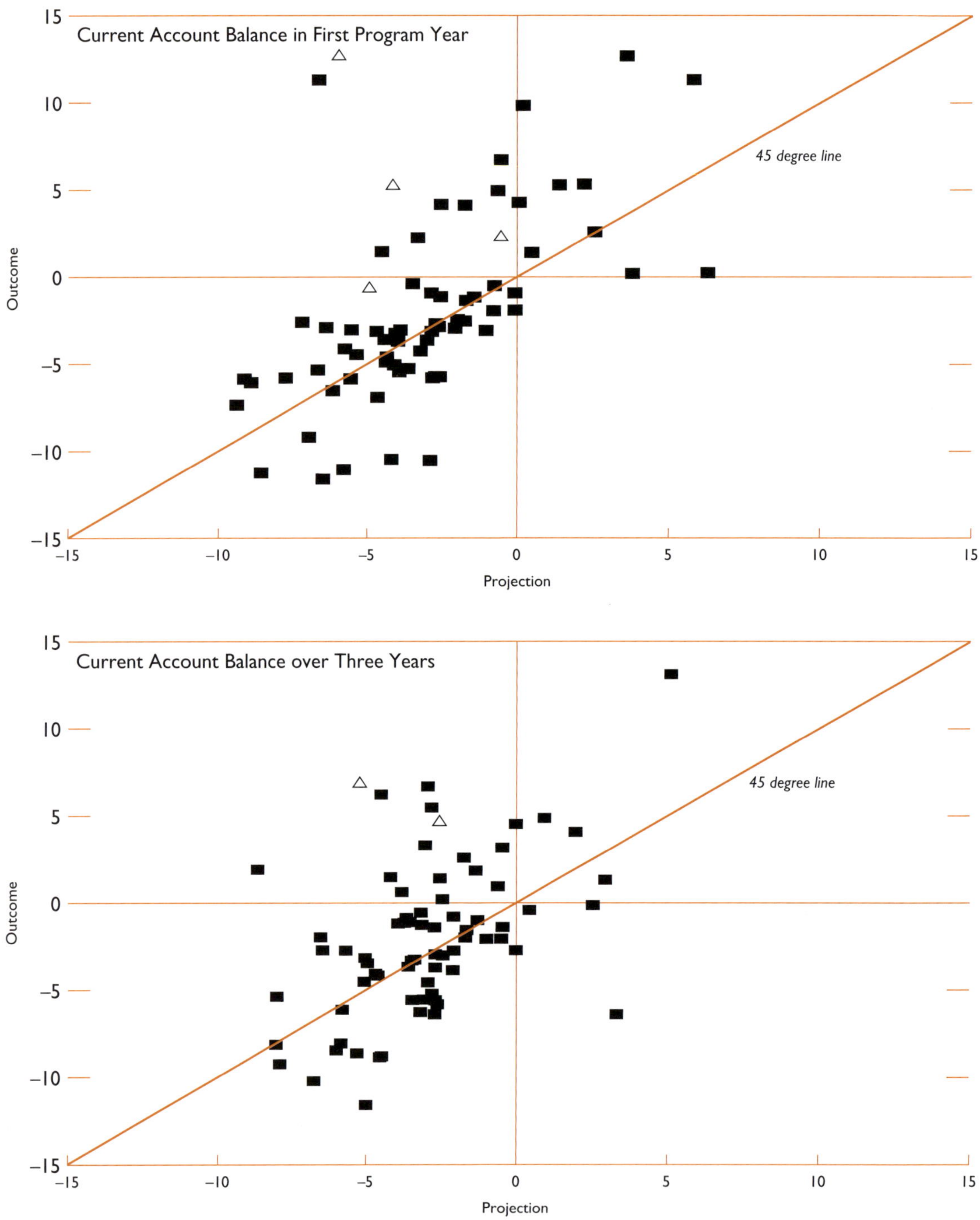

Sources: IMF, MONA and WEO databases; and IMF staff estimates.
Note. See Appendix I for a list of countries.
[1]Capital account crisis countries are depicted by triangles.

crises). This first year projection error is subsequently reversed; over the three-year period, the cumulative difference between the actual and projected current account deficits largely disappears (Figure 2.6, bottom panel). By contrast, precautionary programs saw the first year current account deficit narrow by 0.5 percent of GDP less than originally projected, and, over the three-year period, the deviation remained on average at about 0.5 percent of GDP.

These smaller current account deficits than projected do not reflect unexpectedly tight fiscal policy; on the contrary, the fiscal balance was weaker than targeted by 0.6 percentage point of GDP (Figure 2.7, top panel). The weakness in the fiscal position, however, was more than offset by the shortfall in investment relative to its projection, with the difference averaging about 1.8 percentage points of GDP (Figure 2.7, bottom panel).[26]

Adjustment in Relation to Medium-Term Debt Sustainability

While the comparison between programmed and actual current account balances provides one measure of whether the proper mix between financing and adjustment was achieved, it necessarily relies on the program projection capturing the appropriate extent of adjustment. It is possible, however, that because sufficient financing was not available, the program projection incorporated greater adjustment than was considered economically desirable. It is therefore useful to complement this analysis by considering the current account balance against the metric of medium-term debt sustainability. Although a full assessment of debt sustainability is beyond the scope of this paper, a useful benchmark is the debt-stabilizing balance. For countries starting with high levels of external debt, a larger balance (than the debt-stabilizing balance) would be called for in order to lower the debt ratio and reduce future vulnerability, although the proper pace—and thus the appropriate current account balance—is unclear. Stabilizing the debt ratio should suffice for countries with moderate levels of external debt,[27] while for countries with low initial external debt ratios, it would not be necessary to stabilize the debt ratio immediately. These considerations imply that the current account balance (relative to the debt-stabilizing balance) should be an increasing function of the initial external debt ratio.

Figure 2.8 (top panel) plots the difference between the programmed and debt-stabilizing current account balance[28] (and in percent of GDP) net of foreign direct investment (FDI) during the first program year against the initial external debt (as a percent of GDP). As suggested by considerations of debt sustainability, a positive (and statistically significant) relationship exists between the programmed current account balance (relative to the debt-stabilizing balance) and the initial debt ratio. The relationship implies that, for example, a program in a country with an initial external debt ratio of 50 percent of GDP would seek to reduce the debt ratio to 40 percent of GDP within five years.

The bottom panel of Figure 2.8 reports outcomes. As indicated in the panel, in three-quarters of the 75 GRA-supported programs, the current account balance was larger than would have been necessary to stabilize the external debt ratio given the historical performance of the economy (i.e., these observations lie above the horizontal axis). Again, there is a positive and statistically significant relationship between the actual current account balance (relative to the debt-stabilizing balance) and the initial external debt ratio. Reflecting the finding above that GRA-supported programs, on average, run larger current account balances than programmed, both the slope and intercept of the line are higher than the programmed relationship. While it is difficult to establish precise thresholds at which debt levels may become problematic, the existing empirical literature suggests that there is an appreciable increase in the likelihood of a debt crisis at external debt ratios above 40–60 percent of GDP.[29] At an external debt ratio of 40 percent, the actual current account balance is larger than the debt-stabilizing balance by some 2¾ percent of GDP. Of course, this estimate is heavily influenced by the capital account crisis countries and by

[26]While macroeconomic policies were arguably insufficiently strong, thereby failing to engender a return of confidence, the issue of policy appropriateness remains an open question. Benelli (2003) has found that the disparity between projections and realizations of capital flows is positively associated with the size of financial assistance and negatively associated with policy adjustment, but this finding only suggests that the amount of financing and the type of policy choices were associated with differences in projection errors and were not necessarily related to actual movements in capital flows.

[27]Stabilizing the external debt ratio implies intertemporal solvency; though solvency does not require a stable debt ratio—see IMF (2002).

[28]The debt-stabilizing current account balance (in percent of GDP) is given by $ca^* = -gd$, where g is the medium-term growth rate of the U.S. dollar value of GDP (calculated as the five-year average of the growth of U.S. dollar value of GDP), and d is external debt (in percent of GDP) averaged over end-period t and end-period t+1. Although FDI does not incur additional debt, it is a liability for the recipient country that will eventually need to be serviced in the form of repatriated profits.

[29]For convenience, the range from 40 percent to 60 percent of GDP is shaded in the figure. For a discussion of external debt thresholds see IMF (2002 and 2003a), and Reinhart, Rogoff, and Savastano (2003). On thresholds for public debt, see IMF (2003a and 2003b).

Figure 2.7. Fiscal Balance and Investment in GRA-Supported Programs: Projections and Outcomes[1]
(In percent of GDP)

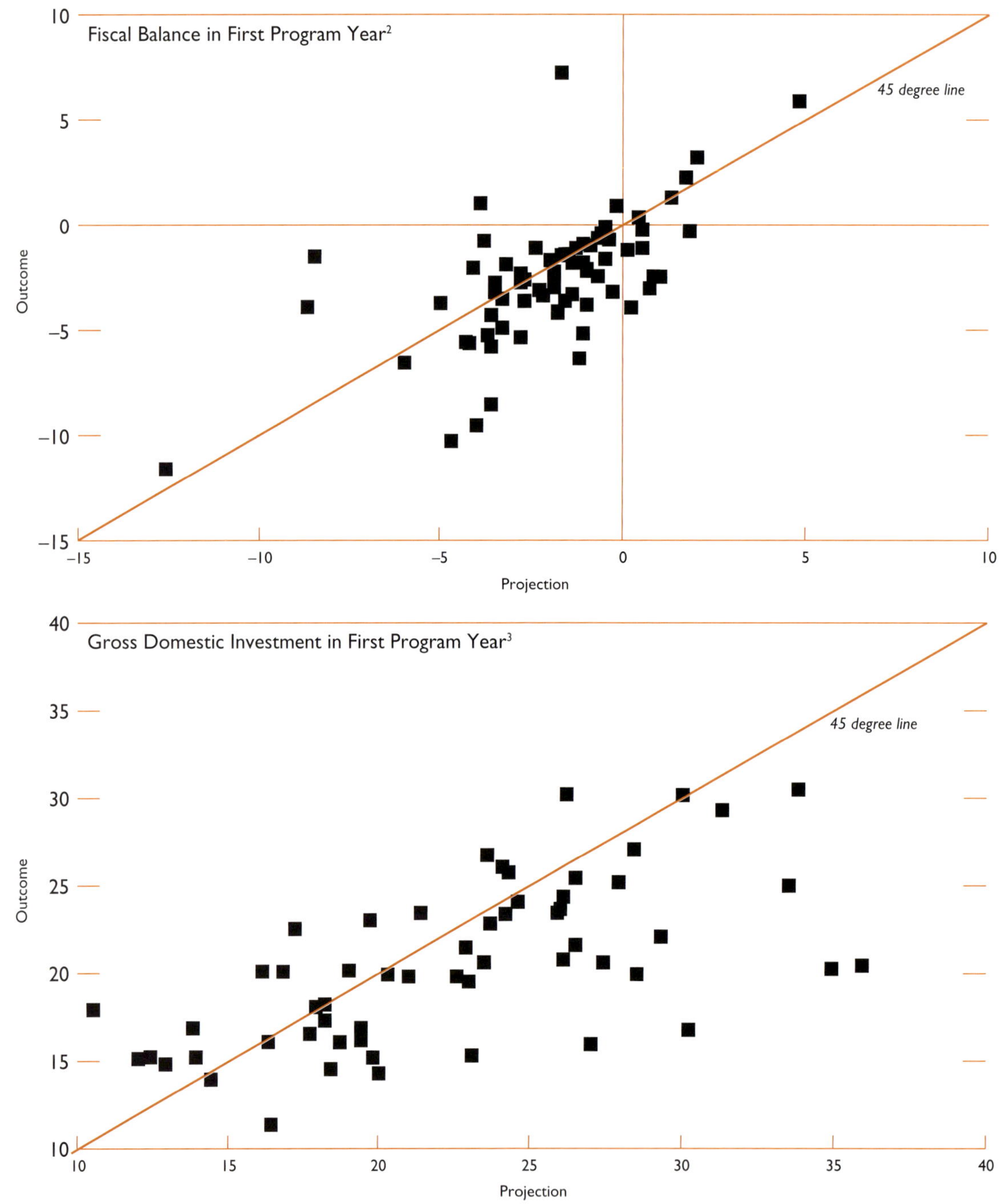

Sources: IMF, MONA and WEO databases; and IMF staff estimates.
Note. See Appendix I for a list of countries.
[1]Fiscal balance includes grants.
[2]Not shown is Gabon 2000 (16.2 percent of GDP, projection).
[3]Not shown are Lesotho 1995 (59.9 percent of GDP, actual) and Lesotho 1996 (52.2 percent of GDP, actual).

Figure 2.8. Projected, Actual, and Debt-Stabilizing Current Account Balances in GRA-Supported Programs[1]

(In percent of GDP)

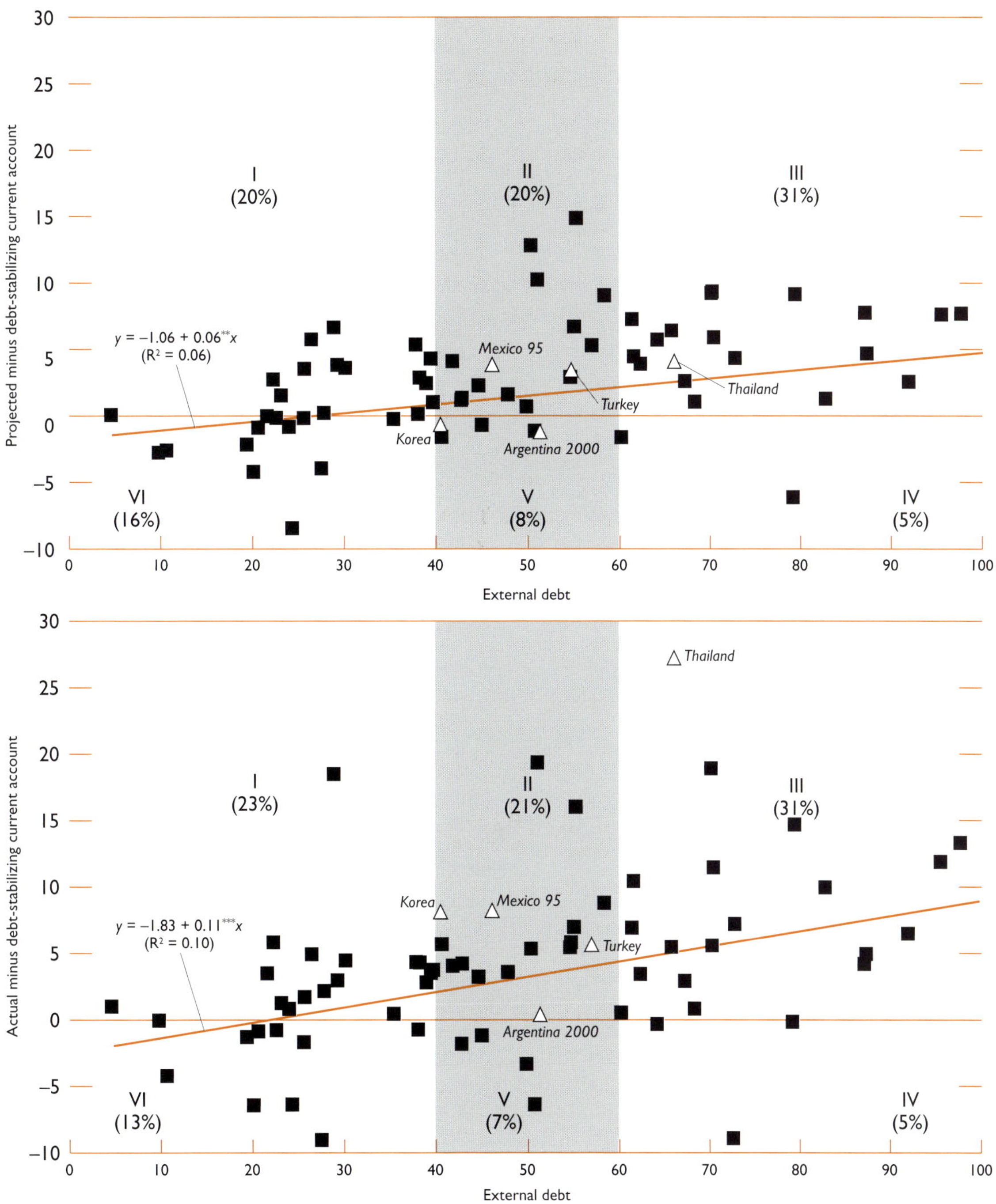

Sources: IMF, MONA and WEO databases; and IMF staff estimates.
Note. See Appendix I for a list of countries.

countries that experienced positive external shocks over this period. Excluding both of these categories (defining positive external shocks as positive changes in oil exports) reduces this difference to slightly above 1 percent of GDP, for the remaining GRA-supported programs.

A useful way to characterize the results is to divide Figure 3.3 into six segments, according to the initial debt ratios and whether the current account balance exceeds the debt-stabilizing balance. For observations in Section I (23 percent of the GRA-supported programs, 40 percent of which were precautionary), the current account balance exceeds the debt-stabilizing balance even though the initial debt ratio, at less than 40 percent of GDP, is relatively low.[30] A further 20 percent of programs (40 percent of precautionary programs) are in the intermediate range for external debt (Section II, with debt ratios of 40–60 percent of GDP), including some notable capital account crises such as Korea (1997) and Mexico (1995), whose initial debt levels were 41 percent and 46 percent of GDP, respectively. These countries have current account balances that would reduce their debt ratios over the medium term although the debt ratios are in a gray zone. While a reduction in their debt ratios may be considered appropriate for such countries, it is unclear that this reduction—as opposed to simply stabilizing the debt ratio—should take place immediately. Countries in Section III (32 percent of the total) are generating larger current account balances than would stabilize debt but they start from debt levels that are high so that there is a strong case for a decline in the debt ratio to reduce vulnerability to an external debt crisis.

Countries in Sections IV, V, and VI have current account balances that are smaller than the debt-stabilizing balances. For 15 percent of cases (Section VI), the low initial debt ratio (below 40 percent of GDP) meant that there was no pressing need to reduce the country's external indebtedness. A further 11 percent of such cases were in the gray zone (i.e., an initial debt ratio of 40–60 percent of GDP) and only 5 percent of programs (Section IV) had current account balances that were clearly insufficient given their high initial external debt ratio. All of these findings are robust to alternative assumptions underlying the calculations for the debt-stabilizing balance (Appendix II).

Overall, the results suggest that external adjustment was largely consistent with that required by medium-term sustainability of external debt. As noted above, however, the actual current account position was better than necessary to stabilize the external debt ratio despite initial debt ratios that were either low or in the gray zone. In part, national authorities may have chosen to run larger current account balances to reduce vulnerability to future liquidity crises by accumulating foreign exchange reserves. However, for countries with debt ratios below 40 percent of GDP, the difference between the actual and debt-stabilizing balance amounted to 2.8 percent of GDP against a programmed increase in reserves of 1.5 percent of GDP (Table 2.2 and Figure 2.9). For countries whose initial debt ratios were in the gray zone of 40–60 percent of GDP, the difference between the current account balance and the debt-stabilizing balance is 8.7 percent of GDP—against a programmed increase in reserves of 1.6 percent of GDP. This suggests that, in these cases, capital outflows were underestimated in the original program design. At the same time, it is noteworthy that national authorities chose to accumulate more reserves than originally programmed—by about 0.2 percent of GDP for countries with low initial debt ratios but almost 1 percent of GDP for countries whose initial debt was 40–60 percent of GDP. This may have reflected a need to accumulate reserves in order to restore confidence as well as differences in the precise timing between current account adjustment and reserve accumulation.[31]

Economic Impact of External Adjustment

Beyond the extent of external adjustment, it is also important to consider the economic impact of that adjustment. In particular, for a given improvement of the current account balance, does IMF support help mitigate the negative impact on growth of expenditure reducing policies? There are at least a couple of reasons for believing it might do so. One possibility is that the member makes better policy choices when undertaking adjustment under an IMF-supported program. For instance, to the extent that some fiscal expenditures are less productive, achieving the necessary current account improvement through adjustment in the public rather than private sector may be less harmful to growth. Another mechanism is the policy credibility that IMF support might impart. Efficient external adjustment requires domestic factors of production—capital and labor—to move from the nontradable to the tradable sector. The willingness of these factors to shift will likely depend on their confidence in the government's intention to carry

[30]In a few of these cases in Section I, however, the current account balance reflected positive terms of trade shocks rather than import compression. Specifically, about a quarter of these cases are associated with positive terms of trade shocks, positive real GDP growth, and constant or rising imports.

[31]For example, Korea underwent a sharp adjustment of its current account balance in late 1997 and early 1998 in the face of capital outflows, accumulating more foreign exchange reserves than programmed in the latter half of 1998 as capital inflows resumed.

Table 2.2. Indicators of GRA-Supported Countries with External Debt Below 60 Percent of GDP and Current Account Balances Above the Debt-Stabilizing Value

	Debt Ratio Less Than 40 Percent		Debt Ratio Between 40 and 50 Percent		Debt Ratio Between 50 and 60 Percent	
	Mean	Median	Mean	Median	Mean	Median
In percent of GDP						
A. Actual minus debt-stabilizing current account	2.8	2.2	8.7	3.7	5.6	4.2
B. Programmed increase in reserves	1.5	1.3	1.6	1.5	1.0	0.7
C. Actual increase in reserves	1.7	2.4	2.5	1.8	2.5	1.9
A – B	1.4		7.1**		4.7**	
C – B	0.2		0.9*		1.5**	
Proportion of countries with positive values						
Programmed increase in reserves	92.3		92.3		88.9	
Actual increase in reserves	69.2		77.8		88.9	
A – B	69.2		88.9		77.8	
C – B	61.5		66.7		77.8	

Sources: IMF, WEO and MONA databases; and IMF staff estimates.

Note. * indicates significance at the 10 percent level; ** indicates significance at the 5 percent level.

through the planned adjustment and sustain it, making expenditure-switching policies more effective. The precommitment that IMF support and conditionality afford, in turn, can help solve time-consistency problems and provide the additional confidence. Whatever the precise mechanism, preliminary findings (documented in Box 2.5) suggest that, controlling for movements in the current account balance and of the real exchange rate, countries with IMF-supported programs grow by about 1 percentage point a year faster than countries undertaking the same current account adjustment (with the same real exchange rate movement) without the benefit of an IMF-supported program. While these results are robust (estimated using instrumental variables, including fixed effects, and controlling for transition countries), the problem of endogeneity in program participation remains,[32] and therefore the results must be viewed with caution.

In sum, consistent with considerations of debt sustainability and reducing vulnerabilities in future crises, both programmed and actual current account balances are higher relative to their debt-stabilizing levels, the greater the initial external debt ratio. Preliminary evidence suggests that more efficient policy choices and program credibility that IMF support affords help mitigate the impact on growth of current account adjustment, subject to the qualifiers mentioned above regarding the endogeneity of the sample. However, on average, current account balances initially improve by more than programmed (although fiscal balances are weaker than programmed), and for a significant portion (23 percent) of GRA-supported programs, current account balances were larger than necessary to stabilize the initial debt ratio even when that ratio was relatively low. Moreover, in a further 20 percent of cases, including some notable capital account crises, countries are in a gray zone (debt ratios between 40 percent and 60 percent of GDP) with current account balances larger than necessary for stabilizing the external debt ratio.

ESAF- and PRGF-Supported Programs

Use of IMF Resources

IMF disbursements in relation to GDP for PRGF countries broadly correspond to the magnitude of IMF disbursements in GRA-supported programs, amounting to about 0.9 percent of GDP (17 percent of the current account deficit) and, in about 80 percent of the cases, the program targeted an increase in *net* international reserves of about 1.3 percent of GDP (Table 2.1).

IMF support has an important catalytic role in low-income countries, albeit on official rather than

[32]That is, countries better able to adjust externally through the choice of appropriate policies may be more likely to seek IMF support.

Figure 2.9. Decomposition of Actual Minus Debt-Stabilizing Current Account
(In percent of GDP)

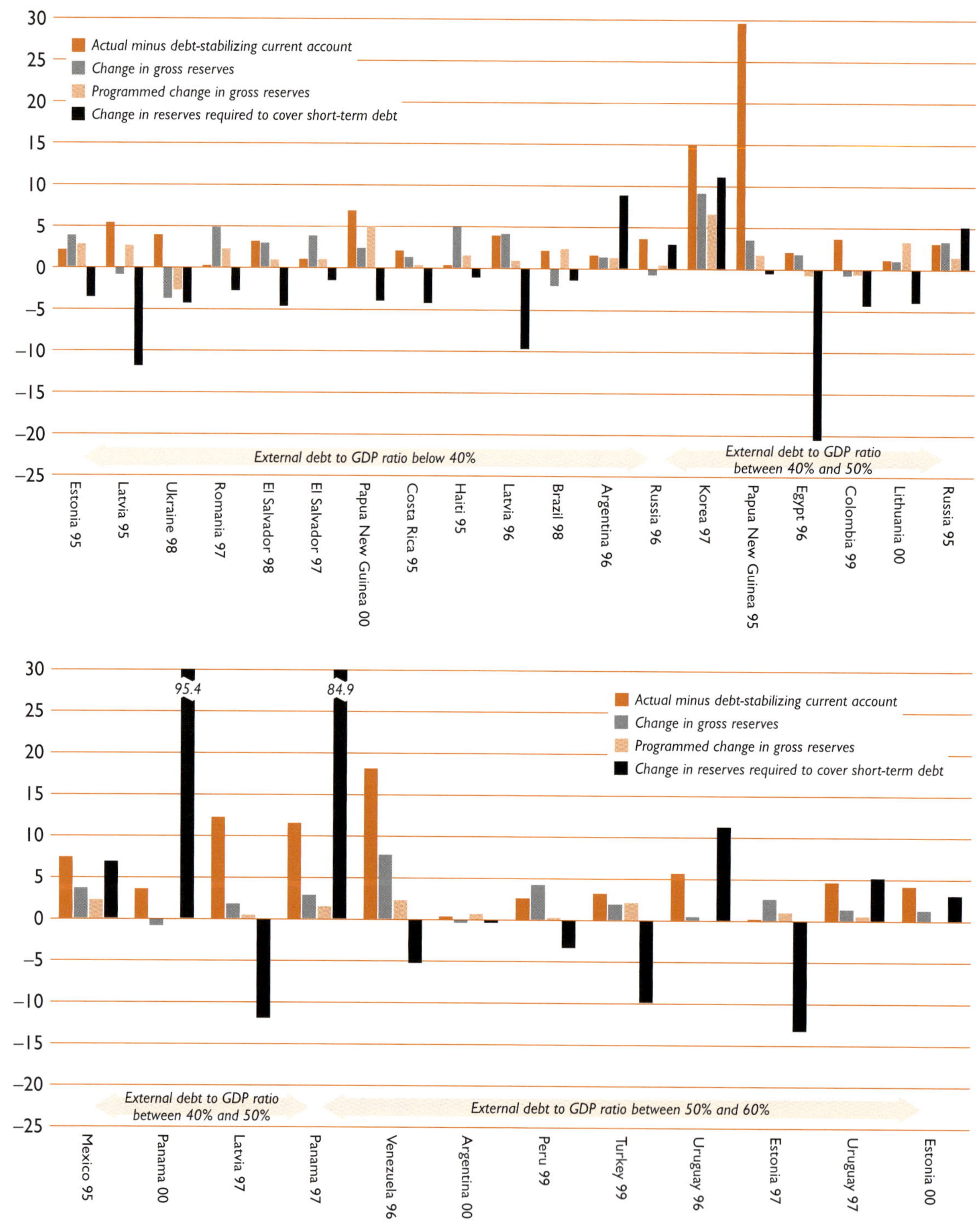

Sources: IMF, MONA, and WEO databases; and IMF staff estimates.

Box 2.5. Economic Impact of External Adjustment

IMF-supported programs may have an effect on the economic impact of any given adjustment, for instance, because the program results in better policy choices or has other beneficial confidence effects.

Consider a standard model for the current account in which the current account balance is posited to depend negatively on income (since higher income raises demand for imports and thus causes the current account balance to deteriorate) and positively on the real exchange rate (where an increase is a depreciation of the real exchange rate) through competitiveness effects: $ca = ca(y, q)$, $ca_y < 0$, and $ca_q > 0$. Differentiating:

$$dy = \frac{dca}{ca_y} - \frac{ca_q dq}{ca_y} \qquad (1)$$

Therefore, a given improvement in the current account $dca < 0$ will be associated with lower activity or growth except to the extent that the country takes part of the adjustment through a real exchange rate depreciation $dq > 0$. The model, as stated, does not allow for any effects of policies or IMF support on the economic impact of a given external adjustment. To examine this possibility, the empirical analog to (1) is estimated, controlling for whether the country undertook the external adjustment in the context of an IMF-supported program. Specifically, a regression of the change in growth rates among middle-income countries on the changes in the current account balance and the real effective exchange rate (both of which are instrumented by their lagged values to address problems of endogeneity), as well as a dummy for an IMF-supported program is estimated. The dependent variable is defined as the change in growth rates between period t+1 and period t–1 to avoid problems of the exact timing of the program.

The econometric results suggest that the existence of an IMF-supported program eases the impact on real growth. This is reflected in the sign and statistical significance of the program dummy. The coefficient is also economically significant: an IMF-supported program leads to growth rates in period t+1 that are, on average, 1 percentage point higher than would have prevailed for a similar external adjustment without an IMF-supported program.

Economic Impact of External Adjustment[1]

Dependent variable: change in growth between t–1 and t+1	(1)	(2)
Change in current account	–0.0021**	–0.0018*
	(–2.07)	(–1.91)
Change in real effective exchange rate	0.5010*	0.4216*
	(1.90)	(1.75)
Program dummy	0.0129***	0.0093***
	(3.02)	(2.66)
Change in growth of major trading partners		0.5626***
		(8.49)
Constant	0.0029	0.0029
	(0.52)	(0.57)
Number of observations	682	670
F statistic	5.8***	31.3***
Standard error of the regression	0.058	0.058

[1]An heteroscedastic error structure is assumed (GLS regression). The t-statistics are in parentheses. Significance at *** 1 percent, ** 5 percent, and * 10 percent levels.

on private flows. In particular, official creditors and donors often rely on the IMF for an assessment of the member's macroeconomic policies, and condition their support on adherence to the policies set under the IMF-supported program. As with private capital flows, however, uncertainty remains about the exact magnitude and timing of official transfers, either because the country does not fulfill the associated policy conditions (including instances where the IMF-supported program goes off-track) or because of shifting priorities of donors or their own budgetary constraints.

Adjustment in Relation to Medium-Term Debt Sustainability

As highlighted earlier, in PRGF-supported programs, the structural transformation of the economy and the promotion of growth and of poverty reduction are key objectives, with the need to maintain external viability acting as an overarching constraint. This is underscored by the inclusion in the programs of some measures such as liberalizing import restrictions that tend to widen the current account deficit in the short run but that help put the economy on a more sustainable path for growth and the balance of payments over the longer term. Outcomes for the external balance in these countries must be viewed in light of these considerations.

Indeed, in terms of the comparison between projections and outcomes for the current account balance, the results for Heavily Indebted Poor Countries (HIPCs) stand in sharp contrast to the experience of GRA-supported programs.[33] The current account bal-

[33]There were six PRGF-supported programs with non-HIPCs, of which, three had current account balances similar to the HIPCs.

ance is generally weaker than projected (about 60 percent of observations are below the 45 degree (line). In the first program year, the difference amounts to 1.7 percent of GDP (Figure 2.10, top panel). Moreover, in contrast with the GRA-supported programs, the difference increases with the time horizon; by the third year it is over 3 percent of GDP. Therefore, averaged over the three program years (Figure 2.10, bottom panel), the current account balance is 2.6 percent of GDP weaker than expected (deficit outcome of 9.2 percent of GDP against a projected deficit of 6.5 percent of GDP).

In large part, the current account balance is weaker than projected because official grants that were expected at the time of the original program failed to materialize in the amounts originally envisioned, although debt-creating official flows were correspondingly higher than expected.[34] Indeed, averaged over the three-year period, the shortfall of official grants to HIPCs amounted to 1.7 percent of GDP a year. This cumulative shortfall was about 1 percentage point of GDP less than the error in projecting the cumulative current account deficits. Thus, notwithstanding a shortfall in official grants, these countries were able to run larger current account deficits than programmed through accumulating external debt.[35]

The larger current account deficit than projected among the PRGF countries resulted from larger government deficits rather than from higher private investment. The difference between the actual and projected fiscal balance amounted to 1.1 percent of GDP, while the domestic investment rate was about ½ percent of GDP lower than programmed, partly offsetting the effects on the current account of the worse-than-expected fiscal position (Figure 2.11). Since the current account shortfall between programmed and actual amounts was estimated at 2.6 percent of GDP, these figures imply that private saving was likely lower than projected.

This finding of weaker external adjustment than programmed is reinforced by the comparison of the projected and debt-stabilizing current account balances (Figure 2.12, top panel).[36] These programs did not envisage generating current account balances that could be expected—given the historical performance of the economy—to stabilize the external debt ratio. Indeed the relationship between initial external debt and projected (or actual) current account adjustment is actually negative, and these results are robust to changes in assumptions (Appendix II). A comparison of the actual and debt-stabilizing current account balances likewise shows that about one-third of HIPCs failed to generate current account balances sufficient to stabilize the external debt ratio (most observations are below the horizontal axis), even though the external debt ratio was already at elevated levels (Figure 2.12, bottom panel).[37] This negative relationship for programs with HIPCs contrasts with the positive relationship for GRA-supported programs. It could be argued, of course, that these calculations do not incorporate anticipated external debt relief under the HIPC Initiative which could be the prime vehicle for achieving external debt stability over this period.[38]

This raises the question of whether IMF-supported programs have paid sufficient attention to debt dynamics. Indeed, even controlling for the debt relief associated with the HIPC Initiative by taking an NPV debt estimate as of end-2004, the results are unchanged. Current account deficits among HIPCs were too large to stabilize their external debt ratios at the lower levels that would prevail following HIPC debt relief, assuming unchanged concessionality rates (Figure 2.13, top panel).[39] On the other hand, if the degree of concessionality rises following the HIPC completion point, the NPV of debt would decline (see Appendix III for more details).

Accordingly, while external debt stocks for PRGF-eligible countries have been declining in relation to GDP during the past decade, this is mostly because of debt relief and debt reductions. The bot-

[34]Of the 1.7 percent of GDP larger than projected current account deficits, 1 percent of GDP is financed by greater borrowing and 0.7 percent of GDP by lower accumulation of reserves than programmed.

[35]If this grant shortfall is viewed as temporary—for instance, a delay in disbursement because of administrative reasons—then a correspondingly larger current account deficit would be warranted as the country borrows against this temporary negative shock. In fact, countries ran a current account deficit that was larger than the shortfall in grant disbursements.

[36]Figure 2.12 is based on the current account balance that stabilizes the face value, rather than the net present value (NPV) of debt. It can be shown, however, that under the assumption that the grant element on the existing stock of debt is approximately constant between two periods, the face-value-stabilizing balance will equal the NPV-stabilizing balance (see Appendix III).

[37]Empirical studies have found that, on average, low-income countries face an increased risk of debt distress at an NPV debt to GDP ratio of 45 percent (IMF, 2004). Assuming an average grant element of 40 percent, this roughly corresponds to a nominal debt ratio of about 80 percent of GDP. This is shown as a vertical line in the figure, though—as with market borrowers—a range of debt levels, rather than a specific level, might be more appropriate given the difficulties of establishing precise thresholds at which debt distress is likely to occur.

[38]The HIPC Initiative was launched in September 1996. As of end-December 2004, 15 countries had reached completion point under the enhanced HIPC Initiative.

[39]For this purpose, the actual debt ratio is replaced by debt ratio after relief in calculating the debt-stabilizing balance, $CA^* = -g^*\overline{npv}$, where g^* is the historical growth rate of the U.S. dollar value of GDP, and where $\overline{npv}$ is the debt ratio that will prevail following debt relief.

Figure 2.10. Current Account Balance in PRGF-Supported Programs: Projections and Outcomes[1]

(In percent of GDP)

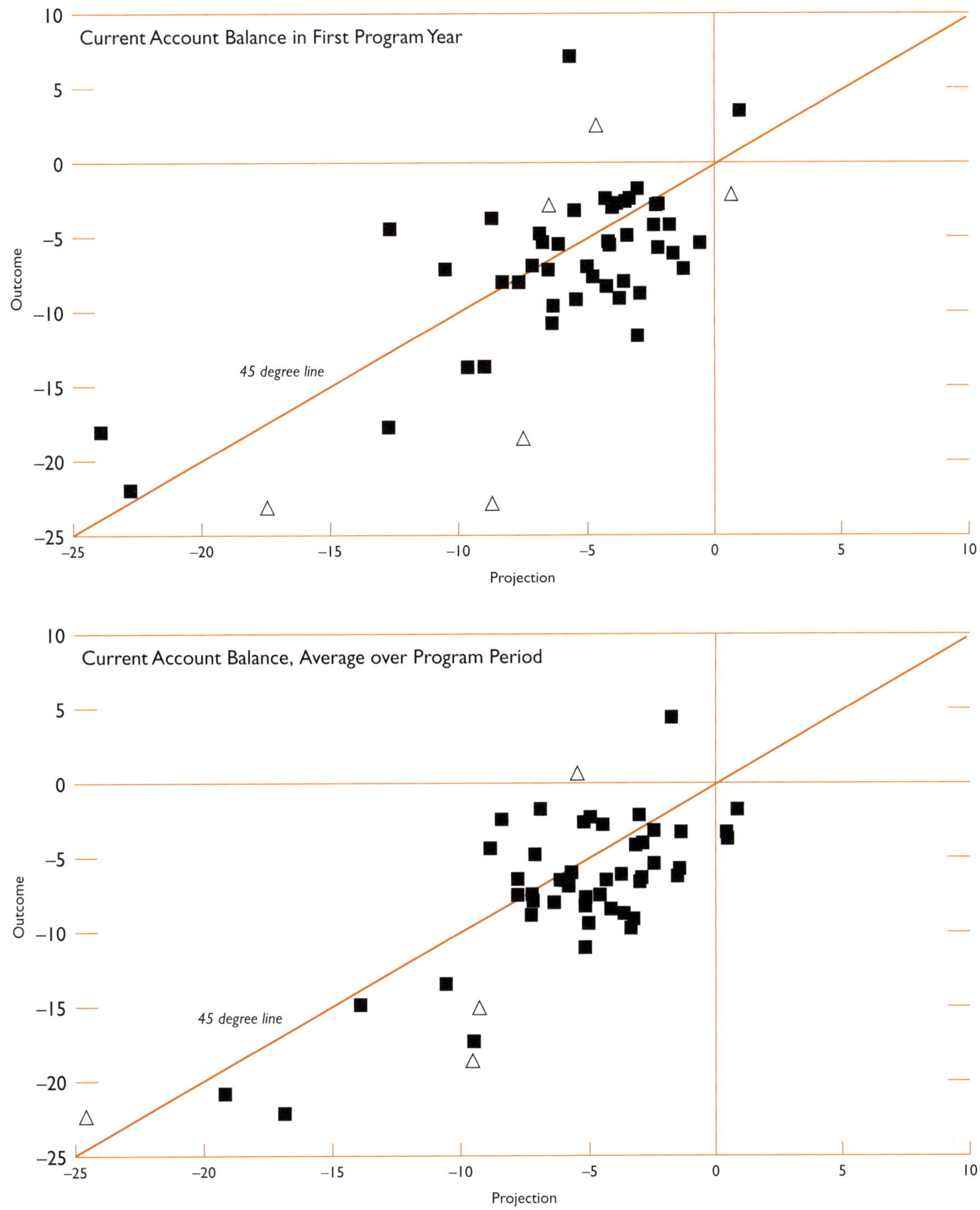

Sources: IMF, MONA and WEO databases; and IMF staff estimates.
Note. See Appendix I for a list of countries.
[1]Non-HIPCs are depicted by triangles.

Figure 2.11. Fiscal Balance and Investment in PRGF-Supported Programs: Projections and Outcomes[1]
(In percent of GDP)

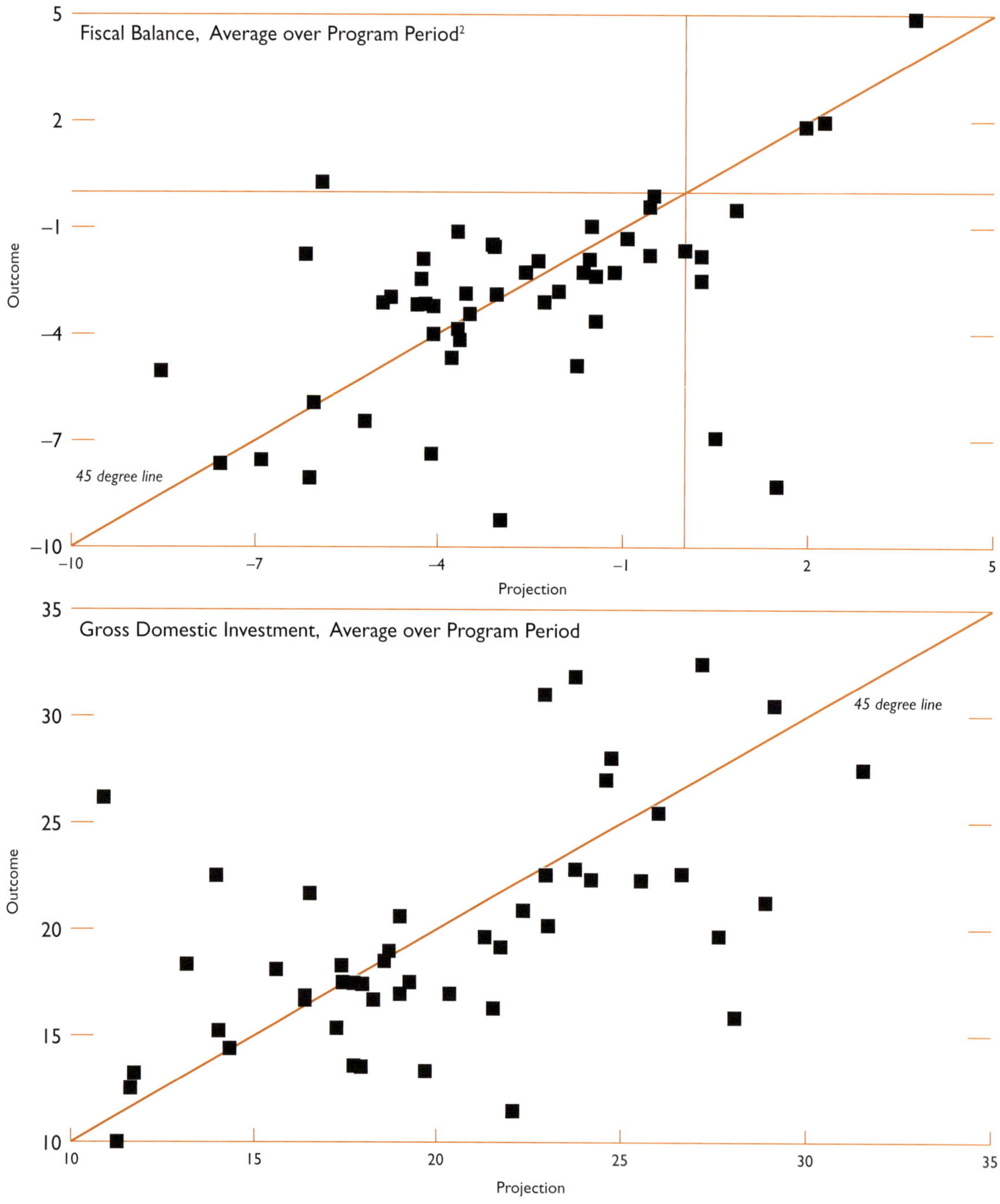

Sources: IMF, MONA and WEO databases; and IMF staff estimates.
Note. See Appendix I for a list of countries.
[1]Fiscal balance includes grants.
[2]Not shown is São Tomé and Príncipe (–21.6 percent of GDP, actual)

Figure 2.12. Projected, Actual, and Debt-Stabilizing Current Account Balances in PRGF-Supported Programs[1]
(In percent of GDP)

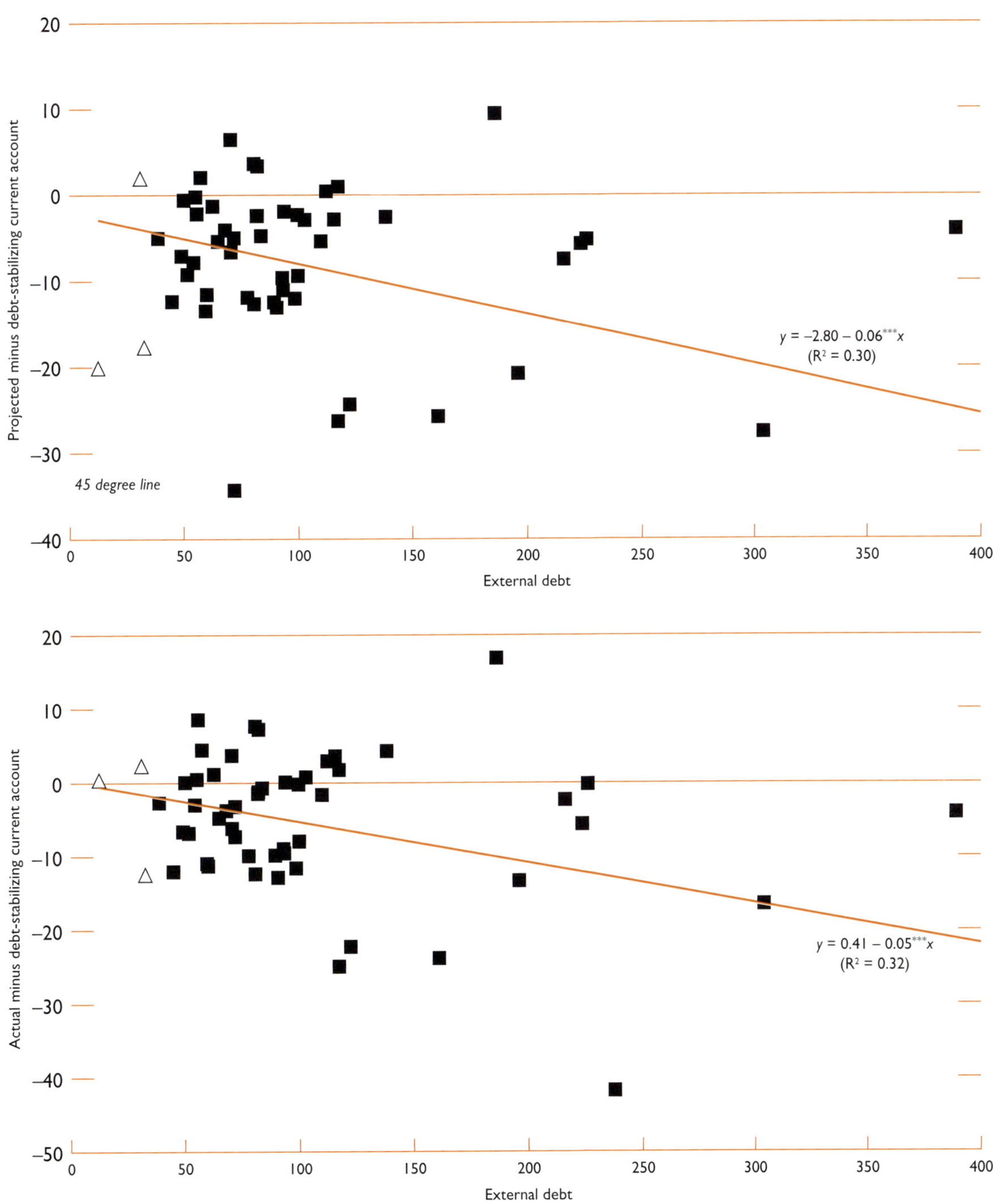

Sources: IMF, MONA and WEO databases; and IMF staff estimates.
Note. See Appendix I for a list of countries.
[1]Non-HIPCs are depicted by triangles; ***significant at 1 percent level.

Figure 2.13. External Adjustment and Debt Relief in PRGF-Supported Programs
(In percent of GDP)

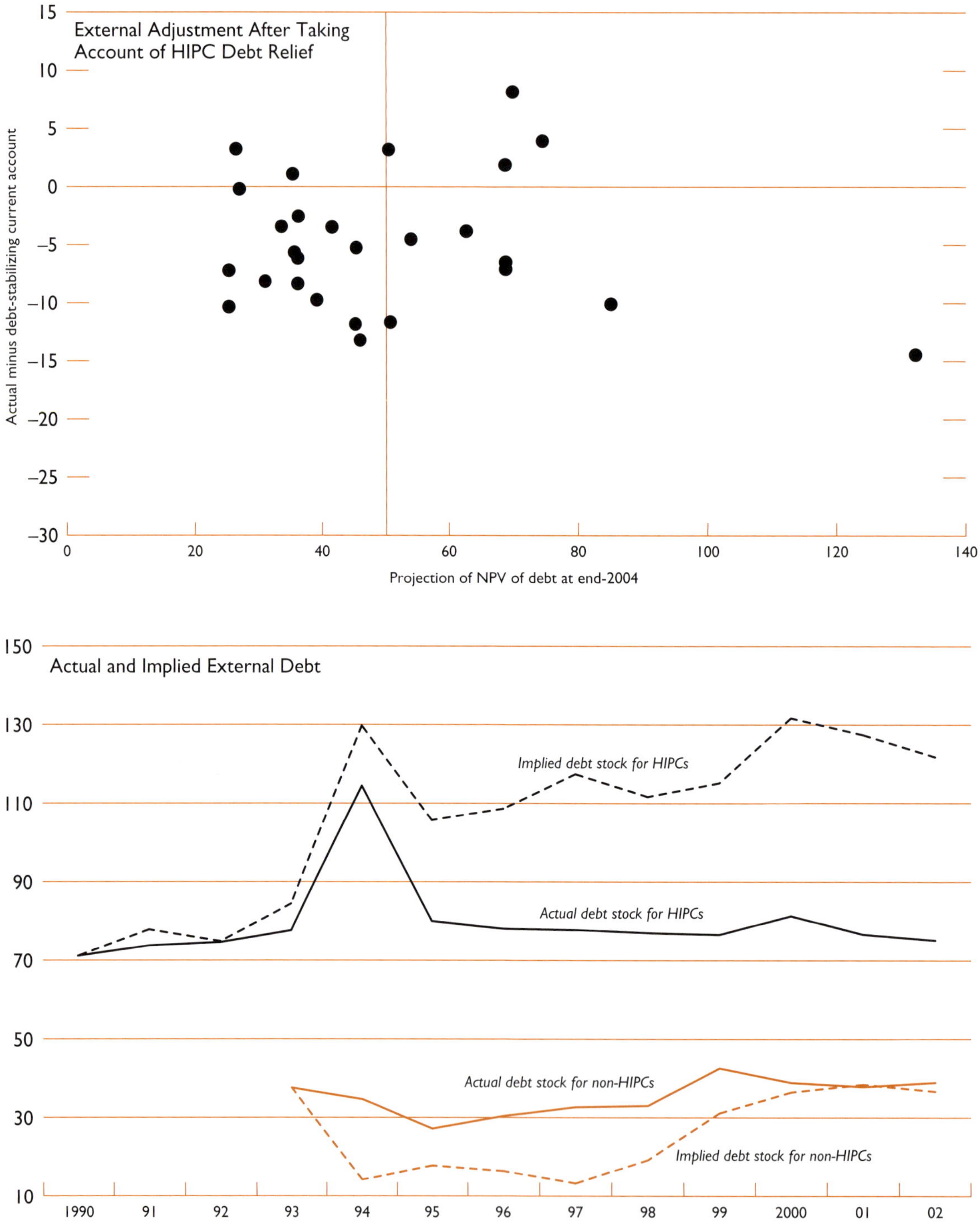

Sources: IMF, MONA and WEO databases; and IMF staff estimates.
Note. See Appendix I for a list of countries.

tom panel of Figure 2.13 compares the actual external debt stock averaged across PRGF countries to the external debt stock implied by cumulating current account deficits (net of FDI)—that is, abstracting from the effects of debt reschedulings or debt relief.[40] For HIPCs, the difference amounts to over 50 percent of GDP by 2002—thus, in absence of debt relief, debt ratios would, on average, have been at least 50 percent of GDP higher. For non-HIPCs with PRGF-supported programs, both the actual debt stock and the implied debt stock follow each other closely.[41]

[40]Indeed, even this counterfactual calculation underestimates the buildup of debt that would have occurred in the absence of debt relief because it is based on actual current account balances rather than the balances that would have prevailed had interest payments been made as scheduled.

[41]Likewise, the difference between the implied and actual debt stock for GRA countries is only 6 percent of GDP, and has remained fairly constant since 1993.

IV Other Macroeconomic Objectives

External adjustment is only one objective—albeit a crucial one—of IMF-supported programs. National authorities, in formulating their reform or adjustment program, may have a variety of other macroeconomic objectives. In some cases, these are directly related to the country's external viability. More generally, however, the authorities' objectives may contribute only indirectly to the external objective, or may actually put additional strain on it. Since these objectives differ across IMF facilities, it is convenient to consider them—and success toward achieving them—separately.[42]

GRA-Supported Programs

An analysis of letters of intent and staff reports suggests that (following external viability) reducing inflation is the most common macroeconomic objective of programs supported by the GRA. Inflation control has been a paramount objective in several Latin American countries (notably Mexico, 1995; Ecuador, 2000; El Salvador, 1995, 1997, and 1998; Uruguay, 1996, 1997, and 1999), as well as in Turkey (1999) and in various transition economies. For programs explicitly attempting to disinflate, inflation declines dramatically from an average of about 600 percent a year (and a median of about 390 percent a year) prior to the program to 25 percent a year during the first program year.

Only four GRA-supported programs (fewer than 10 percent of the total) list growth as one of the program's explicit objectives. These were IMF-supported programs for member countries that were in the lower half of the middle-income group (Egypt, Jordan (2), and Panama—each of which had per capita GDP below $4,000 in the mid-1990s) and each aimed at maintaining GDP growth at about 6 percent a year. Success proved elusive, in that the difference between the preprogram and program period growth rate, while positive, was statistically insignificant, and the actual growth rate was well short of the program target. However, this result needs to be viewed cautiously in light of the small sample size.

Going beyond the immediate program period (and programs that explicitly targeted either disinflation or growth), it is useful to examine more formally the legacy of IMF-supported programs on macroeconomic performance. In doing so, a natural temptation is to try to attribute success or failure in achieving these macroeconomic objectives to whether the program was supported by the IMF. While the academic literature on program evaluation often tries to do so, this runs into some fundamental identification problems because the counterfactual is unknown. In particular, it is difficult to establish whether the authorities would have adopted the same (or similar) policies in the absence of IMF support. Although the literature has attempted various ways of addressing this problem, including the use of control groups, before-and-after comparisons, generalized evaluation estimators, and instrumental variables, none of them is especially convincing.[43] The problem is particularly acute in low-income countries, which typically have successive IMF-supported programs, making it more difficult to identify the policies they would have adopted, and the economic performance that they would have achieved, in the absence of IMF support. Yet, unless the counterfactual can be convincingly established, it is impossible to claim credit or lay blame on the IMF's support of the au-

[42]For the purposes of this section a GRA-supported program applies to countries that were not PRGF eligible as of mid-2003 (and vice versa for PRGF-supported programs). The distinction between "GRA-supported" and "non-PRGF eligible" arises because, particularly in the early 1990s, some low-income countries had either stand-alone Stand-By Arrangements or simultaneous Stand-By and ESAF/PRGF programs. The discussion in this section and the results presented in Table 2.3 classifies these countries as PRGF-supported programs—the assumption is made that the objectives pursued are closer to those of other low-income countries despite their support from GRA resources.

[43]Empirical studies face a number of other problems; Appendix IV surveys the literature.

Table 2.3. Macroeconomic Performance of Countries with IMF-Supported Programs[1]

	Number of Observations	Three Years Before Program	Program Period[2]	Three Years After Program
PRGF-eligible countries				
Inflation[3]				
1980–91	169	68 n.a.	26	73
1992–2002	62	28 n.a.	16*	8***
Real GDP growth[3]				
1980–91	169	2.1 n.a.	2.6	2.4
1992–2002	62	2.4 n.a.	4.1***	3.4*
Standard deviation of growth				
1980–91	169	3.9	3.4	3.2
1992–2002	62	3.0	3.0	2.4
Non-PRGF-eligible countries				
Inflation[3]				
1980–91	104	42 n.a.	72	55
1992–2002	51	80 n.a.	39	27*
Real GDP growth[3]				
1980–91	104	2.7 n.a.	2.0	3.1
1992–2002	51	3.6 n.a.	2.7	3.4
Standard deviation of growth				
1980–91	104	3.7	n.a.	3.5
1992–2002	51	3.0	n.a.	3.0

Sources: IMF, *World Economic Outlook;* and IMF staff estimates.

[1]Average annual growth rates over three-year periods unless otherwise specified.

[2]PRGF-eligible countries: program period is three years and includes the year when the program begins. Non-PRGF-eligible countries: program period is one year—the year the program begins.

[3]Statistical significance of the average rate relative to the preprogram average rate; *** at 1 percent level and * at 10 percent level; n.a. not applicable.

thorities' program. For these reasons, the approach taken here is to try to answer a simpler—and, ultimately, more relevant—question of whether member countries have been broadly successful in achieving macroeconomic goals under their IMF-supported programs, without getting into the finer debate of whether success or failure should be attributed directly to IMF support.

Inflation and growth performance in the three years prior to an IMF-supported program and three years following the completion of an IMF-supported program over the period 1980–2002 are presented in Table 2.3. The sample is split in 1991 because that year corresponds to the end-year of the previous conditionality study. This longer horizon provides a better control for initial conditions which, at least in previous studies, were found to play a major role in the assessment of the effects of IMF-supported programs. One drawback of this methodology is that there may be overlapping IMF arrangements—that is, the postprogram period of one arrangement coincides with the preprogram period of the successor arrangement. While such cases are relatively rare for GRA-supported programs (as defined earlier, i.e., non-PRGF-eligible countries), such overlaps are common for PRGF-supported countries; accordingly, the following analysis treats each program as an individual observation.

During the period 1980–91, GRA-supported programs are associated with a modest sustained increase in growth—from an average of 2.7 percent a year in the three years prior to the program to 3.1 percent a year in the three years following the program—but reflecting the fact that countries often came to the IMF from initial positions of deep macroeconomic distress, there was a marked dip in the growth rate of ¾ percentage point during the first program year (Table 2.3).[44] The experience in the 1990s is broadly similar. The growth rate remains largely the same prior to and following the

[44]This finding is consistent with the Schadler and others (1995).

program at about 3½ percent a year, though again growth dipped (by ¾ percentage point) during the first year of the program. A notable difference to bear in mind is that real growth during the program period was ¾ percentage point higher during 1992–03 than it was during 1980–91.

These GRA-supported programs also made important progress in achieving disinflation. Over the period 1992–2002, inflation fell in the non-PRGF-eligible sample from 80 percent a year during the three years prior to the program to an average of 27 percent a year in the three years following the program. This improved inflation performance is statistically significant. This outcome contrasts with the experience during 1980–91 when inflation rose during the program period before falling back to its preprogram level.

Finally, among the set of GRA countries, a number of recent programs have focused on enhancing policy credibility with a view to achieving sustainability of public debt dynamics, in part because of the potential for a funding crisis to spill over to the balance of payments even if there are no immediate external financing difficulties. IMF support of a member's program (including through conditionality) may enhance policy credibility that, in turn, is likely to be reflected in lower interest rates and spreads, making it easier to achieve debt sustainability. Nevertheless, credibility cannot substitute for adjustment and consistency of policies with program objectives. By underscoring the commitment of the authorities, it can, however, complement their adjustment efforts, lending credibility to their intentions to carry through the necessary adjustment.

Turkey (1999) and Brazil (2002) are cases in point. In both countries, the authorities undertook to carry out the requisite fiscal adjustment to achieve primary surpluses that were expected—under reasonable assumptions about growth and interest rates—to stabilize the public debt ratio (Box 2.6). On the other hand, the experience of Argentina points to some drawbacks of trying to use IMF support to enhance the credibility of the authorities' policies. In particular, the possibility exists that the IMF's "seal of approval" may lead markets to underestimate risks and to continue to provide financing even in the absence of sufficient adjustment.

ESAF- and PRGF-Supported Programs

PRGF programs target a number of country-specific intermediate objectives (including those identified by the Poverty Reduction Strategy Paper), but the key underlying objective is to raise growth and reduce poverty. IMF-supported programs in the transition economies likewise targeted an improvement in the long-run growth performance of the economy (Box 2.7). While it is difficult to assess systematically progress in poverty reduction without time series on household surveys, recent research suggests that real GDP growth provides a reasonable proxy.[45]

During the 1980s, IMF-supported programs among (ESAF-) PRGF-eligible countries were not associated with a durable increase in growth. Growth fluctuated between 2 percent and 2¼ percent in the three years prior to an IMF-supported program and three years following the program (Table 2.3). During the 1990s, however, this relationship has changed significantly—the growth rate has risen dramatically from 2½ percent to over 4 percent a year during IMF-supported programs. Moreover, only some of this gain appears to dissipate after the three-year program period, since growth remains as much as 1 percentage point above its preprogram rate. The increase relative to the preprogram period is statistically significant. As discussed below, the improved growth performance likely reflects both better macroeconomic policies and a more benign domestic and external environment.

Inflation in countries with PRGF-supported programs declined from an average of 28 percent a year in the three years preceding the program to 16 percent during the program period and to 8 percent a year following the program (Table 2.3). This improved inflation performance is statistically significant and is likely to have resulted in an improvement in income distribution as well as a boost to growth.[46]

[45]For instance, Deininger and Squire (1996) and Dollar and Kraay (2001) argue that the poor benefit more from increasing aggregate output than by reducing inequality through redistribution. Moreover, Ravaillon and Chen (1997) have found that changes in inequality are uncorrelated with changes in average living standards. Quah (2001) argues, based on an analysis of India and China, that improvement in living standards due to aggregate economic growth overwhelms any deterioration due to increases in inequality. To evaluate the association between real GDP and poverty, the poverty indicator based on the fraction of the population living on less than $2 a day was correlated with the level of real GDP per capita in 1995. When purchasing power parity deflators are used for the real GDP calculation, the correlation coefficient is –0.7, whereas when the current exchange rate is used, the correlation coefficient is –0.6. Either measure of real output therefore appears to be (inversely) related to poverty.

[46]This inverse relationship between inflation and income inequality is documented in Bulíř and Gulde (2000) and Bulíř (2001).

As discussed above, it is difficult to establish whether this improvement in growth should be attributed to the IMF-supported programs. A more modest goal is to try to understand the factors behind this improved performance using a regression of the change in real per capita GDP growth on a number of variables typically found in growth regressions—indicators of initial conditions, and changes in exogenous shocks, macroeconomic policies, and structural reforms. This analysis (Table 2.4) suggests that macroeconomic policies played an important role in the increase in growth during the 1990s, notably through improvements in the fiscal balance during the program period and continued disinflation over the longer term. It appears that internal and external shocks have also been supportive of growth in developing countries during the 1990s. These results are subject to the usual caveats: problems of potential endogeneity in the country's participation in an IMF-supported program and the omission of sufficient controls. However, the decomposition of the improvement in growth is robust to the use of country effects. Notwithstanding these qualifiers, the results suggest that IMF-supported programs have at least provided a framework for sound macroeconomic management, contributing to the better growth performance.[47]

[47]A similar equation for upper- and lower-middle-income countries (non-PRGF countries) with IMF-supported programs yields slightly larger coefficients for growth of G-7 countries and for macroeconomic indicators. The coefficients on the effects of internal and external shocks are similar to those of PRGF-eligible countries, but they appear to play a less important role in explaining changes in growth. This may reflect a more diversified structure of the economy.

Box 2.6. Policy-Credibility Programs: The Cases of Turkey (1999) and Brazil (2002)

There have been a few cases of IMF-supported programs whose primary purpose is to bolster the credibility of authorities' efforts in achieving public debt sustainability rather than external adjustment. Among these are Turkey (1999) and Brazil (2002). In Turkey's case, the commitment entailed in signing a letter of intent and seeking IMF financial support elicited a very favorable market response even before the actual policies were put in place. Upon signing of the letter of intent (which specified, inter alia, a significant fiscal adjustment) interest rates on treasury bills fell markedly from about 95 percent a year prior to program discussions to 75 percent at the signing of the letter and to 50 percent by the time of Board approval (see figure). Interest rates continued their downward trajectory, aided by the quasi-currency-board arrangement, until the November 2000 banking-cum-currency crisis when the credibility of the whole program was called into question. The sharp decline in interest rates implied significant fiscal savings to the government and contributed to putting the public debt dynamics on a sounder footing. While it is difficult to prove that the decline of interest rates stemmed from the IMF's imprimatur on the authorities' program, it is noteworthy that an earlier attempt at disinflation in 1998—without the umbrella of an IMF arrangement—had resulted in very high ex post real interest rates that compounded adverse debt dynamics and low growth, as the authorities' program lacked credibility.

Brazil's experience, while similar, is rather less clear-cut. The announcement of the new program in early August 2002 led to some improvement in the authorities' credibility that they intended to continue prudent fiscal policies, including under a scenario in which the administration might change at the forthcoming election (it is noteworthy that all four presidential candidates endorsed the IMF-supported program, albeit with somewhat different degrees of commitment). The positive effect proved short-lived, however, and market concerns were rekindled in late September and early October 2002, when a change of administration became increasingly apparent. A durable reduction in spreads only happened as markets gained confidence in the new administration's commitment to adhere to the primary surplus target of 3¾ percent of GDP. Again, the effects of IMF support are difficult to gauge, but the markets seemed to attach at least some importance to the fact that the new program, announced in August 2002, would cover 2003, the first year of the new administration.

In contrast, it is likely that the IMF's continued engagement with Argentina undermined its own credibility. It is noteworthy that Argentina's sovereign bond spreads and the differential between on-shore peso and dollar deposits began to widen appreciably only in 2001—long after fiscal and current account targets had been repeatedly breached. Continued financing by the capital markets allowed for a buildup of debt and vulnerabilities, raising the ultimate cost of the crisis when it erupted. These developments led to questions about the IMF's own credibility, perhaps impinging on the beneficial confidence effects that IMF support will be able to provide in future programs.

Box 2.6 *(concluded)*

Interest Rates, Spreads, and Implied Probability of Sovereign Defaults: Brazil and Turkey

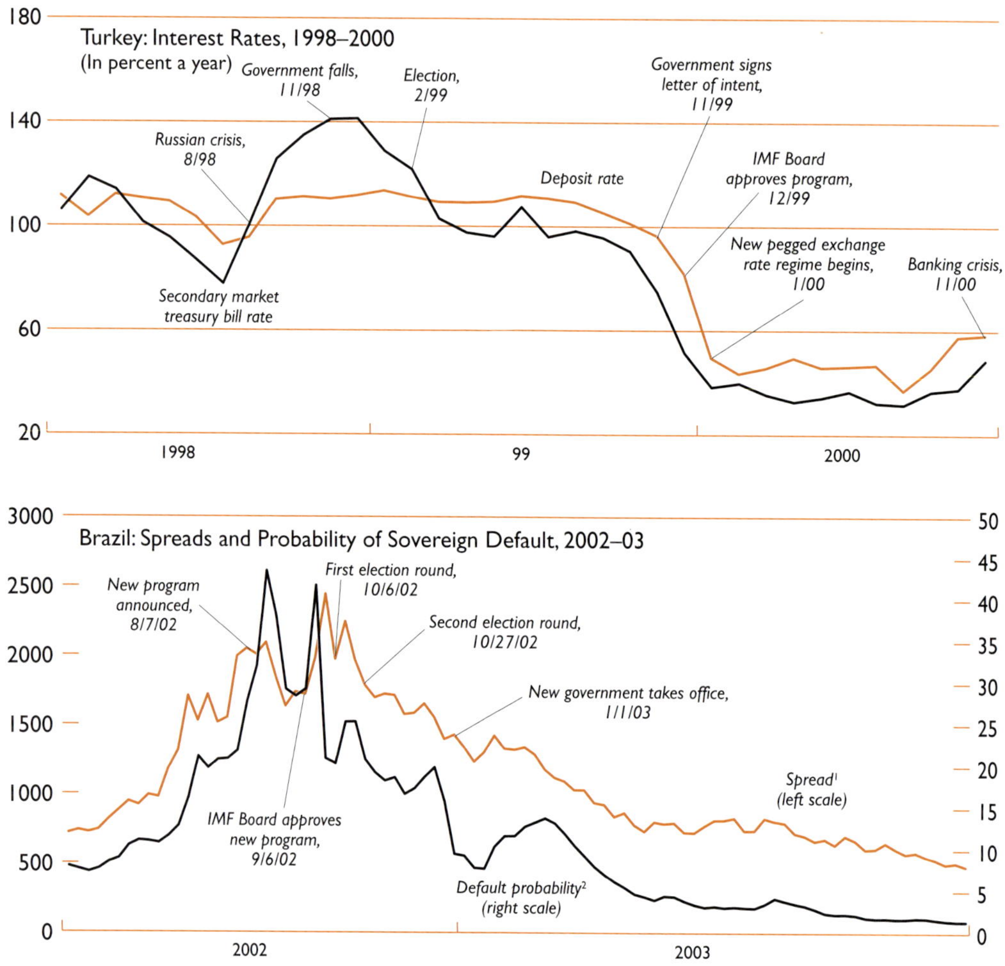

Sources: IMF, WEO database and *International Financial Statistics;* and IMF staff estimates.
[1]Brazil EMBI in basis points.
[2]One-year ahead implied probability of default in percent.

Box 2.7. Growth and External Viability in Transition Economies

Prior to the initiation of IMF-supported programs with transition countries, economic conditions in these countries had been deteriorating for some time. As a result, standard measures of success based on performance before and after IMF-supported programs are inadequate. Since the ultimate objective is to help economies wean themselves off the need for IMF financial support, one yardstick of success is to identify how many of them had stopped requiring IMF financial assistance over the past decade. Another yardstick of success is the extent to which these countries have returned to the output levels that they started with when they initiated the process of reform and, in particular, if they have done so without building up excessively their debt levels.

On the first yardstick of success, six transition countries have not required IMF support since 2001; these countries are the Czech Republic, Hungary, Poland, and the three Baltic states (Estonia, Latvia, and Lithuania). Output has rebounded in most of these countries to or above the level of output recorded in 1991, when many of these countries initiated their reforms (see figure). The two exceptions are Latvia and Lithuania, though growth performance in these countries has picked up over the past few years. Moreover, all six countries have similar levels of GDP per capita and all entered the European Union in May 2004.

On the second measure—reaching the original output level without sacrificing debt sustainability—the results are mixed. Among countries with stable debt levels are Albania, Belarus, Romania, Turkmenistan, and Uzbekistan, all of which have been successful in overcoming the initial output losses.[1] In contrast, while Armenia, Azerbaijan, Bulgaria, Kazakhstan, Russia, and Ukraine have achieved debt sustainability, they have not been able to recover all of the initial output losses. A sharper contrast is observed among countries that have built up large debts over the past decade, mainly to the international financial institutions, and now must adopt tight economic policies—in fact, this tightening has led to a downward debt trajectory since 1999. These countries include Georgia, the Kyrgyz Republic, Moldova, and Tajikistan, which are among the poorest transition economies.

[1]It is arguable whether Uzbekistan's debt-to-GDP ratio is stable, since it has been rising continuously since the mid-1990s but it is still below the standard sustainability thresholds.

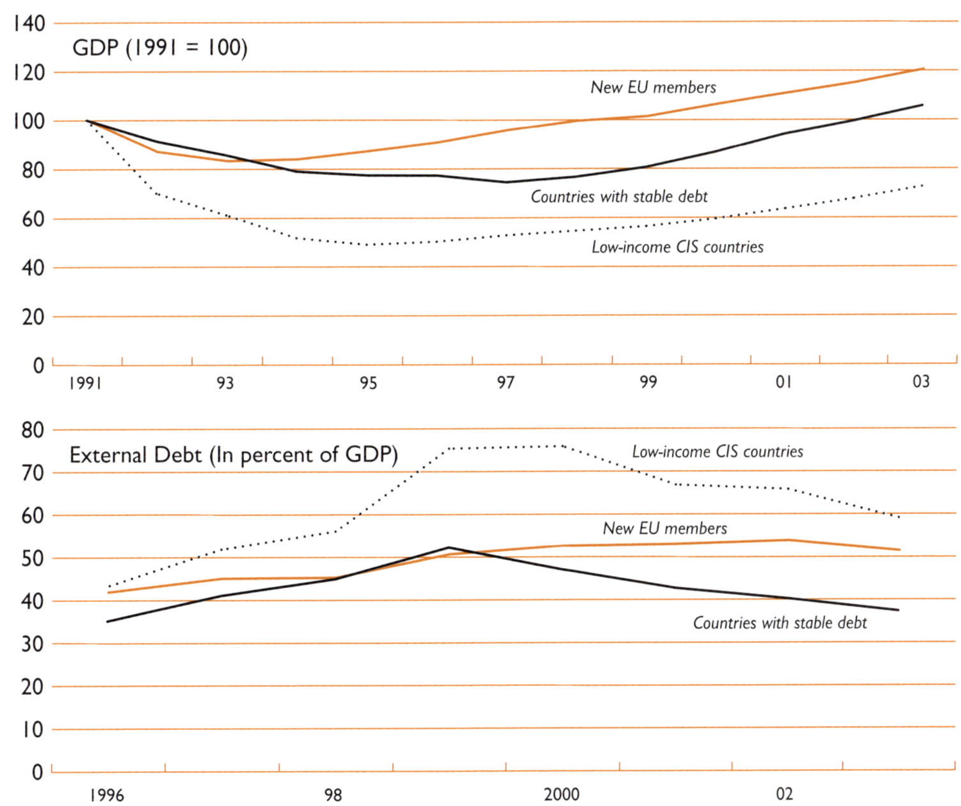

Table 2.4. Explaining Growth in PRGF Countries, 1992–2002
(Average annual growth rates)

	Coefficient Estimates	Three Years Preceding Program		Three-Year Program		Three Years Following Program
Real GDP per capita growth		–0.56		1.34		0.68
Change in per capita growth			1.90		–0.66	
Contributing factors						
G-7 real GDP growth	0.6828***		0.50		0.10	
Initial conditions						
Of which						
Initial income level	–0.0595***		–0.27		–0.37	
Fertility rates	–0.0090		0.25		0.24	
Macro policies						
Of which						
Inflation	–0.0376***		0.02		0.22	
Fiscal balance	0.1360***		0.29		–0.01	
Structural reforms	0.0285**		0.08		0.01	
Shocks (internal and external)						
Of which						
Domestic shocks	–0.0409***		0.50		–0.06	
Terms of trade	0.0247		0.08		–0.02	
Constant	0.0052*		0.52		0.52	
Unexplained			–0.08		–1.29	
Number of observations	162		46		46	
Number of countries	46		31		31	
R-squared adjusted	0.23					
F statistic	26.21***					
Standard error of regression	0.039					

Sources: IMF, *World Economic Outlook;* and IMF staff estimates.
Note. Asterisks indicate statistically significant coefficient estimates; *** at 1 percent, ** at 5 percent, and * at 10 percent levels.

V Conclusions

The original conception of an IMF-supported program was to solve temporary balance of payments problems in a world of limited capital mobility and fixed exchange rates. The main objective of these programs is thus restoring external viability, a precondition for reducing inflation and restoring macroeconomic stability and growth. While this traditional adjustment paradigm remains relevant for many IMF-supported programs, the past decade has seen important evolutions in the objectives and design of IMF-supported programs. Capital account crises have brought external adjustment into sharper relief and called for a flexible policy response as the priority shifts from inducing adjustment to preventing excessive adjustment. For low-income countries supported by PRGF resources, as well as the early transition economy programs, the emphasis has been more on structural transformation, poverty reduction, and growth promotion than on external adjustment.

Since the use of IMF resources adds to the country's obligations, the purpose of IMF financial support is to achieve an appropriate time profile of external adjustment, trading off the short-run impact on output and activity against longer-term considerations of debt sustainability. Experience differs between GRA- and PRGF-supported programs.

Overall, among GRA-supported programs, the results suggest that external adjustment was consistent with that required by medium-term debt sustainability. There is a positive relationship between the degree of external adjustment and the initial level of the external debt-to-GDP ratio. Some countries, however, adjusted by more than envisaged by the program or than indicated by consideration of debt sustainability as capital inflows failed to materialize in the short run and the availability of official financing was limited. While in some cases this adjustment was partly directed at building up reserves, in others, the external adjustment was considerably higher than the reserves buildup. This external adjustment generally reflected investment and output compression. Nevertheless, tentative findings suggest that countries managed to achieve a given improvement in the current account at lower cost to growth than countries adjusting outside of an IMF-supported program.

For PRGF-supported programs in HIPCs, current account balances have fallen well short of the balances necessary to stabilize debt ratios, implying significantly higher debt ratios in the absence of debt relief. Moreover, the positive relationship between initial debt ratios and both programmed and actual current account balances evident in GRA-supported programs does not hold for these countries. Among these countries, the PRGF-supported programs have been geared more toward achieving external viability over the longer term, including by removing trade distortions and fostering growth.

Turning to other objectives, countries have seen marked and durable reductions in inflation under GRA- and PRGF-supported programs in contrast to the experience in the 1980s. Moreover, countries with PRGF-supported programs in the 1990s have also seen significant improvements in growth performance, attributable to better macroeconomic policies and to faster growth in major industrial countries.

The findings of this paper raise questions about the success of IMF-supported programs in achieving an appropriate balance between financing and adjustment. For GRA-supported countries, there have been a number of cases—most notably capital account crises—where external adjustment was more abrupt than anticipated, including because the authorities' policy response was insufficient to engender a rapid return of confidence and reflow of capital. For PRGF-supported programs, the focus on improved growth performance rather than on current account adjustment has been reflected in a sustained rise in the growth rate but at the cost of requiring debt relief to keep external debt to manageable levels. In future, maintaining this growth performance without a buildup of debt will likely require policies focused on strengthening the current account position and greater concessionality of official flows.

Appendix I IMF-Supported Programs, 1995–2000

IMF-Supported Programs: General Resources Account, 1995–2000

Country	Arrangement Type	Approval Date	End Date
GRA-Supported Nontransition Countries			
Algeria	EFF	May 1995	May 1998
Argentina	SBA	Apr. 1996	Jan. 1998
Argentina	EFF	Feb. 1998	Feb. 2001
Argentina	SBA	Mar. 2000	Mar. 2003
Brazil	SBA	Dec. 1998	Dec. 2001
Cape Verde	SBA	Feb. 1998	Apr. 1999
Colombia	EFF	Dec. 1999	Dec. 2002
Costa Rica	SBA	Nov. 1995	Feb. 1997
Ecuador	SBA	Apr. 2000	Apr. 2001
Egypt	SBA	Oct. 1996	Sep. 1998
El Salvador	SBA	July 1995	Sep. 1996
El Salvador	SBA	Feb. 1997	Apr. 1998
El Salvador	SBA	Sep. 1998	Feb. 2000
Gabon	EFF	Nov. 1995	Nov. 1998
Gabon	SBA	Oct. 2000	Apr. 2002
Indonesia	SBA	Nov. 1997	Nov. 2000
Indonesia	EFF	Aug. 1998	Nov. 2000
Indonesia	EFF	Feb. 2000	Dec. 2002
Jordan	EFF	Feb. 1996	Feb. 1999
Jordan	EFF	Apr. 1999	Apr. 2002
Korea	SBA	Dec. 1997	Dec. 2000
Lesotho	SBA	July 1995	June 1996
Lesotho	SBA	Sep. 1996	Sep. 1997
Mexico	SBA	Feb. 1995	Aug. 1996
Mexico	SBA	July 1999	Nov. 2000
Nigeria	SBA	Aug. 2000	Aug. 2001
Panama	SBA	Nov. 1995	Mar. 1997
Panama	EFF	Dec. 1997	Dec. 2000
Panama	SBA	June 2000	Feb. 2002
Papua New Guinea	SBA	July 1995	Jan. 1997
Papua New Guinea	SBA	Mar. 2000	May 2001
Peru	EFF	July 1996	Mar. 1999
Peru	EFF	June 1999	May 2002
Philippines	SBA	Apr. 1998	Mar. 2000
Thailand	SBA	Aug. 1997	June 2000
Turkey	SBA	Dec. 1999	Dec. 2002
Uruguay	SBA	Mar. 1996	Apr. 1997
Uruguay	SBA	June 1997	Mar. 1999
Uruguay	SBA	Mar. 1999	Mar. 2000
Uruguay	SBA	May 2000	Mar. 2002
Venezuela	SBA	July 1996	July 1997
Zimbabwe	SBA	June 1998	June 1999
Zimbabwe	SBA	Aug. 1999	Oct. 2000

Country	Arrangement Type	Approval Date	End Date
GRA-Supported Capital Account Crises Countries			
Argentina	SBA	Apr. 1996	Jan. 1998
Argentina	SBA	Mar. 2000	Mar. 2003
Brazil	SBA	Dec. 1998	Dec. 2001
Indonesia	EFF	Aug. 1998	Nov. 2000
Korea	SBA	Dec. 1997	Dec. 2000
Mexico	SBA	Feb. 1995	Aug. 1996
Thailand	SBA	Aug. 1997	Jun. 2000
Turkey	SBA	Dec. 1999	Dec. 2002
GRA-Supported Transition Countries			
Belarus	SBA	Sep. 1995	Sep. 1996
Bulgaria	SBA	July 1996	Mar. 1998
Bulgaria	SBA	Apr. 1997	June 1998
Bulgaria	EFF	Sep. 1998	Sep. 2001
Croatia	EFF	Mar. 1997	Mar. 2000
Estonia	SBA	Apr. 1995	July 1996
Estonia	SBA	July 1996	Aug. 1997
Estonia	SBA	Dec. 1997	Mar. 1999
Estonia	SBA	Mar. 2000	Aug. 2001
Hungary	SBA	Mar. 1996	Feb. 1998
Kazakhstan	SBA	June 1995	June 1996
Kazakhstan	EFF	July 1996	July 1999
Kazakhstan	EFF	Dec. 1999	Dec. 2002
Latvia	SBA	Apr. 1995	May 1996
Latvia	SBA	May 1996	Aug. 1997
Latvia	SBA	Oct. 1997	Apr. 1999
Latvia	SBA	Dec. 1999	Apr. 2001
Lithuania	SBA	Mar. 2000	June 2001
Macedonia, FYR	SBA	May 1995	June 1996
Macedonia, FYR	EFF	Nov. 2000	Nov. 2003
Romania	SBA	Apr. 1997	May 1998
Romania	SBA	Aug. 1999	Mar. 2000
Russia	SBA	Apr. 1995	Mar. 1996
Russia	EFF	Mar. 1996	Mar. 1999
Russia	SBA	July 1999	Dec. 2000
Ukraine	SBA	Apr. 1995	Apr. 1996
Ukraine	SBA	May 1996	Feb. 1997
Ukraine	SBA	Aug. 1997	Aug. 1998
Ukraine	EFF	Sep. 1998	Sep. 2001
Uzbekistan	SBA	Dec. 1995	Mar. 1997

IMF-Supported Programs: Poverty Reduction and Growth Facility, 1995–2000

Country	Arrangement Type	Approval Date	End Date
PRGF-Supported Nontransition Countries			
Benin	ESAF	Aug. 1996	Aug. 1999
Benin	PRGF	July 2000	July 2003
Bolivia	ESAF	Sep. 1998	Sep. 2001
Burkina Faso	ESAF	June 1996	June 1999
Burkina Faso	ESAF	Sep. 1999	Sep. 2002
Cambodia	ESAF	Oct. 1999	Oct. 2002
Cameroon	ESAF	Aug. 1997	Aug. 2000
Cameroon	PRGF	Dec. 2000	Dec. 2003
Central African Rep.	ESAF	July 1998	July 2001
Chad	ESAF	Sep. 1995	Aug. 1998
Chad	PRGF	Jan. 2000	Jan. 2003
Congo, Rep. of	ESAF	June 1996	June 1997
Côte d'Ivoire	ESAF	Mar. 1998	Mar. 2001
Djibouti	PRGF	Oct. 1999	Oct. 2002
Ethiopia	ESAF	Oct. 1996	Oct. 1999
Gambia, The	ESAF	June 1998	June 2001
Ghana	ESAF	June 1995	June 1998
Ghana	ESAF	May 1999	May 2002
Guinea	ESAF	Jan. 1997	Jan. 2000
Guinea-Bissau	ESAF	Jan. 1995	Jan. 1998
Guinea-Bissau	PRGF	Dec. 2000	Dec. 2003
Guyana	ESAF	July 1998	July 2001
Haiti	ESAF	Oct. 1996	Oct. 1999
Honduras	ESAF	Mar. 1999	Mar. 2002
Kenya	ESAF	Apr. 1996	Apr. 1999
Kenya	PRGF	Aug. 2000	Aug. 2003
Madagascar	ESAF	Nov. 1996	Nov. 1999
Malawi	ESAF	Oct. 1995	Oct. 1998
Malawi	PRGF	Dec. 2000	Dec. 2003
Mali	ESAF	Apr. 1996	Apr. 1999
Mali	ESAF	Aug. 1999	Aug. 2002
Mauritania	ESAF	Jan. 1995	Jan. 1998
Mauritania	ESAF	July 1999	July 2002
Mozambique	ESAF	June 1996	June 1998
Mozambique	ESAF	June 1999	June 2002
Nicaragua	ESAF	Mar. 1998	Mar. 2001
Niger	ESAF	June 1996	June 1999
Niger	PRGF	Dec. 2000	Dec. 2003
Pakistan	ESAF	Oct. 1997	Oct. 2000
Rwanda	ESAF	June 1998	June 2001
São Tomé and Príncipe	PRGF	Apr. 2000	Apr. 2003
Senegal	ESAF	Apr. 1998	Apr. 2001
Tanzania	ESAF	Nov. 1996	Nov. 1999
Tanzania	PRGF	Mar. 2000	Mar. 2003
Uganda	ESAF	Nov. 1997	Nov. 2000
Yemen, Rep. of	ESAF	Oct. 1997	Oct. 2000
Zambia	ESAF	Dec. 1995	Dec. 1998
Zambia	ESAF	Mar. 1999	Mar. 2002

Country	Arrangement Type	Approval Date	End Date
PRGF-Supported Transition Countries			
Azerbaijan	ESAF	Dec. 1996	Dec. 1999
Georgia	ESAF	Feb. 1996	Feb. 1999
Kyrgyz Republic	ESAF	June 1998	June 2001
Moldova	PRGF	Dec. 2000	Dec. 2003
Mongolia	ESAF	July 1997	July 2000
Tajikistan	ESAF	June 1998	June 2001

Appendix II Robustness of the Analysis of the Debt-Stabilizing Current Account

Figures 2.8 and 2.12 of the text compare actual and debt-stabilizing current account balances for GRA- and PRGF-supported countries. This appendix elaborates on those results. The appendix first discusses the robustness of the results under alternative assumptions underlying the calculation of the debt-stabilizing balance as well as excluding transition economies.

Robustness of Calculation of the Debt-Stabilizing Balance

In the calculations underlying the debt-stabilizing current account, long-run growth is estimated as the historical average of growth in U.S. dollars for the five years prior to the commencement of the IMF-supported program. To ascertain whether this result is robust to changes in assumptions, alternative debt-stabilizing current account estimates are derived based on four specifications:

- Using a 10-year average for growth centered on the first year of the program;
- Using a 10-year historical average for growth;
- Limiting the sample to nontransition countries; and
- Using a 3-year average for the actual current account in percent of GDP.

As shown in Figure 2.A1, the proportion of observations in each of the six categories (classified according to the initial level of debt and whether the current account balance exceeds the debt-stabilizing balance) is very similar to the proportions reported in Figure 2.8 of the text. As such, the broad conclusions about adjustment reported in the text appear robust to alternative assumptions for the underlying calculations.

For the PRGF countries, an alternative debt-stabilizing current account estimate is derived based on a 10-year average for growth centered on the first year of the program. As for the GRA programs, the results of the baseline scenario are robust to changes in the assumptions since the negative relationship between the current account overadjustment and the external debt ratio remains (Figure 2.A2).

Figure 2.A1. Sensitivity Analysis on Debt-Stabilizing Current Account Balances in GRA-Supported Programs[1]

(In percent of GDP)

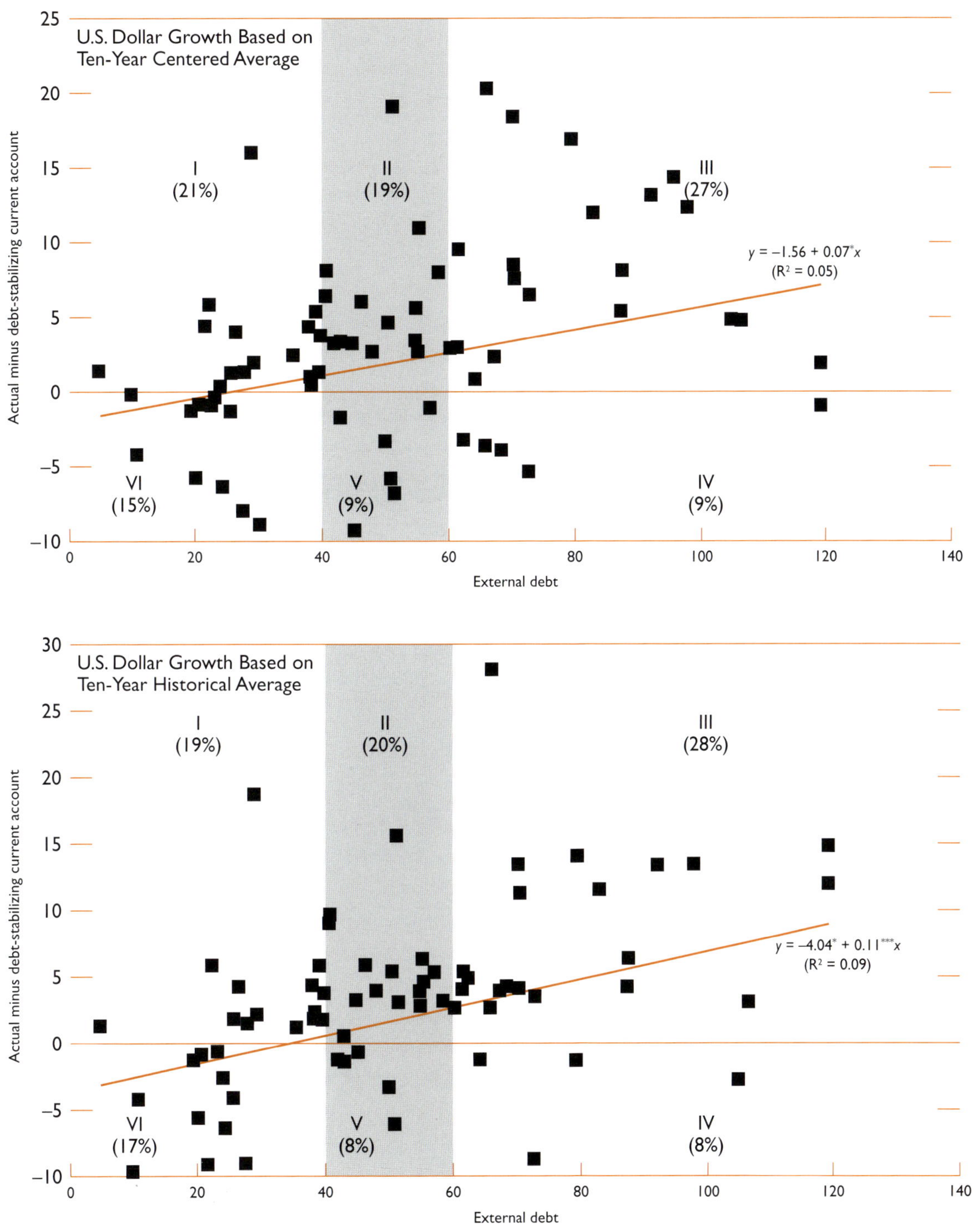

Figure 2.A1 (*concluded*)

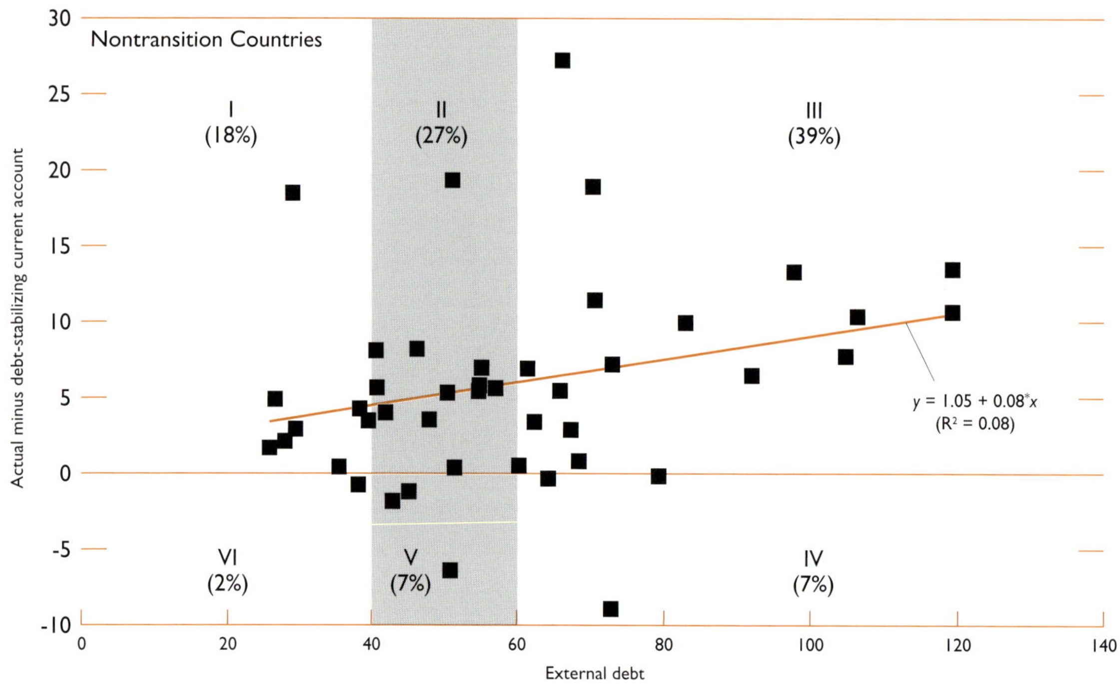

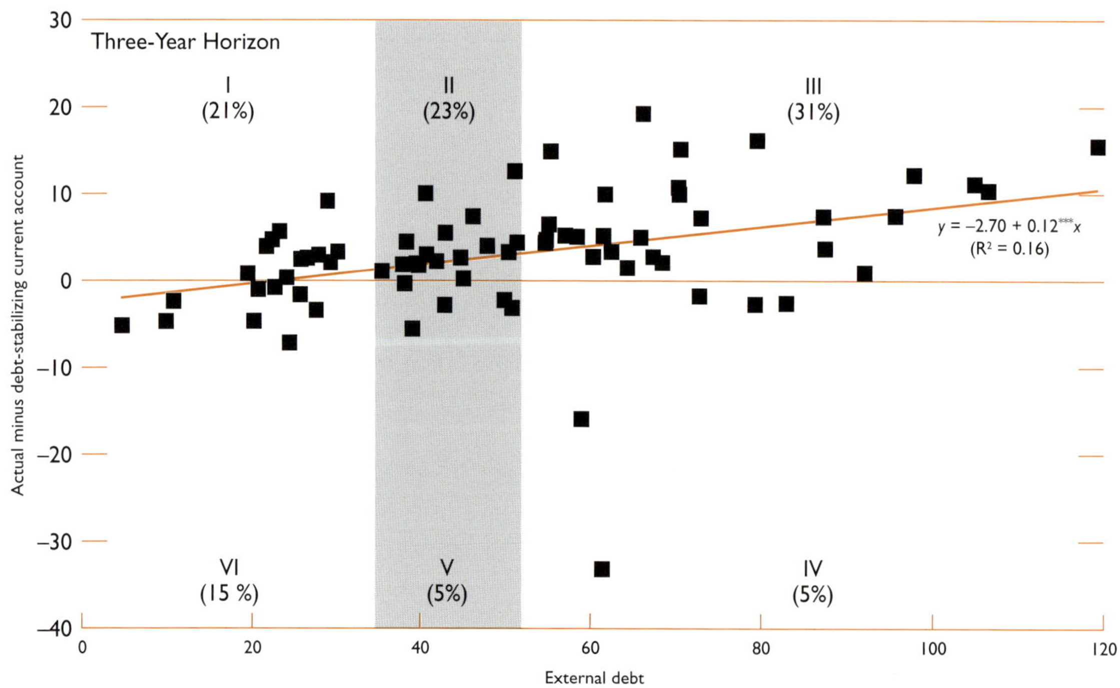

Sources: IMF, MONA and WEO databases; and IMF staff estimates.
Note. See Appendix 1 for a list of countries.
[1]*significant at 10 percent level and ***significant at 1 percent levels.

Figure 2.A2. Sensitivity Analysis on Debt-Stabilizing Current Account Balances in PRGF-Supported Programs[1]
(In percent of GDP)

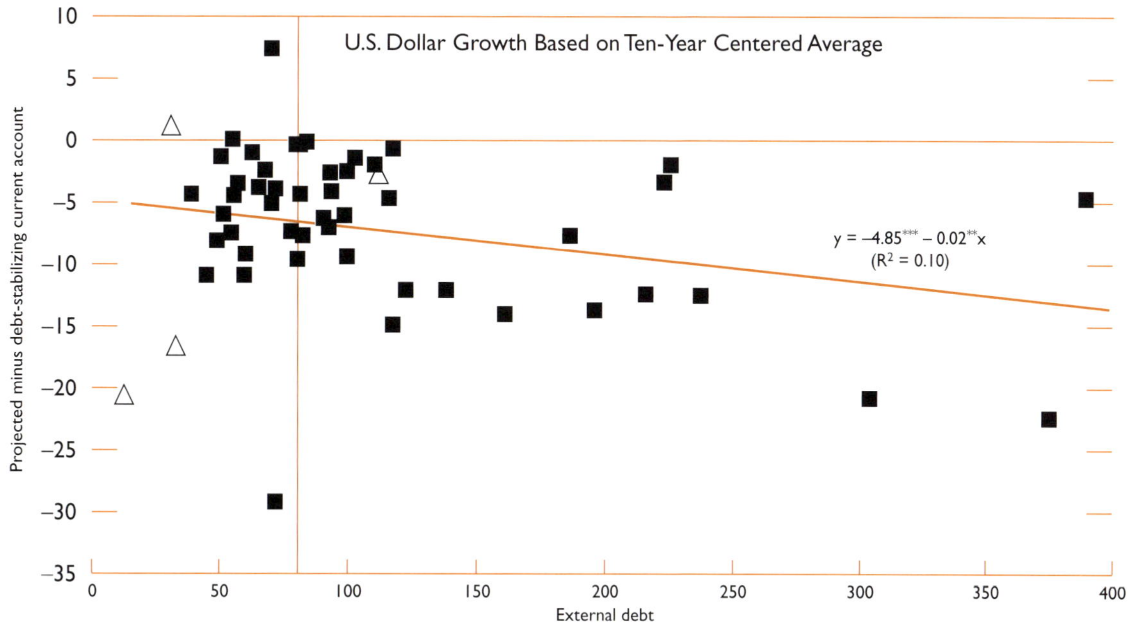

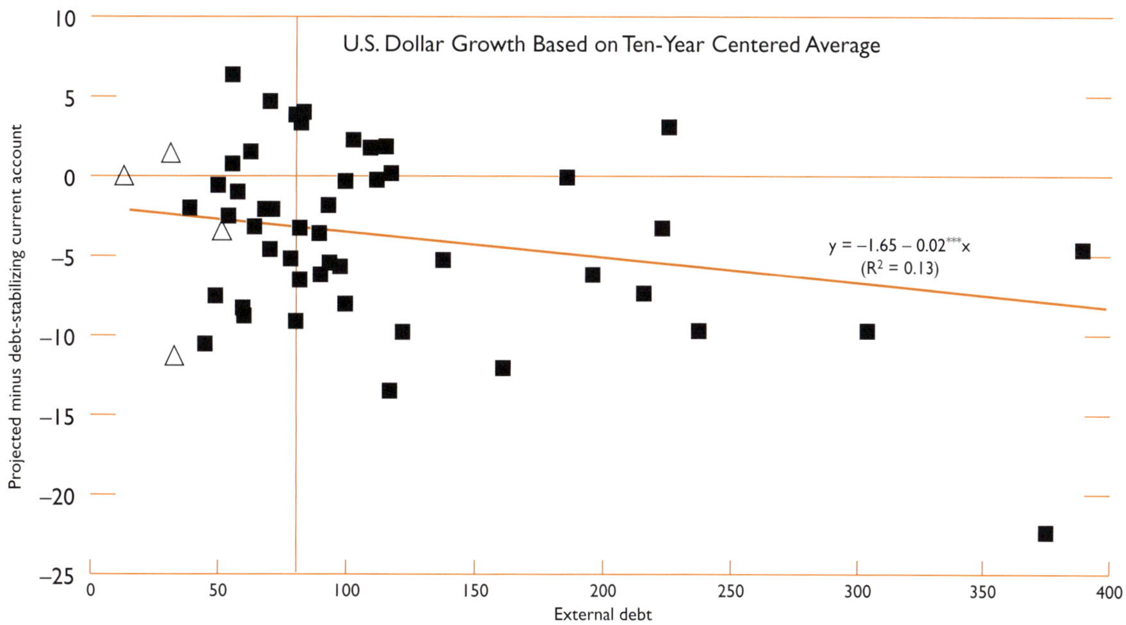

Sources: IMF, MONA and WEO databases; and IMF staff estimates.
Note: See Appendix I for a list of countries.
[1]Non-HIPC countries are depicted by triangles; ** significant at 5 percent, *** significant at 1 percent levels.

Appendix III Face-Value-Stabilizing and NPV-Stabilizing Current Account Balances

In the text, it is claimed that the face-value-stabilizing and NPV-stabilizing current account balances are the same under the assumption that the grant element on the outstanding stock of debt is approximately constant between two periods.

Face-Value-Stabilizing Balance

Debt dynamics are given by:

$$D_{t+1} = D_t - CA_t, \tag{1}$$

where D is the face value of debt and CA is the current account balance. As a ratio to GDP:

$$d_{t+1}\,(1 + g) = d_t - ca_t \tag{2}$$

$$d_{t+1} - d_t = -gd_{t+1} - ca_t. \tag{3}$$

The face-value-stabilizing current account balance, ca^*, has the property $d_{t+1} = d_t$:

$$ca^* = -gd_{t+1}. \tag{4}$$

NPV-Stabilizing Balance

Starting from the face value dynamics:

$$D_{t+1} = D_t - CA_t, \tag{5}$$

which can be written in NPV terms as:

$$\frac{NPV_{t+1}}{(1 - GE_{t+1})} = \frac{NPV_t}{(1 - GE_t)} - CA_t, \tag{6}$$

where GE is the grant element. Then, as a ratio to GDP:

$$\frac{NPV_{t+1}}{(1 - GE_{t+1})Y_{t+1}}\,\frac{Y_{t+1}}{Y_t} = \frac{NPV_t}{(1 - GE_t)Y_t} - \frac{CA_t}{Y_t} \tag{7}$$

$$\frac{npv_{t+1}}{(1 - GE_{t+1})}(1 + g) = \frac{npv}{(1 - GE_t)} - ca_t. \tag{8}$$

Now assume that $GE_{t+1} \approx GE_t$:

$$\frac{npv_{t+1} - npv_t}{(1 - GE)} = -g\,\frac{npv_{t+1}}{(1 - GE)} - ca_t. \tag{9}$$

The NPV-stabilizing current account balance, ca^{**}, has the property that $npv_{t+1} = npv_t$:

$$ca^{**} = -g\,\frac{npv_{t+1}}{(1 - GE)}, \tag{10}$$

which is the same as the debt-stabilizing current account balance since $d_{t+1} = npv_{t+1}/(1 - GE)$:

$$ca^{**} = -g\,\frac{npv_{t+1}}{(1 - GE)} = -gd_{t+1} = ca^*. \tag{11}$$

Appendix IV Confronting the Counterfactual: Estimating the Effects of IMF-Supported Programs

Various approaches have been used to estimate a country's expected gain from participation in an IMF-supported program. Each approach tries to measure the impact of IMF-supported programs by comparing the actual result with a counterfactual using either country data or information from a sample of countries (Table 2.A1); the key difficulty that all studies face lies in constructing a convincing counterfactual.

Before-after calculations compare the performance of the program country in the program period with its own performance in the period before partic-

Table 2.A1. Summary of Empirical Evaluations of the Effect of IMF-Supported Programs

	Time Period	Number of Programs	Number of Countries	Effects on: Balance of payments	Current account	Inflation	Growth
Before-after							
Reichman and Stillson (1978)	1963–72	79	. . .	0	. . .	0	+
Connors (1979)	1973–77	31	23	0	0	0	0
Killick (1984)	1974–79	38	24	0	0	–*	0
Zulu and Nsouli (1985)	1980–81	35	22	. . .	0	0	0
Goldstein and Montiel (1986)	1974–81	68	58	–	–	–	–
Pastor (1987)	1965–81	. . .	18	+*	0	0	0
Khan (1990)	1973–88	259	69	+	+*	–	–
Killick, Malik, and Manuel (1992)	1979–85	. . .	16	+*	+*	–*	+*
Schadler and others (1993)	1983–93	55	19	+	–	–	+
Simulation/estimation							
Khan and Knight (1981)	1968–75	. . .	29	+	+	–	–
Khan and Knight (1985)	1968–75	. . .	29	+	+	–	–
Control group							
Donovan (1981)	1970–76	12	12	. . .	. . .	–	+
Donovan (1982)	1971–80	78	44	+	+	–	–
Goldstein and Montiel (1986)	1974–81	68	58	–	+	–	+
Gylfason (1987)	1977–79	32	14	+*	. . .	0	0
Loxley (1984)	1971–82	38	38	0	0	–*	0
Khan (1990)	1973–88	259	69	+*	+*	–	+
Przeworski and Vreeland (2000)	1951–90	226				0	–*
Generalized evaluation							
Goldstein and Montiel (1986)	1974–81	68	58	–	–	+	–
Khan (1990)	1973–88	259	69	+*	+*	–	–*
Conway (1994)	1976–86	217	73	. . .	+*	–	–, +*
Bagci and Perraudin (1997)	1973–92	. . .	68	+*	+*	–	+*
Dicks-Mireaux and others (2000)	1986–91	88	74	. . .	. . .	–	+*

Sources: Conway (1998) and IMF staff updates.

Note. * indicates statistically significant results.; 0 indicates that the results of the various studies were inconclusive; + indicates a positive effect on the variable indicated; and – indicates a negative effect on the variable indicated.

ipation. This method suffers from biases associated with a change in the economic structure of the country or shocks between both periods that are unrelated to the decision to participate in a program. *Estimation and simulation* can be used to address the bias in the first method either by: (1) estimating the economic model and policy reaction function of the participating country before and during the IMF-supported program; or (2) pairing the program country with one or more nonprogram countries and attributing differences in performance to program participation. This modification (*control group comparison*) may not lead to an improvement because of cross-country differences in exogenous shocks, in economic structures, and in the participation decision. For example, the choice of participating in an IMF-supported program can lead to its own biases because of the unique features of this choice and requires its own controls. These concerns may be reduced, however, by assembling data for a large group of countries, dividing the countries into participants and nonparticipants, controlling for the choice of an IMF-supported program, and testing for statistical significance of differences in average macroeconomic performance and policy. The *generalized evaluation estimator* removes external influences by estimating the channels through which IMF-supported programs and external shocks affect macroeconomic outcomes in the participating and nonparticipating country.

Academic studies on the effects of IMF-supported programs have used all these methods and have tended to concentrate on broad outcomes during the program period such as improvements in the current account and overall balance of payments, inflation, and economic growth. Studies have generally found that the balance of payments has improved, but while inflation has fallen, the decline is generally not significant, partly because most of these studies were conducted before the sharp decline in inflation in the 1990s. Findings on the effects of IMF-supported programs on growth are mixed. Some studies find a significant positive relationship with respect to growth in the short term (Killick (1995), Bagci and Perraudin (1997), and Dicks-Mireaux and others (2000)) and up to three years after the program (Conway (1994)), whereas other studies, in particular, Khan (1990) and Przeworski and Vreeland (2000) find significant negative growth effects in the short and long term. Conway (2000) shows that the macroeconomic performance of countries under IMF-supported programs declines with the length of time a country spends under such a program. Perhaps surprisingly, in light of the IMF's responsibility for external sustainability, no academic study has considered the effects of an IMF-supported program on the evolution of debt.

Traditionally, studies have not distinguished between Stand-By, EFF, and PRGF programs although the few studies that have made this separation find sizable differences. Kochhar and Coorey (1999) find that whereas in the early 1980s, ESAF countries grew at about 1 percentage point a year less than non-ESAF poor countries, by the early 1990s, this negative differential had vanished. Barro and Lee's (2002) analysis of SBAs and EFFs showed no growth improvement following IMF-supported programs over the 1970–2000 period.

References

Allen, Mark, Christoph B. Rosenberg, Christian Keller, Brad Setser, and Nouriel Roubini, 2002, "A Balance Sheet Approach to Financial Crisis," IMF Working Paper No. 02/210 (Washington: International Monetary Fund).

Ariyoshi, Akira, Karl Habermeier, Bernard Laurens, Inci Ötker-Robe, Jorge Iván Canales-Kriljenko, and Andrei Kirilenko, 2000, *Capital Controls: Country Experiences with Their Use and Liberalization,* IMF Occasional Paper No. 190 (Washington: International Monetary Fund).

Bagci, P., and W. Perraudin, 1997, "Do IMF Programs Work?" (unpublished); cited in P. Conway, 1998, "Evaluating Fund Programs: Methodology and Empirical Estimates" (unpublished; Chapel Hill, North Carolina: University of North Carolina).

Barro, Robert J., and Jong-Wha Lee, 2002 "IMF Programs: Who Is Chosen and What Are the Effects?" NBER Working Paper No. 8951 (Cambridge, Massachusetts: National Bureau of Economic Research).

Benelli, Roberto, 2003, "Do IMF-Supported Programs Boost Private Capital Inflows? The Role of Program Size and Adjustment," IMF Working Paper No. 03/231 (Washington: International Monetary Fund).

Bird, Graham, 2000, "IMF Programs: Is There a Conditionality Laffer Curve?" (unpublished).

———, and Dane Rowlands, 1997, "The Catalytic Effect of Lending by the International Financial Institutions," *World Economy*, Vol. 20 (November), pp. 967–91.

Bordo, Michael D., Ashoka Mody, and Nienke Oomes, 2004, "Keeping Capital Flowing: The Role of the IMF," IMF Working Paper No. 04/197 (Washington: International Monetary Fund).

Bredenkamp, Hugh, and Susan Schadler, eds., 1999, *Economic Adjustment and Reform in Low-Income Countries: Studies by the Staff of the International Monetary Fund* (Washington: International Monetary Fund).

Bulíř, A., 2001, "Income Inequality: Does Inflation Matter?" *IMF Staff Papers,* Vol. 48, No. 1, pp. 139–59.

———, and A. Gulde, 2000, "Inflation and Income Inequality: Further Evidence on Empirical Links," *Finance a Uver*, Vol. 50.

Bulíř, A., and J. Hamann, 2003, "Aid Volatility: An Empirical Assessment," *IMF Staff Papers*, Vol. 50, No. 1, pp. 64–89.

Bulíř, A., and T. Lane, 2002, "Managing the Fiscal Impact of Aid," *Finance & Development*, Vol. 39, No. 4, pp. 28–30.

Burnside, Craig, and David Dollar, 1998, "Aid, the Incentive Regime, and Poverty Reduction," Policy Research Working Paper No. 1937 (Washington: World Bank).

———, 2000, "Aid, Policies, and Growth," *American Economic Review,* Vol. 90, No. 4 (September), pp. 847–68.

Chinn, Menzie D., 1999, "Before the Fall: Were East Asian Currencies Overvalued?" NBER Working Paper No. 6491 (Cambridge, Massachusetts: National Bureau of Economic Research).

Collier, Paul, and Jan Willem Gunning, 1999, "The IMF's Role in Structural Adjustment," *Economic Journal,* Vol. 109 (November), pp. F634–F651.

Collier, Paul, David Dollar, and Nicholas Stern, 2000, "Fifty Years of Development," available at www.worldbank.org/research/abcde/eu_2000/papers_eu2.html.

Connors, Thomas A., 1979, "The Apparent Effects of Recent IMF Stabilization Programs," International Finance Discussion Paper No. 135 (Washington: Board of Governors of the Federal Reserve System).

Conway, Patrick, 1994, "IMF Lending Programs: Participation and Impact," *Journal of Development Economics,* Vol. 45 (December), pp. 365–91.

———, 1998, "Evaluating Fund Programs: Methodology and Empirical Estimates," Working Paper (Chapel Hill, North Carolina: University of North Carolina).

———, 2000, "IMF Programs and External Balance: The Crisis-Participation Dynamic," Working Paper (Chapel Hill, North Carolina: University of North Carolina).

Cottarelli, Carlo, and Giannini Curzio, 2002, "Bedfellows, Hostages, or Perfect Strangers? Global Capital Markets and the Catalytic Effects of IMF Crisis Lending," IMF Working Paper No. 02/193 (Washington: International Monetary Fund).

Daseking, Christina, Atish R. Ghosh, Alun Thomas, and Timothy Lane, 2004, *Lessons from the Crisis in Argentina,* IMF Occasional Paper No. 236 (Washington: International Monetary Fund).

Deininger, Klaus W., and Lyn Squire, 1996, "A New Data Set Measuring Income Inequality," *World Bank Economic Review*, Vol. 10 (September), pp. 565–91.

Dicks-Mireaux, Louis, Mauro Mecagni, and Susan Schadler, 2000, "Evaluating the Effect of IMF Lending to Low-income Countries," *Journal of Development Economics,* Vol. 61 (April), pp. 495–526.

Dollar, David, and Aart Kraay, 2001, "Growth Is Good for the Poor," Policy Research Working Paper No. 2587 (Washington: World Bank).

Dollar, David, and Jakob Svensson, 2000, "What Explains the Success or Failure of Structural Adjustment Programmes?" *Economic Journal,* Vol. 110 (October), pp. 894–917.

Donovan, Donal J., 1981, "Real Responses Associated with Exchange Rate Action in Selected Upper Credit Tranche Stabilization Programs," *IMF Staff Papers,* Vol. 28 (December), pp. 698–727.

———, 1982, "Macroeconomic Performance and Adjustment Under Fund-Supported Programs: The Experience of the Seventies," *IMF Staff Papers*, Vol. 29 (June), pp. 171–203.

Easterly, William, 2000, "The Effect of IMF and World Bank Programs on Poverty," paper presented at the IMF's First Annual Research Conference (November).

Frenkel, Jacob A., and Mohsin S. Khan, 1990, "Adjustment Policies and Economic Development," *American Journal of Agricultural Economics,* Vol. 72, No. 3 (August), pp. 815–20.

Ghosh, Atish, Timothy Lane, Marianne Schulze-Ghattas, Aleš Bulíř, Javier Hamann, and Alex Mourmouras, 2002, *IMF-Supported Programs in Capital Account Crises,* IMF Occasional Paper No. 210 (Washington: International Monetary Fund).

Goldstein, Morris, and Peter Montiel, 1986, "Evaluating Fund Stabilization Programs with Multicountry Data: Some Methodological Pitfalls," *IMF Staff Papers,* Vol. 33 (June), pp. 304–44.

Guitián, Manuel, 1992, *Rules and Discretion in International Economic Policy,* IMF Occasional Paper No. 97 (Washington: International Monetary Fund).

———, 1995, "Conditionality: Past, Present, Future," *IMF Staff Papers,* Vol. 42, No. 4 (December), pp. 792–835.

Gylfason, Thorvaldur, 1987, "Credit Policy and Economic Activity in Developing Countries with IMF Stabilization Programs," Princeton Studies in International Finance No. 60 (Princeton, New Jersey: Princeton University).

Independent Evaluation Office, 2002, *Evaluation of Prolonged Use of IMF Resources* (Washington: International Monetary Fund).

———, 2003a, *The IMF and Recent Capital Account Crises: Indonesia, Korea, Brazil* (Washington: International Monetary Fund).

———, 2003b, *Fiscal Adjustment in IMF-Supported Programs* (Washington: International Monetary Fund).

———, 2004, *The IMF and Argentina, 1991–2001* (Washington: International Monetary Fund).

International Monetary Fund, 1997, *The ESAF at Ten Years,* IMF Occasional Paper No. 156 (Washington).

———, 1998, *External Evaluation of ESAF: Report by a Group of Independent Experts* (Washington).

———, 2001, "Private Sector Involvement in the Prevention and Resolution of Financial Crises—Report of the MD to the IMFC;" available at www.imf.org/external/np/omd/2001/042501.pdf.

———, 2002, "Assessing Sustainability;" available at www.imf.org/external/np/pdr/sus/2002/eng/052802.htm.

———, 2003a, "Sustainability Assessments—Review of Application and Methodological Refinements;" available at www.imf.org/external/np/pdr/sustain/2003/061003.htm.

———, 2003b, "Public Debt in Emerging Markets," *World Economic Outlook, September,* World Economic and Financial Surveys (Washington).

———, 2004, "Debt Sustainability in Low-Income Countries;" available at www.imf.org/external/np/pdr/sustain/2004/020304.pdf.

Kenen, Peter B., 1986, *Financing, Adjustment and the International Monetary Fund* (Washington: Brookings Institution).

Keynes, J.M., 1929, "The German Transfer Problem," *Economic Journal,* Vol. 39, No. 153, pp. 1–7.

Khan, Mohsin, 1990, "The Macroeconomic Effects of Fund-Supported Adjustment Programs," *IMF Staff Papers*, Vol. 37 (June), pp. 195–231.

———, and Malcolm Knight, 1981, "Stabilization Programs in Developing Countries: A Formal Framework," *IMF Staff Papers,* Vol. 28 (March), pp. 1–53.

———, 1985, *Fund-Supported Adjustment Programs and Economic Growth,* IMF Occasional Paper No. 41 (Washington: International Monetary Fund).

Killick, Tony, 1995, *IMF Programmes in Developing Countries: Design and Impact* (London and New York: Routledge).

———, 1997, "Principals, Agents and the Failings of Conditionality," *Journal of International Development,* Vol. 9, No. 4, pp. 483–95.

———, ed., 1984, *The Quest for Economic Stabilization: The IMF and the Third World* (New York: St. Martin's).

———, Ramani Gunatilaka, and Ana Marr, 1998, *Aid and the Political Economy of Policy Change* (London: Routledge).

Killick, T., M. Malik, and M. Manuel, 1992, "What Can We Know About the Effects of IMF Programmes?" *World Economy,* Vol. 15, pp. 575–97.

Kocchar, Kalpana, and Sharmini Coorey, 1999, "Economic Growth and What Has Been Achieved and How?" in *Economic Adjustment and Reform in Low-Income Countries: Studies by the Staff of the International Monetary Fund*, ed. by Hugh Bredenkamp and Susan Schadler (Washington: International Monetary Fund).

Loxley, John, 1984, *The IMF and the Poorest Countries: The Performance of the Least Developed Countries Under IMF Stand-By Arrangements* (Ottawa: North-South Institute).

Marchesi, Sylvia, 2003, "Adoption of an IMF Programme and Debt Rescheduling: An Empirical Analysis," *Journal of Development Economics*, Vol. 70, No. 2 (April), pp. 403–23.

Mody, Ashoka, and Diego Saravia, 2003, "Catalyzing Private Capital Flows: Do IMF-Supported Programs Work as Commitment Devices?" IMF Working Paper No. 03/100 (Washington: International Monetary Fund).

Mussa, Michael, and Miguel Savastano, 1999, "The IMF Approach to Economic Stabilization," IMF Working Paper No. 99/104 (Washington: International Monetary Fund).

Pastor, Manuel, Jr., 1987, "The Effects of IMF Programs in the Third World: Debate and Evidence from Latin

America," *World Development,* Vol. 15 (February), pp. 249–62.

Przeworski, Adam, and James Vreeland, 2000, "The Effect of IMF Programs on Economic Growth," *Journal of Development Economics,* Vol. 62 (August), pp. 215–76.

Quah, D., 2001, "Some Simple Arithmetic on How Income Inequality and Economic Growth Matter," London School of Economics Working Paper (London).

Ravallion, Martin, and Shaohua Chen, 1997, "What Can New Survey Data Tell Us About Recent Changes in Distribution and Poverty?" *World Bank Economic Review,* Vol. 11, No. 2 (May), pp. 357–82.

Reichman, Thomas M., and Richard Stillson, 1978, "Experience with Programs of Balance of Payments Adjustment: Stand-By Arrangements in the Higher Credit Tranches, 1963–72," *IMF Staff Papers,* Vol. 25 (June), pp. 119–39.

Reinhart, Carmen M., Kenneth S. Rogoff, and Miguel A. Savastano, 2003, "Debt Intolerance," *Brookings Papers on Economic Activity: 1* (Brookings Institution), pp. 1–62.

Sachs, J., 1982, "The Current Account in the Macroeconomic Adjustment Process," *Scandinavian Journal of Economics,* Vol. 84, No. 2, pp. 147–64.

Schadler, Susan, Franek Rozwadowski, Siddharth Tiwari, and David Robinson, 1993, *Economic Adjustment in Low-Income Countries: Experience Under the Enhanced Structural Adjustment Facility,* IMF Occasional Paper No. 106 (Washington: International Monetary Fund).

Schadler, Susan, Adam Bennett, Maria Carkovic, Louis Dicks-Mireaux, Mauro Mecagni, James H.J. Morsink, and Miguel A. Savastano, 1995, *IMF Conditionality: Experience Under Stand-By and Extended Arrangements,* IMF Occasional Paper No. 128 (Washington: International Monetary Fund).

Spraos, John, 1986, *IMF Conditionality: Ineffectual, Inefficient, Mistargeted,* Princeton Essays in International Finance No. 166 (Princeton, New Jersey: Princeton University).

Svensson, Jakob, 1999a, "Why Conditional Aid Doesn't Work and What Can Be Done About It," Working Paper (Washington: World Bank).

———, 1999b, "Aid, Growth and Democracy," *Economics and Politics,* Vol. 11, No. 3 (November), pp. 275–97.

———, 2000, "When Is Foreign Aid Policy Credible? Aid Dependence and Conditionality," *Journal of Development Economics,* Vol. 61 (February), pp. 61–80.

Tsikata, Tsidi M., 1998, "Aid Effectiveness: A Survey of the Recent, Empirical Literature, in IMF," *International Economic Policy Review*, Vol. 1.

Ul Haque, Nadeem, and Mohsin S. Khan, 1998, "Do IMF-Supported Programs Work? A Survey of the Cross-Country Empirical Evidence," IMF Working Paper No. 98/169 (Washington: International Monetary Fund).

Vreeland, James R., 1999, "The IMF: Lender of Last Resort or Scapegoat?" (unpublished; New Haven, Connecticut: Department of Political Science, Yale University).

Zhang, Xiaoming Alan, 1999 "Testing for 'Moral Hazard' in Emerging Markets Lending," IIF Research Paper No. 99 (Washington: Institute of International Finance).

Zulu, Justin B., and Saleh M. Nsouli, 1985, *Adjustment Programs in Africa: The Recent Experience,* IMF Occasional Paper No. 34 (Washington: International Monetary Fund).

Part III

Policy Formulation, Analytical Frameworks, and Program Design

I Introduction

IMF-supported programs require an analytical basis to ensure that policy advice is coherent, that conditionality comprises measures that are critical for program success, and that the intended objectives will indeed be achieved. While the analytical challenges of setting coherent policies and goals are not unique to IMF-supported programs—national authorities face such challenges on a daily basis, and the IMF always strives to ensure that its policy advice is coherent and apt—they take an added importance in the context of IMF-supported programs for a number of reasons. First, members typically seek IMF support at a times of crisis or when significant external adjustment is required—that is, when a policy response (usually different from the country's previous policies) is required. Second, at such times the economy may be experiencing shifts in existing economic relationships, thus complicating the formulation of economic policies and making it more likely that policymakers will want to draw upon the IMF's advice and expertise. Third, the IMF needs to assess whether the authorities' policy program is likely to achieve its intended objectives, both to ensure that the member country addresses its economic problems and to help safeguard IMF resources.

Therefore, while this paper pertains to economic policy setting in general, it focuses on those economic programs in which a country's authorities request the use of IMF resources.[1] The first part of this paper lays out the process of program design and briefly describes some of the analytical tools—including the *financial programming framework*, the *balance sheet approach*, and the *debt sustainability template*—employed by IMF country teams in advising national authorities on policy formulation. The second part of this paper seeks to assess how well this process works in practice. Since this is difficult to do directly, the approach taken here is to examine whether there are systematic errors in program projections of key near-term macroeconomic variables—output, inflation, and the current account balance—and in the relationships between policies and targets implicit in the design of IMF-supported programs. Turning to longer horizons, the paper examines the record on program projections of real GDP growth and external debt dynamics. It bears emphasizing that the record on the quality of program projections sheds light on how well the analytical tools and approaches to policy formulation work as a modeling process—not on whether program objectives themselves were appropriate and achieved.[2]

The main conclusions are as follows. First, no single model or framework is universally applicable—policy formulation relies on a variety of models, techniques, and economic judgment. A key feature of this eclectic approach is its adaptability to evolving economic conditions, with program reviews providing an opportunity to reassess policies subject to conditionality (see Mussa and Savastano, 1999). In this regard, the role of financial programming is to inform and tie together projections of individual sectors (external, monetary, fiscal) into a coherent macroeconomic framework, rather than to pin down precisely the parameters of the financial program. Second, capital account crises pose challenging analytical problems and the balance sheet approach can help to assess the potential magnitude of capital flows and their implications for the efficacy of policy instruments. Third, analytical tools for understanding the factors driving sustained output growth are limited, and such tools as do exist are not always fully utilized in program design. For example, greater use of cross-country growth models could be

[1]To include both program and postprogram experience, the sample consists of arrangements approved over the period 1995–2000 and supported by the General Resources Account (GRA)—Stand-By Arrangements (SBAs) and Extended Fund Facility (EFF) arrangements—or by concessional facilities—the Enhanced Structural Adjustment Facility (ESAF) prior to 1999/2000, and the Poverty Reduction and Growth Facility (PRGF) thereafter. For simplicity, the term PRGF is used to refer to both ESAF- and PRGF-supported programs. A list of arrangements can be found in Appendix I of "Objectives and Outcomes" (Part II of this occasional paper); individual analyses reported below may use subsamples, depending on data availability.

[2]The latter question is considered in "Objectives and Outcomes" and "Macroeconomic and Structural Policies: Review of Experience" (Parts II and IV of this occasional paper).

helpful in informing and disciplining medium-term growth projections. Fourth, the IMF's debt sustainability template complements the macroeconomic projections underlying IMF-supported programs by articulating their implications for debt dynamics and subjecting these dynamics to systematic stress testing exercises.

These conclusions are reflected in the record of program projections. Projections over the short term are relatively accurate and do not exhibit systematic biases with respect to inflation or output growth (except in capital account crises). This is important in that policies in IMF-supported programs are seldom formulated for more than a few months without an opportunity for revision at the time of quarterly or semiannual reviews. Moreover, the relationships between macroeconomic instruments and targets assumed in programs are generally consistent with the actual relationships. At longer horizons, however, the quality of projections deteriorates markedly, with systematic biases in long-run growth projections that can, in turn, undermine assessments of debt sustainability.

The plan of this paper is as follows. Section II discusses the process of program design and the analytical tools used to help set macroeconomic and structural policies to achieve program objectives. Section III turns to the record on projections of key macroeconomic variables and on relationships between policies and targets assumed in program design. Section IV concludes.

II Analytical Tools for Policy Formulation and Program Design

An IMF-supported program is a package of policy measures which, combined with approved financing, is intended to achieve certain economic objectives.[3] In essence, therefore, a program is defined by its objectives, the link between those objectives and policy instruments, and thus the specification of macroeconomic and structural policies. This section considers the process and analytical tools used for establishing the link between policies and objectives in the formulation of IMF-supported programs.

One approach to policy formulation would be for national authorities and IMF country teams to develop a comprehensive macroeconomic model linking policies to targets. This model could then be inverted to derive the policies necessary to achieve them. If the IMF was confident that the implied policies would be implemented, it would support a program that predicts that sufficiently ambitious targets would be achieved.

While such an approach would have a number of advantages—ensuring consistency, illustrating the effects of alternative policy mixes, and identifying intertemporal trade-offs between financing and adjustment—empirical and practical considerations make the use of comprehensive macroeconomic models implausible in most cases.[4] Instead, therefore, national authorities and IMF country teams typically rely on a variety of approaches to help formulate macroeconomic and structural policies. For the purposes of discussion, it is useful to consider the process of policy formulation for short-run objectives (such as macroeconomic stabilization and external adjustment) separately from the longer-term goals of ensuring debt sustainability, reducing vulnerabilities, and raising the growth potential of the economy—though, of course, these are dynamically linked.

Macroeconomic Stabilization and External Adjustment

In formulating their economic program, national authorities have a number of different instruments—the exchange rate regime, monetary policy, fiscal policy, and structural measures. While such policy prescriptions would be consistent with most open economy macroeconomic models, the specific policy content of the authorities' program naturally depends upon the country's characteristics and the circumstances it is facing. Thus, if Keynesian effects are likely to be important, then the effect of fiscal consolidation on activity and output growth would need to be taken into account. Likewise, the pace at which disinflation should be targeted—and the choice of nominal anchor—should be viewed against the benefits for growth of macroeconomic stability, the possible need to adjust administered prices in the economy, and realistic expectations regarding fiscal policy.[5] Since no single model is universally applicable, national authorities—and IMF country teams in advising them—must draw on an array of small econometric models and single equation estimates (including existing analytical work undertaken by research departments in central banks, ministries of finance, and private think

[3]The objectives typically include promoting external adjustment and macroeconomic stability, of which restoring confidence in capital account crises is an extreme case; fostering growth and poverty reduction; and reducing vulnerabilities. These goals, of course, are not necessarily mutually exclusive—programs often aim at a number of objectives. The emphasis of the program, however, naturally depends upon country-specific circumstances; see "Objectives and Outcomes" (Part II of this occasional paper).

[4]Experience with econometric models in industrial countries suggests that parameter instability is a significant concern especially when policy changes are taking place (Lucas, 1976). This, together with a lack of data or ergodic time series in many countries supported by IMF arrangements, makes the stability of elaborate models suspect. Moreover, without ad hoc adjustments, it is difficult to capture the myriad of circumstance- and country-specific factors, some of which (e.g., the credibility of the program) do not lend themselves easily to formal modeling.

[5]Practical considerations may also constrain monetary and fiscal choices. For example, if the government is locked into high nominal interest rates on long maturity instruments, rapid disinflation—and high real interest rates—may be costly to the government. See Coorey and others (1996) on accommodating administered price changes in inflation targets.

Box 3.1. The Anatomy of Program Design: Indonesia, 2000

Policy formulation for Indonesia's 2000 EFF arrangement provides a typical example of the process of program design. The preparation of a macroeconomic framework started with preliminary output and price projections, followed by projections for the fiscal, external, and monetary sectors. Given the linkages among the various sectors, achieving internally consistent and economically meaningful projections required an iterative rather than a recursive process. The steps involved are summarized below.

Real sector. Projections were expenditure based, with the real GDP growth rate and consumer price inflation assumptions reflecting program objectives. Public consumption and investment were obtained from the fiscal accounts, while private consumption and investment were based on the expected recovery of the banking and corporate sectors. Export and import volume growth rates were obtained from the external accounts, while the change in inventories was derived as a residual.

Fiscal sector. The targeted overall balance (a performance criterion under the IMF-supported program) sought to balance the twin objectives of supporting recovery and reducing the public debt, while being mindful of the available financing (to limit base money growth consistent with the inflation target, the program did not allow for domestic bank financing; the program also established limits on arrears accumulation). On the revenue side, oil and gas revenue projections were derived using the IMF's *World Economic Outlook* oil price assumptions and the assumed program exchange rate. Non-oil revenues were derived from the projected nominal GDP growth with adjustments for policy implementation (such as better revenue collection and higher tax ratios). On the expenditure side, the projections were made using a combination of nominal GDP growth and historical expenditure ratios with adjustments for policy implementation (such as lower payments on subsidies). The projections were also influenced by the upcoming need for implementing fiscal decentralization.

External sector. The components of the external current account were projected based on the *World Economic Outlook* projections for oil prices, import deflators, and trading partners' growth rates; program exchange rate assumptions; and estimates of price and income elasticities for exports and imports. The capital account was derived based on estimates of official capital flows from various multilateral and bilateral sources, estimates of private capital flows (including the projected returns from corporate and bank restructurings), and exceptional financing items. The net international reserves (NIR, performance criterion) accumulation target was set to zero for the first year of the program. A small recovery in NIR was targeted for subsequent years.

Monetary sector. Attempts at estimating traditional money demand functions to arrive at a path for the monetary variables did not yield stable results. Therefore, the monetary projections were based on assumed monetary ratios and historical benchmarks. Among the components of Bank Indonesia's balance sheet, base money (an indicative target) was derived from projections of currency in circulation and deposits (bank and nonbank). Currency in circulation was derived by multiplying the rupiah broad money by the long-term trend of the ratio of currency to rupiah broad money. Bank deposits were derived by applying the reserve requirement ratios to rupiah M2, and nonbank deposits were held constant. On the assets side, consistent with the balance of payments projections, NIR for the initial program year was assumed to be constant so as not to exert an expansionary influence on base money; in the outer years, accumulation was allowed. Net domestic assets (performance criterion) was derived residually from base money and NIR. In the monetary survey, rupiah broad money was derived by applying its trend growth rates, and private credit was assumed to be in line with the nominal GDP growth rate.

---

tanks), as well as economic judgment for formulating macroeconomic and structural policies.

The program thus developed is essentially defined by a core set of macroeconomic projections on real GDP growth, inflation, the current account, and the balance of payments. In turn, these variables both influence, and are influenced by, monetary, exchange rate, and fiscal policy instruments. Thus inflation and growth will be important inputs into fiscal revenue and expenditure projections, but the size of the deficit may have a bearing on economic activity, and its financing on inflation and interest rates. Likewise, the monetary policy stance has implications for prices and output growth, but real growth, in turn, is likely to affect the demand for money.

The mutual dependence of instruments and targets means that the modeling process is usually iterative and often quite complex (Box 3.1). A key concern is ensuring consistency of the macroeconomic framework and coherence of the policy stance across instruments to meet program objectives. Financial programming is used as a general approach[6] to inform

[6]As noted in the text, the financial programming model is seldom used to pin down exact parameters of a program, but to inform and to help ensure consistency across sectors (external, monetary, fiscal). Specifically, the fiscal deficit must match sources of financing. These include: an *external component*, derived from an assessment of the balance of payments (at either a fixed exchange rate or an expected path of a floating exchange rate), the market's

Table 3.1. Projected and Actual Current Account Adjustment in Capital Account Crisis Programs
(In percent of GDP)

	Approval Year	Crisis Year	Current Account Adjustment	
			Projected	Actual
Argentina	2000	2002	0.1	12.0
Brazil	1998	1999	0.6	–0.6
Indonesia	1997	1998	0.5	6.0
Korea	1997	1998	2.5	14.4
Mexico	1995	1995	3.7	6.5
Russia	1996	1999	0.0	12.1
Thailand	1997	1998	2.0	14.8
Turkey	1999	2001	0.3	7.2
Uruguay	2000	2002	0.2	4.4
Average			1.1	8.5

Sources: IMF, MONA and WEO databases; and IMF staff estimates.

and tie together the various sectors in a consistent manner, while incorporating country-specific factors.[7] In this fashion, not only does financial programming serve as an ex ante consistency check on important financial aggregates, it also provides an ex post monitoring tool.[8]

A key characteristic of this approach is that it allows policies to be adjusted and reformulated in a dynamic manner in light of outcomes.[9] Policy formulation thus extends well beyond the Executive Board approval of an IMF arrangement. Indeed, program reviews are intended to offer the opportunity for country authorities and IMF staff to reassess their initial assumptions and the progress achieved during the first few months of the program, including reasons why program objectives may be deviating from targets, with the forward-looking aspect of IMF reviews allowing for policy adjustments to help ensure that program objectives are achieved.[10]

The need for frequent reassessments of policies in light of outcomes is especially acute in capital account crises. Although these programs are, at one level, little different from more traditional programs—typically targeting some external adjustment (on average, about 1.1 percent of GDP; Table 3.1)—their salient feature is the large and sudden capital outflows that force much larger-than-envisaged adjustments of the current account balance (on average, 8.5 percent of GDP), with pervasive macroeconomic consequences.[11] In particular, the timing and magnitude of the capital outflows are very difficult to pre-

appetite for sovereign bonds, external privatization receipts, and expected inflows through the banking system; expected *privatization receipts*; and *government borrowing from the banking system*. The latter is derived from assumptions regarding changes in broad liquidity, which in turn depend on money demand developments (given macroeconomic parameters such as growth and inflation), net foreign assets projections consistent with the balance of payments projections, and assumptions regarding net domestic claims on the private sector that are consistent with the growth projections.

[7]See Polak (1957) and Robichek (1967 and 1971). In its original conception, in a world of low capital mobility, limited recourse to bond financing by the government, and fixed exchange rates, the financial programming model was intended to define the fiscal deficit consistent with a reserves accumulation target. The assumptions underlying the "classic" financial programming model (see Appendix I ("The Financial Programming Model"); Mussa and Savastano, 1999) are unlikely to be fulfilled. These assumptions can be relaxed, however (Khan and Montiel, 1989).

[8]The financial programming framework may therefore be useful for monitoring conditionality, serving as tripwires (ceilings or floors) for identifying instances in which a program is going off-track rather than for specifying the actual policy stance. In particular, the financial programming framework is not intended for setting monetary policy, which typically depends on the country's monetary and exchange rate regime (e.g., a pegged exchange rate, a target for monetary aggregates, an inflation targeting framework, or an interest rate rule).

[9]See Mussa and Savastano (1999).

[10]While staff reports for program reviews usually analyze breaches of conditionality, they do not always analyze the reasons for deviations from broader program objectives.

[11]A further complication in many capital account crises were the concomitant banking crises.

dict—indeed, existing models of capital flows perform very poorly even in noncrisis situations.[12] These flows and the attendant exchange rate movements interact with domestic balance sheet exposures, potentially altering the magnitude, and even the sign, of the effects of economic policies.[13]

Partly in response, the IMF has been developing a balance sheet approach to understand the mechanisms underlying these stock shifts.[14] From the perspective of this approach, a financial crisis occurs when a plunge in demand for financial liabilities takes place in one or more of the sectors—creditors may lose confidence in the sovereign's ability to service its debt, in the banking system's ability to meet deposit outflows, or in corporations' ability to repay bank loans and other debt—ultimately spilling on to the balance of payments. Since most emerging market countries borrow in foreign currency, some sectors in the economy have foreign exchange risk. The key insight is that the maturity structure and distribution of those liabilities across domestic balance sheets, as well as the interrelationships between balances among residents, may have important bearing on the country's vulnerability to a shift in confidence. The balance sheet analysis can help pinpoint the source of balance of payments disequilibrium and, possibly, the form of intervention that might succeed in containing the crisis.

While a useful addition to the analytical toolkit, it is important to recognize the limitations of the approach. First, although it can help identify vulnerabilities, it cannot predict either the timing or the magnitude of a possible crisis and the capital outflows.[15] Second, though some balance sheet structures may be more resilient than others, as long as the country as a whole has foreign exchange exposure, some balance sheet within the economy faces risks that cannot be diversified away. Finally, there are a number of difficulties in the practical application of the framework, particularly related to the availability of data.

Promoting Economic Efficiency and Output Growth

Enhancing economic efficiency and promoting growth are important goals of IMF-supported programs, particularly among low-income countries.[16] Although the economics profession is far from reaching consensus on what drives growth, several conclusions emerge from various studies. First, most studies agree that macroeconomic stabilization is a sine qua non for sustained output growth and for reaping the benefits of any structural reforms, possibly because high and volatile inflation might lessen the value of price signals and distort the allocation of resources.[17] Second, while there is less agreement on

[12]Most models postulate that capital flows depend on relative expected returns. When capital mobility is high—as among industrial countries—capital flows should respond immediately to any perceived differentials in expected rates of return, implying that uncovered interest rate parity (UIP) should hold continuously. In fact, however, empirical evidence suggests that deviations from UIP are pervasive and persistent. In comprehensive literature surveys, Froot and Thaler (1990) and MacDonald and Taylor (1992) report few cases where the interest rate differential has the right value or even the right sign.

[13]For example, Furman and Stiglitz (1998) argue that monetary tightening may even produce a perverse effect on the exchange rate. In their view, tight monetary policies by causing widespread corporate bankruptcies can widen the risk premium, contributing to further outflows and depreciation of the exchange rate. The efficacy of tightened monetary policy in stemming capital outflows may therefore depend on the relative balance sheet exposures of the financial and corporate sector to exchange rate and domestic interest rate risk (see Montiel (2003) for a review of the empirical literature). Aghion, Bacchetta, and Banerjee (2001) develop a model in which balance sheet effects alter the impact of monetary and fiscal policies on the economy. Likewise, the impact of fiscal policy may depend on parameters of the economy that may not be known at the time of a crisis (see Lane and others, 1999, Appendix 7.2 for a model in which the degree of capital mobility and balance sheet effects affect the impact of fiscal policy on output). *IMF-Supported Programs in Capital Account Crises* (Ghosh and others, 2002) discusses how the appropriate response of fiscal policy depends on whether capital outflows represent a supply-side shock (for instance, because the exchange rate depreciation raises the cost of intermediate inputs or leads to widespread bankruptcies due to the corporate sector's foreign exchange exposure) or a demand-side shock. Ultimately, there may be inherent limits to whether the effect of policies on macroeconomic targets can be knowable in crisis situations; such limits have long been recognized in the physical sciences—see Heisenberg (1927).

[14]See "The Balance Sheet Approach and Its Applications at the Fund" (IMF, 2003a); and "Integrating the Balance Sheet Approach into Fund Operations" (IMF, 2004a).

[15]Moody's Macro Financial Risk Model (M*f*Risk) has applied the contingent claim analysis to the whole economy to estimate default and distress probabilities for the sovereign, the banking, and the nonfinancial corporate sectors. This approach is forward looking in that it uses the information contained in financial asset prices to predict default probabilities, while the balance sheet approach relies on past financial statements. Moody's M*f*Risk model also assesses risk transfers from one sector to another (see Gapen and others, 2004). While the model's main application to date has been in the corporate and financial sectors, which are particularly amenable to statistical methods given large samples of data, it is also being used by institutional investors and investment banks to model sovereign risk.

[16]PRGF-supported programs also target poverty reduction; some of these measures, including improving health and education, are likely to have positive growth effects as well.

[17]Most empirical work finds a negative and convex relationship between inflation and growth. The greatest *marginal* loss of growth occurs at low inflation rates—beyond a low inflation "kink" that studies place variously between about 3 percent and 8 percent a year (see Sarel, 1996; IMF, 1997; and Ghosh and Phillips, 1998). Beyond the kink point, each doubling of the inflation rate is associated with ½ percentage point lower per capita growth. As usual there are caveats regarding causal

the best sequence for reforms, a widely accepted view is that stabilization should precede trade[18] or financial sector[19] liberalization, particularly if these can adversely affect stabilization efforts by reducing trade-related revenues or raising the costs of public sector funding. Moreover, domestic financial markets should be liberalized—with well-supervised prudential regulations in place—before the capital account to ensure an efficient allocation of resources and to limit vulnerabilities. Third, a growing body of literature emphasizes the importance of sound institutions for sustained output growth. At the same time, the variety of judicial systems and institutions in strong performing economies belies the idea that any single approach works best in all countries.[20]

Beyond these general prescriptions, there are four main analytical tools for understanding the determinants of activity and output growth. First is the demand side assessment—that is, a decomposition of the expected growth into private consumption, investment, government spending, and the current account balance. While this does not provide a model of potential output, it does provide a check on whether the growth projection is consistent with other program parameters, for instance fiscal adjustment. Second, mechanical univariate approaches, such as Hodrick-Prescott filters, may be useful input to medium-term growth projections.[21] Third, estimating the aggregate production function may also serve to model growth and discipline projections. However, even though this provides a model for potential output growth, it requires data that are not readily available (e.g., capital stock data), as well as assumptions regarding competition in factor markets or estimates of factor utilization; of course, growth of potential output need not translate into actual output growth if demand is lacking or economic inefficiencies abound. Fourth, growth regressions can be used to map country characteristics (including the availability of factors of production, such as physical and human capital, and structural characteristics, economic policies, and institutions) into its expected growth performance based on cross-country experience. Such regressions perform best over medium-term horizons—usually a five-year period—where business cycle movements and the effects of temporary shocks are averaged out. Their major drawbacks are their data requirements, and the inherent difficulties of quantifying some of the explanatory variables, such as the quality of institutions. One approach would be to examine the association between growth and specific measures in similar (possibly neighboring) countries. These comparisons could usefully include data on medium-term growth rates in countries that are facing similar challenges and are situated at similar stages of development, which in turn would serve to further discipline projections.

A growth model would also allow an assessment of whether the assumed acceleration in growth is realistic and whether the structural reforms embodied in the authorities' reform program could plausibly lead to such an acceleration. At the same time, it needs to be recognized that it is enormously difficult to map specific measures into the structural indices typically employed in growth regressions. Moreover, while the authorities may draw on cross-country experience to identify broad areas where reforms could bolster growth, they must rely on their own country-specific knowledge to determine the growth bottlenecks that are critical for their country. Even when there is agreement on which reforms might contribute to better economic performance, a further difficulty lies in determining the impact of these reforms on growth—specifically, whether the beneficial effects are likely to peter out quickly or to have a lasting effect on a country's growth performance. Empirical research suggests that various economic measures—macroeconomic stability, an enabling business environment, trade liberalization, fiscal sustainability, and financial sector development—boost output growth, but in some cases—such as trade liberalization and fiscal sustainability—the long-run effect on the growth rate is weaker (Box 3.2). It would therefore be important to distinguish between immediate and lasting effects on growth rates in assessing the impact of structural reforms on the country's growth performance.

Despite the availability of these analytical tools, and notwithstanding their shortcomings, a review of

interpretations—and high inflation may be capturing macroeconomic dislocation more generally—but the relationship is surprisingly robust to controls for endogeneity and the inclusion of other growth determinants. Evidence on sequencing of reforms presented in Zalduendo (2005) suggests that macroeconomic stabilization is so critical for economic performance that it is a precondition for deriving positive results from structural reforms.

[18]Many authors argue that trade barriers should be dismantled only if alternative revenue sources have been identified (Funke, 1993; and Nsouli and others, 2002). Michaely and others (1990) argue that the benefits of trade liberalization weaken if fiscal imbalances result in a real exchange rate appreciation that erodes the incentive of moving resources to the tradables sector. Others call for the implementation of trade reforms that do not affect the inflation rate—for example, shifting from quantitative restrictions to tariffs (Krueger, 1984).

[19]The timing of financial liberalization should also depend on a country's initial conditions; for example, whether financial repression is used to help finance the public sector.

[20]Mauro (1995); Kaufman, Kraay, and Zoido-Lobatón (1999); and IMF (2003b).

[21]Peak-to-peak (and trough-to-trough) growth developments can help inform projections of potential growth. These tools do not, however, assess determinants of growth and frequently have difficulty in distinguishing between trend and one-time factors.

Box 3.2. Permanent and Temporary Growth Effects from Economic Policies

A cross-country growth equation representing five clusters of economic policies suggests that improving each of these clusters by one standard deviation leads to improvements in growth rates (see Table A) that range from 0.3 percent to 0.6 percent a year (see Zalduendo (2005) for a discussion of the use of factor analysis to capturing different dimensions of economic policy). The five clusters were derived by applying factor analysis to different economic policy indicators. These empirical results use an unbalanced panel of five-year periods between 1981 and 2000. The two clusters of macroeconomic policy are viewed as proxies to economic stabilization and fiscal sustainability. The three clusters of reforms represent trade liberalization policies, financial sector development, and an enabling environment for private sector activity.

Table A. Effects on Growth Rates

	Coefficient	Standard Deviation	Annual Growth Effect
Business environment	0.04	0.14	0.51
Financial sector development	0.02	0.16	0.28
Economic stabilization	0.06	0.07	0.42
Trade liberalization	0.07	0.07	0.49
Fiscal sustainability	0.07	0.08	0.58

Is the growth pay-off from a given improvement in economic policies permanent? The econometric results (see Table B) suggest that growth effects from sound policies are lasting, but that some policies have a more lasting impact than others. This conclusion is derived by comparing three regressions. The first regression includes only contemporaneous measurements of economic policy clusters. The second regression includes only lagged indicators (i.e., the average of the preceding five-year period). The last regression combines contemporaneous indicators and the lagged five-year period for each economic policy regressor. The coefficient estimates in the first equation are positive (better policies support growth) and statistically significant. The conclusions from the second equation are similar, albeit less robust—only lagged macroeconomic stabilization and trade liberalization are statistically important for growth. In contrast, the last equation has positive coefficient estimates on contemporaneous indicators of policy clusters and negative estimates in the lagged indicators. While the sum of the corresponding statistically significant contemporaneous and lagged coefficients is still positive, it is weaker than the contemporaneous effect by itself. More precisely, the combined contemporaneous and lagged coefficients for trade liberalization and fiscal sustainability (equation 3) are smaller than those in the specification that has only contemporaneous regressors (equation 2). In sum, even though the observed growth effects are lasting, in some cases they weaken over time.

a sample of staff reports over a six-year period shows that they typically make limited use of these tools (9 out of 20 staff reports used one or another of the above described techniques, and in almost all cases only once over the six-year period; see Box 3.3). As discussed below, greater use of analytical tools could discipline medium-term growth projections embodied in programs as well as helping to identify some of the impediments to growth pertinent to the particular country.

Medium-Term Debt Sustainability

An important use of medium-term growth projections is to inform debt sustainability assessments. Indeed, going beyond flow balance of payments problems, IMF-supported programs are also intended to reduce vulnerabilities to future crises so that a country should emerge with both its public and external debt dynamics on a sustainable path. To assess debt dynamics, the IMF has developed a standardized debt sustainability template.[22] The template lays bare the key assumptions underlying the debt sustainability analysis so that their realism can be as-

[22]The debt sustainability template (see IMF, 2002 and 2003c) was designed for market borrowers; a similar framework, taking account of factors specific to low-income countries, was approved for analytical work by the Executive Board (see IMF, 2004b).

Table B. Growth Effects[1]
(Dependent variable: growth rate in GDP per capita)

	Equation 1	Equation 2	Equation 3
Economic policy regressors			
Business environment	0.0359***		0.0717***
	(3.40)		(4.44)
Financial sector development	0.0177***		0.0248***
	(2.91)		(3.47)
Economic stabilization	0.0639***		0.0920***
	(4.17)		(4.34)
Trade liberalization	0.0652***		0.1552***
	(3.67)		(4.19)
Fiscal sustainability	0.0720***		0.1108***
	(4.33)		(6.03)
Business environment, lagged		0.0097	–0.0442***
		(0.99)	(–2.96)
Financial sector development, lagged		0.0067	–0.0050
		(1.55)	(–0.60)
Economic stabilization, lagged		0.0680**	–0.0004
		(2.54)	(–0.01)
Trade liberalization, lagged		0.0525***	–0.0998***
		(5.10)	(–2.73)
Fiscal sustainability, lagged		0.0125	–0.0527***
		(0.94)	(–3.11)
Wald statistic	191.57	204.55	271.63
Standard error of regression	0.0213	0.0230	0.0208
R-squared	0.43	0.32	0.45
Number of observations	172		
Number of different countries	61		

Note. *** indicates significance at 1 percent level, and ** indicates significance at 5 percent level; *t*-statistics are in parentheses.
[1]Regression includes a number of nonpolicy regressors, such as initial income level, terms of trade shocks, and indicators of domestic shocks. Some of these regressors serve to control for differences in initial conditions.

sessed against a country's historical experience. The template also applies stress tests to the baseline projection to examine its resilience to shocks and serves to anchor near-term policy recommendations.

Some of the debt sustainability template's features and limitations are also worth noting, however.[23] First, the template articulates debt dynamics under the baseline and stress scenarios, and thus helps arrive at judgments about the sustainability of a given path of debt, but cannot replace the need for such judgments. Second, the template is intended to take account of the main shocks—such as poor growth performance or real exchange rate depreciations—that could result in an unsustainable increase in debt, but not to model the crisis itself. Thus, while the template tracks gross financing needs, it is not well-suited to modeling how liquidity crises manifest since it focuses only on the country's aggregate net external debt and capital flows. Third, although the template helps discipline projections, it does not specify a particular model or method that country teams should use in making program projections; ultimately, debt sustainability assessments will only be as good as the macroeconomic projections, including for output growth, underlying it.

[23]See IMF (2003c) for a discussion of the issues that arise in the practical application of the template; for instance, choosing the appropriate window of historical data for the calibration of shocks is particularly difficult when countries are undergoing rapid structural change.

Box 3.3. The Treatment of Growth in Staff Reports: Theory and Practice

Even though growth projections are not intended to be forecasts (they are conditioned, inter alia, on policy implementation, and reflect a mix of quantitative analysis and judgment reached during discussions between country authorities and IMF staff), the existence of systematic biases are problematic because they provide a poor basis for choosing the macroeconomic policies and distort the assessment of debt sustainability.

What options are available when preparing growth projections?

The options depend on the length of the projection period and the availability of data. One-time factors, sector-specific issues, and cyclical factors play an important role when preparing short-term growth projections. Unfortunately, many of these factors do not lend themselves easily to formal modeling. A detailed demand-side analysis also provides a useful perspective when preparing growth projections. The range of options broadens for medium-term projections: mechanical univariate approaches (HP-type filters), production function approaches, and growth equations. However, these options also have limitations. Univariate-based assessments have difficulty in distinguishing between trend and one-time factors. Production function approaches are intensive on data that are frequently not available, such as capital stock data, or based on accounting exercises that depend heavily on assumptions regarding factor utilization and production function parameters. Growth equations lack a theoretical foundation. An additional difficulty relates to the quantification of the effects of structural reforms on growth. In fact, it is fair to say that individual reforms might have a limited effect on output. More likely, it is the accumulation of sound economic management and structural reforms that strengthens a country's growth prospects.

A review of selected IMF reports (20 staff reports for Article IVs and use of IMF resources programs, as well as selected issues papers; see table) covering the period 1995–2000 reveals that:

- Almost half of the reports utilized at least once during the six-year period an analytical framework for growth projections—HP filters and incremental capital output ratio (ICOR) relationships were the most frequently employed techniques;
- On slightly over half of the sample analytical work was not feasible or not explicitly described in the reports;
- Links between reforms and growth are rarely analytical, perhaps reflecting the quantification difficulties mentioned above;
- Most reports provide a demand-side assessment based on a S-I discussion, though these assessments are not always fully explained;
- Commodity-based countries provide a supply-side analysis (weather and positive shocks); and
- Other supply-side assessments refer to sector-specific factors, such as developments in the oil sector.

Use of Analytical Growth Frameworks

	Year	HP Filter	Growth Equation	Production Function: Growth accounting	Production Function: Derivative of production function	Other
Argentina	1996	x				
Armenia	1996					x[1]
Central African Republic	1998					x[1]
Congo, Rep. of	1996					x[2]
Côte d'Ivoire	1998				x[3]	
Ghana	1999					x[1]
Guinea-Bissau	1995				x[3]	
Guinea-Bissau	2000					x[1]
Guyana	1998					x[4]
Jordan	1998				x	
Kenya	2000			x		
Kyrgyz Republic	2000	x	x		x	
Macedonia, FYR	1997					x[1]
Madagascar	1996				x[3]	
Malawi	2000					x[1]
Niger	2000					x[2]
Philippines	1999	x	x	x		
Senegal	1998					x[1]
Vietnam	1999	x				
Zambia	1995					x[1]

Source: IMF Staff Reports, 1995–2000.

[1]Ad hoc (e.g., increase savings and investment through program reforms).

[2]Underlying population growth and total productivity assumptions.

[3]Based on ICOR assumptions.

[4]Report mentions rise in productivity, though no model is discussed.

III Performance of Analytical Frameworks and Program Design

The preceding discussion outlined the processes and analytical tools that national authorities—and IMF country teams in advising them—use to formulate policies in IMF-supported programs. This section seeks to examine how well these tools perform in practice, with a view to assessing the performance of the modeling process rather than evaluating the outcomes of programs.[24] Since this is difficult to do directly—and since a program is in essence defined by its intended outcomes—the tack taken here is to examine whether there are systematic errors in projections for key objectives, including real GDP growth, inflation, and the current account balance (see the section "Near-Term Macroeconomic Projections").

An important question is the horizon over which such projections should be assessed. On the one hand, most countries set budgets annually (though there may be supplemental budgets).[25] On the other hand, in IMF-supported programs, policies (and particularly program targets) are seldom set for more than one or two quarters ahead without at least some opportunity to reconsider them, in light of developments, at the time of the quarterly or semiannual program reviews. This suggests that, for assessing the analytical underpinnings of policy formulation, short horizons of one year or less (referred to as year t) are the most relevant, which in turn are affected by what is known regarding period $t-1$.[26] In this regard, the deviations between estimates and actuals in year $t-1$ show that both GRA- and PRGF-supported programs underestimate growth (Box 3.4). The current account balance is also underestimated in GRA-supported programs in spite of the overestimation of the fiscal balance, while the opposite is the case among PRGF-supported programs. Although, on average, these deviations are generally not statistically significant, their magnitude (as measured by the root mean squared error) suggests that policy settings and projections for the program period might have been different had the assessment of prevailing economic conditions been more accurate.

Examining projection errors for the year following program approval ($t+1$) is also important inasmuch as they capture whether the program's broad objectives are being met, even if there may be an opportunity to adjust policies in light of evolving developments afterwards. The evidence on projection errors mingles the effects of modeling errors, exogenous shocks, and, possibly, uneven (or even no) policy implementation. For the purposes of policy formulation, however, it is important that national authorities and country teams understand the relationships between macroeconomic policies and program objectives. In this regard, identifying appropriate corrective measures requires understanding whether targets were missed because of modeling errors, exogenous shocks, or policy slippages. In addition, even if projection errors turn out to be small, knowing how to adjust policies in light of evolving developments requires an understanding of the underlying macroeconomic model. The section "Actual and Programmed Relationships Between Policies and Targets," therefore, examines whether systematic biases exist in the relationships between macroeconomic policies and targets being assumed.

While near-term projections are the most relevant for formulating the appropriate macroeconomic policy response, member countries should also emerge from their IMF-supported programs with sustainable external debt positions.[27] Such assessments re-

[24]Outcomes and experience with IMF-supported programs are discussed in greater detail in "Objectives and Outcomes" and "Macroeconomic and Structural Policies: Review of Experience" (see Parts II and IV of this occasional paper).

[25]Some countries prepare medium-term budget frameworks, typically covering three-year periods, but these are often mainly indicative—much of the focus of economic policies is on the budget for the upcoming fiscal year.

[26]As noted above, a key component of program design is the scope for introducing adjustments to program targets and policies at the quarterly and semiannual reviews.

[27]Indeed, IMF resources cannot be provided if the country's external debt is not expected to be sustainable.

Box 3.4. Impact of Data Revisions for Year *t*–1

Estimates of previous years' outturns are preliminary at best when authorities are formulating their economic policies. In turn, different initial conditions might call for different policy choices.[1] How large are data revisions in practice? The accompanying table provides the average deviations (and standard deviations) of some key macroeconomic variables across program types between the revised (actual) data and the original program estimates for period *t*-1. The main results that emerge are as follows:

- Real GDP growth in the previous period is underestimated across all program types by over ¼ percent—however, this underestimation is not statistically significant;
- The current account balance is underestimated by about a ½ percentage point of GDP in GRA-supported programs (i.e., the deficit outturn in *t*-1 is smaller than estimated), but overestimated by ¾ percentage point in PRGF-supported programs—the former is statistically significant while the latter is not; and
- The overall fiscal balance in GRA-supported programs was overestimated by 0.4 percentage point of GDP (i.e., the deficit in *t*–1 turns out to be larger than considered at the time of the program approval), while the fiscal balance deviation in PRGF-supported programs was underestimated by about the same amount—neither is statistically significant.

[1]For a discussion, see Morgenstern (1950).

Data revisions, even if not statistically significant, might have modified policy setting. Furthermore, the projections for periods *t* and *t*+1 are also likely to have been different if the actual *t*–1 data were available at the time of program design, which could possibly reduce the projection errors.

Average Deviations[1]

(In percentage points)

	t–1	Root Mean Squared Error
Real GDP growth	0.29	3.28
EFF/SBA	0.31	4.01
SAF/ESAF/PRGF	0.26	1.94
Current account balance		
(in percent of GDP)	–0.07	2.51
EFF/SBA	0.46*	1.80
SAF/ESAF/PRGF	–0.74	3.09
Overall fiscal balance		
(in percent of GDP)	0.00	3.99
EFF/SBA	–0.40	4.65
SAF/ESAF/PRGF	0.40	2.96

Sources: IMF, MONA and WEO databases; and IMF staff calculations.

Note. * implies *t*-statistic significant at the 5 percent level.

[1]Actual minus program estimate.

quire a longer horizon and corresponding projections for the evolution of the external balance, real exchange rates, and output growth. These are examined in the section "Medium-Term Growth and Debt Sustainability."

Near-Term Macroeconomic Projections

Output Growth

On the whole, near-term projections in IMF-supported programs—reported in Table 3.2—are relatively good. In GRA-supported programs, excluding a handful of capital account crisis programs, the average bias in year *t* was not statistically significant (Figure 3.1, left panel).[28] In contrast, for capital account crisis cases, growth rates were overpredicted—on average 9¼ percentage points, a statistically significant bias. In PRGF-supported programs, growth in the year of program approval is overpredicted by 0.4 percentage points a year—a magnitude that is insignificant in relation to the volatility of growth (Figure 3.1, right panel).[29] Indeed, the root mean squared error (RMSE) of the projection is 2¼ percent a year against a standard deviation of growth of 2¾ percent a year.[30]

At the one-year horizon (i.e., growth between the year of program approval, *t*, and the next year, *t*+1) growth projections do not fare as well. The bias

[28]This result is consistent with the findings of Musso and Phillips (2001).

[29]For programs approved in the fourth quarter of year *t*, this projection refers to year *t*+1. In practice, given the time required for program discussions, the outturn for the first quarter may not even be available during negotiations of an arrangement approved at mid-year.

[30]The RMSE gives a measure of how large the typical error is without allowing for positive and negative errors across programs to cancel out each other.

Table 3.2. Statistical Characteristics of Program Projection Errors[1]

	Number of Observations	Period *t* Mean error	Period *t* RMSE	Period *t*+1 Mean error	Period *t*+1 RMSE	ρ(error *t*; error *t*+1)
Real GDP growth						
PRGF-supported programs	56	–0.4	2.2	–1.2***	3.1	0.49***
GRA-supported programs						
Transition[2]	27	0.1	3.7	–0.7	4.4	0.65***
Nontransition[2]	35	–0.3	2.7	–0.7	4.4	0.37**
Capital account crises	9	–9.3***	10.7	–0.9	5.0	–0.13
Inflation						
PRGF-supported programs	47	0.9	8.1	4.0**	13.0	0.59***
GRA-supported programs						
Transition[2]	21	0.3	12.6	5.4	16.5	0.52**
Nontransition[2]	25	1.5	12.4	1.8	11.5	–0.29
Capital account crises	6	16.1	19.7	4.9	8.6	–0.08
Current account balance						
PRGF-supported programs	48	–1.5**	4.9	–1.9***	4.8	0.64***
GRA-supported programs						
Transition[2]	24	0.4	2.5	–0.4	2.3	0.15
Nontransition[2]	28	2.4***	4.6	2.7***	5.2	0.79***
Capital account crises	8	5.6**	7.2	6.5**	8.7	0.62*

Sources: IMF, MONA and WEO databases; and IMF staff estimates.

Note. * significant at 10 percent level, ** significant at 5 percent level, and *** significant at 1 percent level .

[1]Data transformed so that they map into the interval (–100, 100) percent. Errors defined as actuals minus projections. Table constructed using a data set of countries with available information for year *t*, *t*+1, *t*+2, and *t*+3.

[2]Excludes capital account crises.

among PRGF-supported programs is about 1.2 percentage points, a statistically significant error with a RMSE of 3.1 percentage points a year. For GRA-supported programs, the bias increases to 0.7–0.9 percentage points, though these errors remain not statistically significant. Moreover, errors are serially correlated, implying that countries for which growth is overpredicted in one year are more likely to be overpredicted the following year as well.

These findings could reflect the tension that arises from using real GDP growth both as a key variable that requires realism for program design purposes and as a political objective.[31] Yet, empirical evidence suggests that upward biases are no larger when a member has an IMF-supported program than when it does not.[32] In addition, given that these growth projections are predicated on the full implementation of the authorities' intended policies, some optimistic bias could be expected.

Inflation

Inflation tends to be underpredicted in the year of program approval, but this bias is not statistically significant (Figure 3.2).[33] More precisely, inflation in the year of program approval is, on average, underpredicted by 1 percentage point a year in PRGF-supported programs and by a similar margin in GRA-supported programs (transition and nontransition combined, excluding capital account crises), but neither of these deviations is statistically significant. Among capital account crises, projection errors average 16 percentage points (while the error among capital account crises is large, it is not statistically significant, mainly on account of the small number of observations).[34]

[31]This may be particularly pertinent in low-income countries, where overly conservative growth projections may be interpreted as constraining countries' development potential.

[32]See Joshi and Ghosh (2003) for an analysis using projections undertaken for the World Economic Outlook exercise (see also IMF, 1996).

[33]The data set is mapped into the interval (–100, 100) percent to reduce the incidence of outliers.

[34]The RMSEs are also large, ranging from 8 percentage points in PRGF-supported programs to 12½ points in GRA-supported programs (and about 20 points in capital account crises).

Figure 3.1. Real GDP Growth: Projections and Outcomes[1]
(X-axis, projections; Y-axis, outcomes)

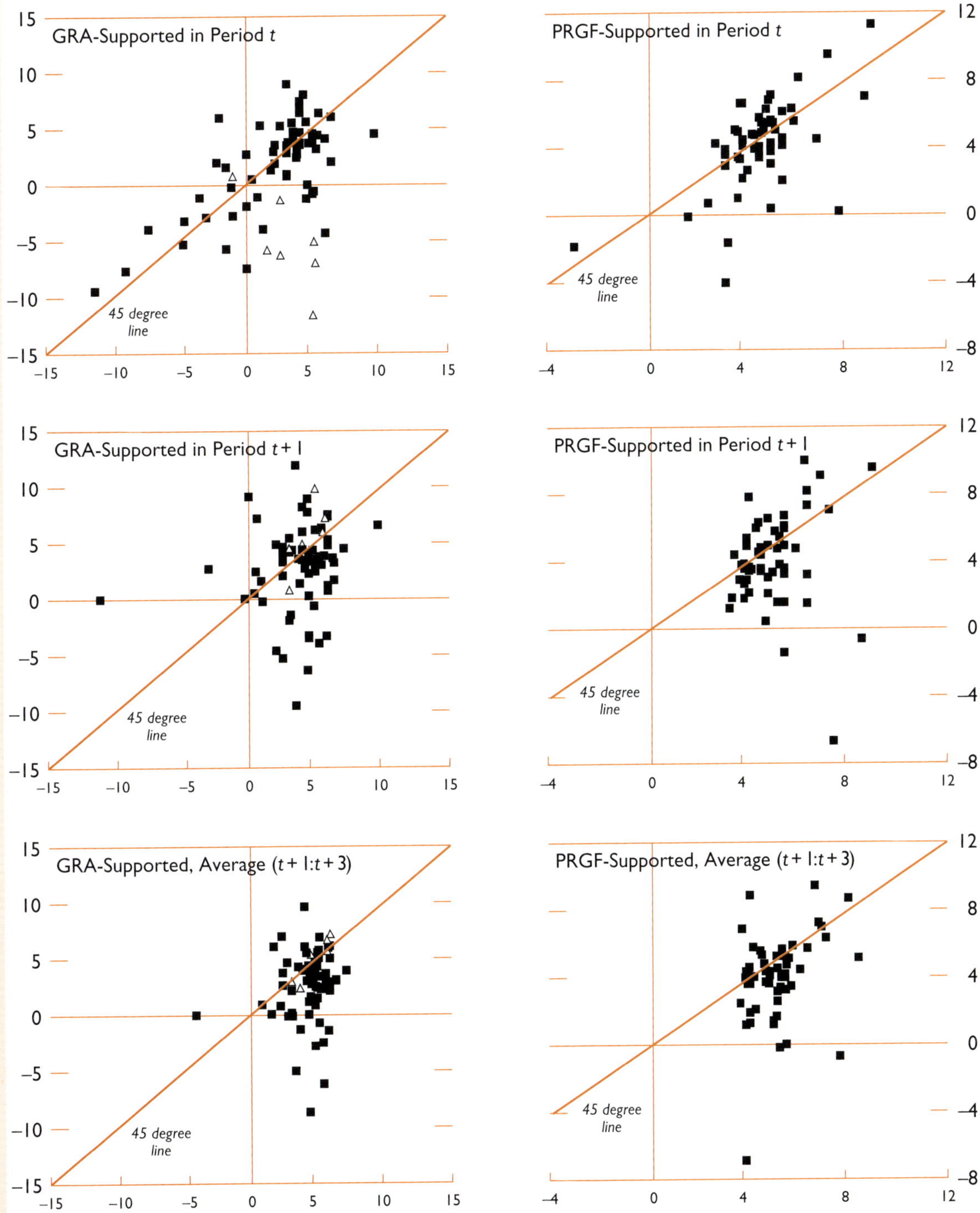

Sources: IMF, MONA and WEO databases; and IMF staff estimates.
Note. Data mapped into the interval (–100, 100) percent.
[1]Capital account crisis countries are depicted by triangles.

Figure 3.2. Inflation: Projections and Outcomes[1]
(X-axis, projections; Y-axis, outcomes)

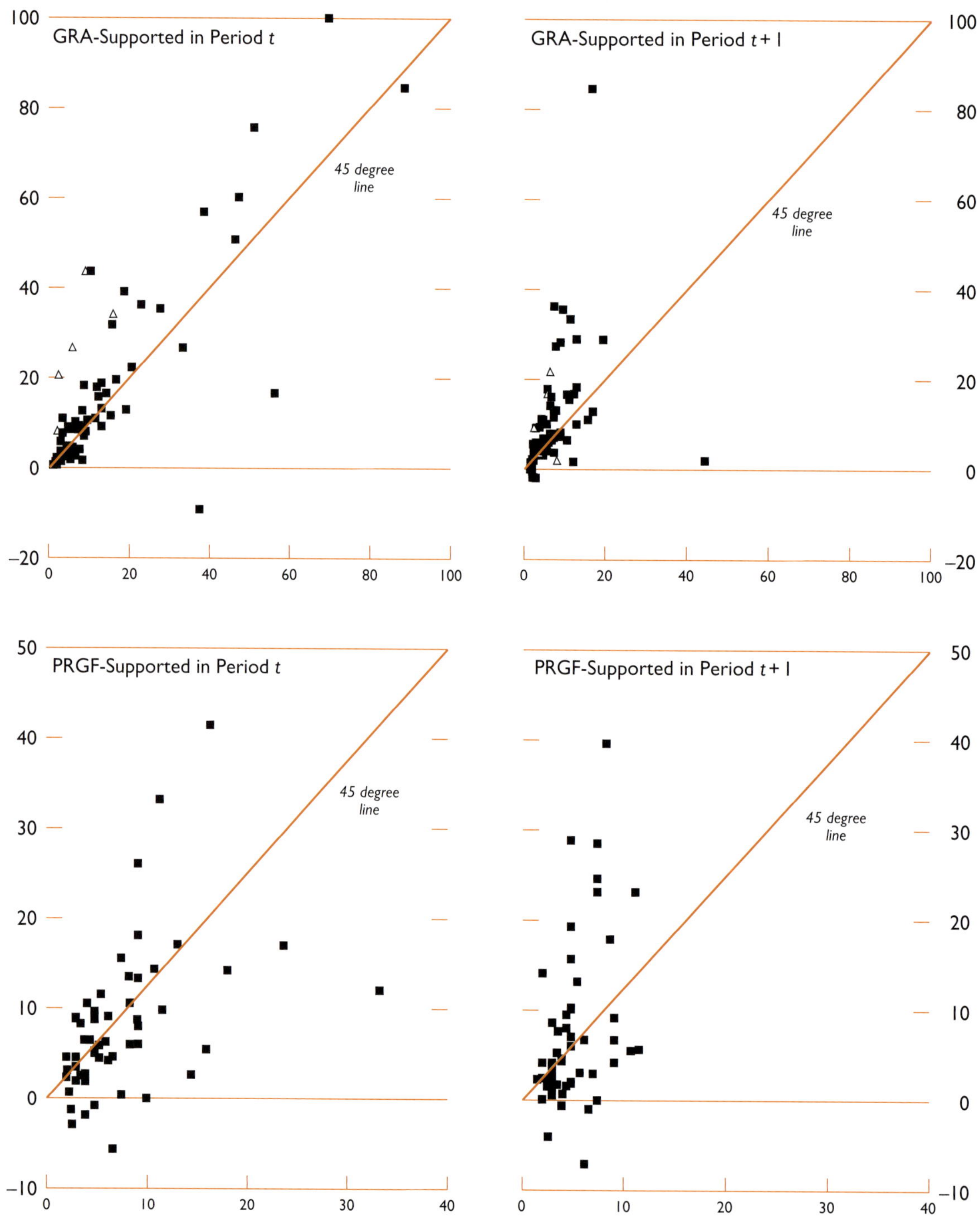

Sources: IMF, MONA and WEO databases; and IMF staff estimates.
Note. Data mapped into the interval (–100, 100) percent.
[1]Capital account crisis countries are depicted by triangles.

Projection errors for inflation in the year following program approval tend to be much larger—except among capital account crises countries—and, once again, underpredicted.[35] However, only the projection errors in PRGF-supported programs are statistically significant. The deviations may reflect unrealistic targets for disinflation rather than genuine projection errors owing in part to the tension between the realism of projections and the highly political role played by some of these economic indicators. Although the projection errors are serially correlated in PRGF-supported programs (with a statistically significant coefficient), they are generally not correlated in the GRA sample (except in transition economies).

Current Account Balance

Among GRA-supported countries, the current account in the year of program approval turns out to be stronger than expected (a larger surplus or a smaller deficit)—by about 2½ percent of GDP among nontransition economies, which is a statistically significant difference (Figure 3.3). These projection errors are particularly large, of course, for capital account crises. The comparable projection error for transition economies was not statistically significant. Among PRGF-supported programs, by contrast, current account deficits are larger than projected—by about 1½ percentage points of GDP.[36] In fact, statistically significant biases are recorded in the first few years that follow the implementation of a IMF-supported program. Projection errors are also serially correlated—if adjustment is overpredicted in one year, it is likely to be overpredicted in the following year.

Actual and Programmed Relationships Between Policies and Targets

As noted above, projection errors for key macroeconomic variables potentially mix a number of different effects—modeling errors, exogenous shocks, and weak policy implementation.[37] Program documents, however, seldom articulate explicitly the underlying framework (they simply report projections for macroeconomic variables), thus making it difficult to test whether the framework itself is correct. The approach taken here, therefore, is to consider whether the relationships between policies and targets (fiscal balance and growth; fiscal expenditures and growth; fiscal balance and the current account balance; and money growth and inflation) implicitly assumed in programs are consistent with the actual (ex post) relationships. It bears emphasizing that the issue of interest here is the bivariate interaction between the variables (for instance, the fiscal balance and growth), without any causal interpretation; as such, econometric simultaneity is not a concern.

Specifically, to test whether programmed and actual relationships differ, a bivariate regression was estimated (for instance, between the fiscal balance and output growth) on data for both actual and programmed variables, with an interactive dummy to distinguish those observations that pertain to the programmed relationship.[38] If this interactive dummy is statistically significant, then the relationship (say, between the fiscal balance and output growth) assumed in programs differs significantly from the actual relationship.[39] Controls are added for the type of IMF-supported program and other group-specific characteristics (such as capital account crisis and transition economy programs); these allow for the different *average* projection errors identified above.[40]

From Table 3.3, the null hypothesis of equality between programmed and actual relationships cannot be rejected in two instances: the effects of an increase in fiscal expenditures on growth (negative correlation; Regression [1]) and of broad money growth on inflation rates (positive correlation;

[35]See "Macroeconomic and Structural Policies: Review of Experience" (Part IV of this occasional paper) for a discussion of the reasons why inflation diverged from program targets.

[36]See "Objectives and Outcomes" (Part II of this occasional paper) for a discussion of the contrasting external adjustment patterns in GRA- and PRGF-supported programs.

[37]If the target, y, is a function of policies, x, other variables, z, and a random shock, ε: $y = \alpha + \beta x + \gamma z + \varepsilon$, then the projection error can be written as:

$$y - \hat{y} = \underbrace{(\alpha - \hat{\alpha}) + (\beta - \hat{\beta})\hat{x} + (\gamma - \hat{\gamma})\hat{z}}_{\text{Model error}} + \underbrace{\beta(x - \hat{x})}_{\text{Policy slippage}} + \underbrace{\gamma(z - \hat{z}) + \varepsilon}_{\text{Shock}}.$$

The analysis in the section "Near-Term Macroeconomic Projections" considered the full program projection error $(y - \hat{y})$, while this section focuses on whether the analytical frameworks employed in program design get the policy multipliers $(\beta - \hat{\beta})$, right. "Macroeconomic and Structural Policies: Review of Experience" (see Part IV of this occasional paper) examines the role of policy implementation in accounting for slippages in targets. See also Baqir, Ramcharan, and Sahay (2004).

[38]An alternative approach would be to estimate these regressions separately for programmed and actual data and use a Wald test statistic to test for the equality of the relationships across the two samples.

[39]These relationships pertain to variables in the year of program approval (or the following calendar year for programs approved in the fourth quarter) and year $t+1$.

[40]For example, in the current account balance regression, the dummy corresponding to PRGF-supported programs is negative, reflecting the lower-than-projected external balances in these countries. Conversely, the capital account crisis dummy is positive, reflecting the greater-than-programmed current account adjustment.

Figure 3.3. Current Account Balance: Projections and Outcomes[1]

(X-axis, projections; Y-axis, outcomes)

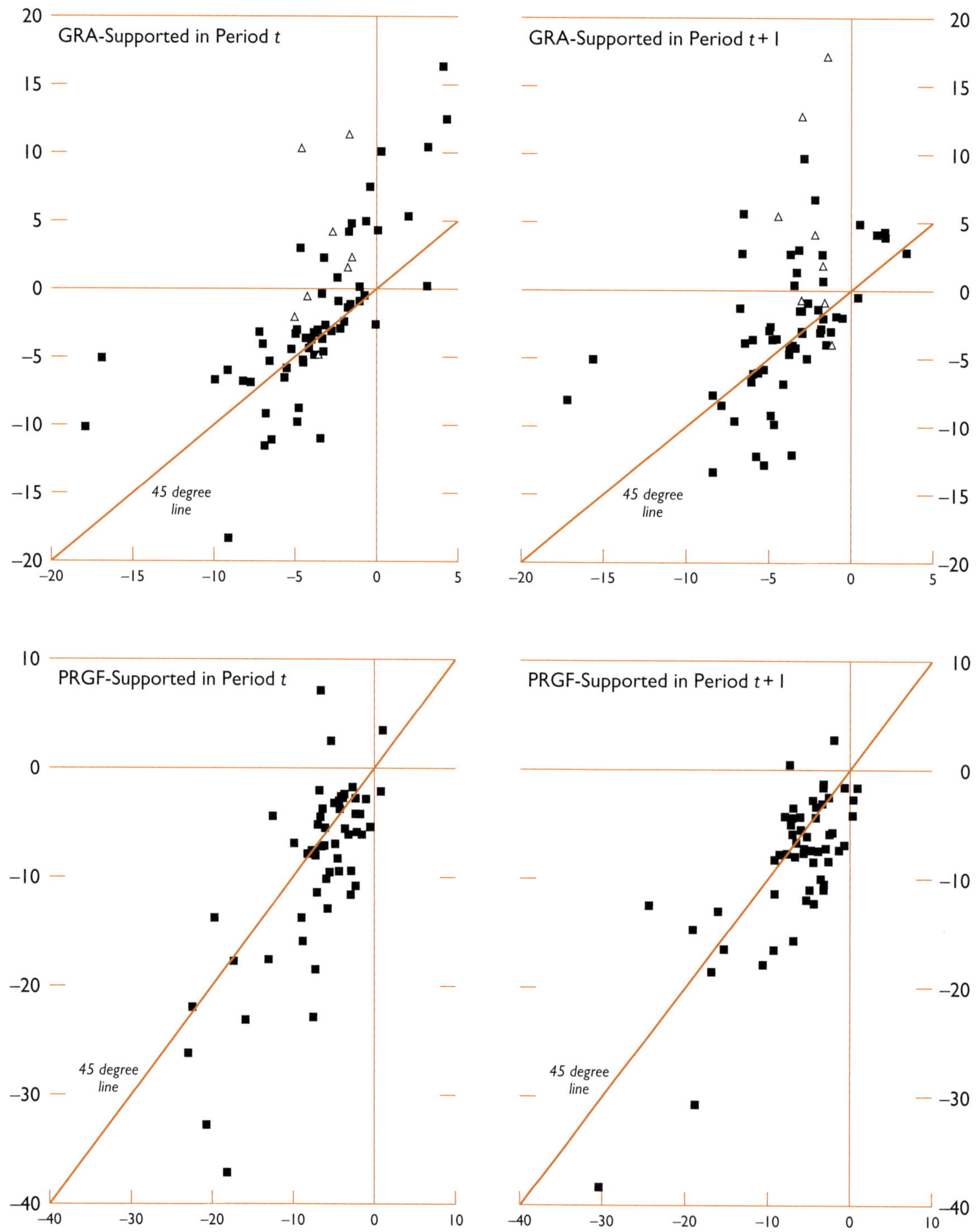

Sources: IMF, MONA and WEO databases; and IMF staff estimates.

[1]Capital account crisis countries are depicted by triangles.

Table 3.3. Programmed and Actual Relationships Between Policies and Targets[1,2]

Regression [1]		Regression [2]	
Dependent variable		Dependent variable	
Real GDP growth		Inflation	
Regressors		Regressors	
Fiscal expenditures	–0.06***	Broad money growth	0.67***
Fiscal expenditure times projection dummy	**0.03**	**Broad money growth times projection dummy**	**0.03**
Projection dummy	0.16	Projection dummy	–1.70
PRGF dummy	1.51***	PRGF dummy	–2.24**
Transition economy dummy	–0.27	Transition economy dummy	2.98**
CAC dummy[3]	2.61***	CAC dummy[3]	3.13
Intercept	3.41***	Intercept	0.31
Number of observations	365	Number of observations	397
R squared	0.19	R squared	0.53

Regression [3]		Regression [4]	
Dependent variable		Dependent variable	
Current account balance		Real GDP growth	
Regressors		Regressors	
Fiscal balance	0.48***	Fiscal balance	0.25***
Fiscal balance times projection dummy	**–0.32***	**Fiscal balance times projection dummy**	**–0.17****
Projection dummy	–1.34**	Projection dummy	0.37
PRGF dummy	–4.56***	PRGF dummy	2.06***
Transition economy dummy	–1.00	Transition economy dummy	–0.09
CAC dummy[3]	2.75**	CAC dummy[3]	–1.64***
Intercept	–1.62*	Intercept	2.25***
Number of observations	443	Number of observations	452
R squared	0.26	R squared	0.20

Sources: IMF, MONA and WEO databases; and IMF staff estimates.

Note. * significant at 10 percent level, ** significant at 5 percent level, and *** significant at 1 percent level.

[1]Pooled OLS regressions with year dummies.

[2]Panel data set for period *t* and period *t*+1.

[3]CAC stands for capital account crisis program.

Regression [2]).[41] Underlying the reduced form relationship between inflation and money growth is the behavior of money demand. It is noteworthy in this regard that the projected relationship between lower inflation and remonetization does not differ much from the actual relationship (Box 3.5).

In contrast, the improvement in the current account balance and the fiscal balance reveals a statistically significant difference; projections assume a weaker relationship between the fiscal balance and the current account balance than is (ex post) present in the data (see Regression [3]). Specifically, a 1 percent of GDP fiscal tightening was expected to be associated with a 0.16 percent of GDP improvement in the current account balance; in fact, it would have been associated with a 0.48 percent of GDP improvement in the current account balance.[42]

Finally, in light of concerns about the impact on growth of fiscal tightening, the relationship between

[41]As may be expected, the actual relationships, while statistically significant, are quite weak (low R^2), reflecting the diversity of country-specific characteristics. The issue of interest, however, is whether policy formulation in programs assumes a relationship that is different from the actual relationship. For example, Keynesian effects—the relationship between output and either the fiscal balance or government expenditure—may happen to be weak in countries seeking IMF support, in which case it would be important for national authorities not to assume strong Keynesian effects since the policy prescription would inappropriately call for a fiscal loosening. Conversely, if Keynesian effects are in fact strong but are ignored in program design, then the program may call for a fiscal tightening without considering the impact on growth.

[42]The multiplier implied by the program projection is given by the sum of the coefficient on the fiscal balance (0.48) and the coefficient on the interactive program dummy (–0.32).

Box 3.5. Inflation and Money Demand: Program Versus Actual Remonetization

Underlying the relationship between money growth and inflation projected in the program are assumptions about the behavior of money demand. In particular, programs often assume that the lower inflation expected under the program will result in remonetization—that is, a decrease in velocity. This raises the question of how the response of velocity to inflation embodied in the program compares to the actual relationship.

To examine this, the table below reports estimates of a money demand function that relates velocity growth to change in income and inflation (both instrumented by their own lags and terms of trade growth) for a panel of 59 nontransition economies (that had IMF-supported programs at some point during 1995–2000) over the period 1994–2003.

There is a positive relationship between velocity and expected inflation: since higher inflation reduces money demand, lower inflation should raise money demand and reduce velocity (column (1)). By this metric (Δv^B), programs are conservative: on average, whereas the estimate would suggest that velocity should decrease by 3½ percent a year in GRA-supported programs (given their programmed decrease in inflation), in fact programs assumed that velocity would remain largely unchanged (a change of only 0.1 percent a year), resulting in a statistically significant difference of 3.4 percentage points a year (see accompanying table). Likewise, the difference in PRGF-supported program was 1.7 percentage points a year.

The actual relationship between remonetization and inflation is more complex however, and suggests a ratchet effect on money demand (column (2)): higher inflation *(DPOS)* increases velocity, but a decrease in inflation *(DNEG)* does not lead to a corresponding decrease in velocity. Taking account of this statistically significant ratchet effect, the remonetization assumed in GRA-supported programs due to disinflation is largely in line with the estimated empirical relationship (a deviation of 0.3 percentage points a year), while PRGF-supported programs are marginally more conservative (corresponding to higher velocity growth of about 1½ percentage points a year than would be implied by the empirical relationship)—but neither of these deviations is statistically significant.

[1]The money demand function takes the form $m - p = \alpha y - \beta \pi^e$. Taking first differences and rearranging gives: $\Delta v \equiv \Delta m - \pi - \Delta y = (\alpha - 1)\Delta y - \beta \Delta \pi^e$.

Velocity and Inflation: Panel Regression Results[1]

Dependent Variable: Velocity Growth	Nontransition GRA-Supported (1)	Nontransition GRA-Supported (2)	Nontransition PRGF-Supported (1)	Nontransition PRGF-Supported (2)
Real GDP growth[2]	0.112	–0.047	0.399*	0.451**
Change in inflation[2]	0.531*	. . .	0.335***	. . .
$\Delta\pi$*DPOS*[2]	. . .	0.909**	. . .	0.433***
$\Delta\pi$*DNEG*[2]	. . .	–0.106	. . .	0.169
R^2	0.106	0.118	0.213	0.217
Number of observations	250	250	340	340
Program versus benchmark velocity growth[3]				
$\Delta v^P - \Delta v^B$	3.4*	2.2	1.7	1.1
$\Delta v^{P-} - \Delta v^{B-}$	. . .	0.3	. . .	1.5

Sources: IMF, MONA and WEO databases; and IMF staff estimates.

[1]All regressions include country dummies; significant at *** 1 percent, ** 5 percent, and * 10 percent levels.

[2]*DPOS* and *DNEG* are dummy variables that equal 1 if $\Delta\pi>0$ and $\Delta\pi<0$, respectively, and 0 otherwise, where $\Delta\pi$ stands for change in inflation; all regressors are instrumented by their own three lags and the terms of trade growth; real GDP growth and inflation are transformed to be mapped into an interval (–100, 100) percent to reduce the influence of outliers.

[3]Δv^P refers to programmed velocity growth; Δv^B is the benchmark velocity growth constructed by using the estimated coefficients and programmed change in inflation ($\Delta\pi^P$) and real GDP growth (Δy^P); Δv^{P-} and Δv^{B-} represent, respectively, the values of Δv^P and Δv^B for disinflation programs (with $\Delta\pi^P<0$) only.

the fiscal balance and growth is examined (Regression [4]).[43] Program projections implied that a 1 percent of GDP fiscal tightening would be associated with a 0.08 percentage point increase in growth; in fact, it would have been associated with a 0.25 percentage point increase in growth.[44] The difference is also statistically significant.

While caution is required in any causal interpretation since these estimates do not correct for potential

[43]See Independent Evaluation Office (2003).

[44]The multiplier implied in this case is given by the sum of the coefficient on the fiscal balance (0.25) and the coefficient on the interactive program dummy (–0.17).

Table 3.4. Medium-Term Program Projection Errors[1]

	Number of Observations	Average Period $t+1:t+3$	
		Mean error	RMSE
Real GDP growth			
PRGF-supported programs	56	–1.3***	2.8
GRA-supported programs			
Transition[2]	27	–0.5	2.9
Nontransition[2]	35	–2.4***	4.3
Capital account crises	7	–0.4	2.3
Current account balance			
PRGF-supported programs	48	–2.2***	4.1
GRA-supported programs			
Transition[2]	24	–0.8	2.6
Nontransition[2]	28	1.6***	3.2
Capital account crises	. . .	. . .	. . .

Sources: IMF, MONA and WEO databases; and IMF staff estimates.

Note. * significant at 10 percent level, ** significant at 5 percent level, and *** significant at 1 percent level.

[1]Data transformed so that they map into the interval (–100, 100) percent. Errors defined as actuals minus projections. Table constructed using a data set for countries with available information for year t, $t+1$, $t+2$, and $t+3$.

[2]Excludes capital account crises.

endogeneity of the fiscal balance (e.g., endogeneity could arise from higher growth raising revenues and improving the fiscal balance), these findings suggest that programs project too large a negative impact on growth and too small a positive impact on the current account balance of a given fiscal tightening.[45]

Medium-Term Growth and Debt Sustainability

Recent debt crises in emerging market economies as well as the need for debt relief for low-income countries have underscored the importance of accurate debt sustainability analyses. As discussed above, the IMF's debt sustainability template is intended to bring greater discipline to such projections. Building on results for errors in projecting medium-term growth and the current account balance, this section considers the sources of errors in projecting external debt ratios, while noting that the sample covered (1995–2000) precedes the introduction of standardized debt sustainability templates.

Medium-Term Growth

With the exception of the capital account crises, the medium-term growth projection error averaged over the three years following program approval is as large as, or larger than, the error in the year of program approval (Table 3.4). Among both GRA- (excluding transition economies and capital account crises) and PRGF-supported programs the average errors are statistically significant, raising questions about the accuracy of these medium-term growth projections.

In fact, with the exception of the industrial countries, preliminary results suggest that projections from a cross-country growth model could outperform medium-term projections contained in staff reports (Box 3.6). Medium-term growth projections could be enhanced in a number of ways. One possibility would be to generate growth projections centrally using a cross-country growth model.[46] However, this may be too mechanical and would need to be informed by additional information available to the country authorities and desk economists. A variant of this approach would be to estimate the cross-country model, but use its projections as a reference point and "reality check" for the projections prepared by national authorities and IMF country teams. Significant deviations from the pro-

[45]One explanation may be that the economy is assumed to be more closed than it is in reality, leading to the overestimation of the implicit Keynesian multiplier. Evidence presented in "Macroeconomic and Structural Polices: Review of Experience" (Part IV of this occasional paper) using instrumental variable estimation (i.e., controlling for endogeneity), however, also finds a positive relationship between the fiscal balance and growth among IMF-supported programs.

[46]The models could also be estimated for different types of countries to capture, for example, region-specific or economic structure-specific aspects that may have implications for growth.

Box 3.6. Medium-Term Growth Projections Using Cross-Country Growth Models

IMF growth projections tend to be overly optimistic as documented in a number of reports and forums; for example, the PRSP/PRGF reviews and PRSP progress report, the IEO's reports on prolonged users of IMF resources and on fiscal adjustment in IMF-supported programs, and reports on IMF projections prepared outside the institution (such as the U.S. General Accounting Office (2003) and the Heritage Foundation (see Beech and others, 1999)). As discussed elsewhere in this paper, the one- and three-year-ahead projection errors average about 1¼ percent a year. Similar biases apply to five-year-ahead projections.

Can these projections be improved?

Improving growth projections is not an easy task, in part because they are conditional on the implementation of policies and on the absence of shocks. Still, a number of analytical methods are available. One method is reduced form growth equations. While these equations have many recognized weaknesses (e.g., unstable coefficient estimates and lack of a theoretical foundation), they also have advantages, in particular the drawing together of cross-country information. Although these equations are ill-suited for short-term projections, working backwards they serve to cap overoptimistic tendencies. In addition, they offer a benchmark against which to argue about a country's growth potential.

To this end, a cross-country growth equation is estimated for the five-year periods between 1981 and 1995 and one out-of-sample projection is carried out for 1996–2000. The projections are based on historical trends for the right-hand variables in the equation and on projections for the two macroeconomic indicators in the equation (inflation and fiscal balance). The latter serves as control for the macroeconomic (but not the structural) aspects on which country projections are based.

What are the results?

The results, which focus on the projection accuracy (Theil U-statistic: the ratio of the root mean square errors of the model projections relative to those derived by country desks, with a value less than one implying that the model is more accurate), suggest that the model outperforms projections in developing countries, but performs very poorly among high-income countries. The differences in the model and projections are, on aggregate, statistically significant. These results must be qualified, however, by the fact that the results apply to only one out-of-sample forecast period (1996–2000).

Medium-Term Growth Projections, 1996–2000

	Value	Number of Countries
Error in country projections	1.37	109
Average error in growth equation projections	0.36	109
Total Theil U	0.85	109
High-income	1.22	14
Upper middle-income	0.99	20
Lower middle-income	0.91	32
Low-income	0.77	43

Source: Batista annd Zalduendo (2004).

jections implied by the cross-country growth model would warrant closer scrutiny. This could include an analysis of the explanatory variables expected to generate the faster growth, a more detailed understanding of the country's own past growth performance vis-à-vis the model, or a comparison of the model's projections for a particular country relative to those of neighboring countries facing similar economic challenges. Even a discussion of why the cross-country growth model may be performing poorly for a given country could be revealing and may help identify specific growth bottlenecks facing a country.

Debt Sustainability

Both errors in projecting output growth and in projecting the current account balance feed into projections errors for the external debt ratio.[47] Regarding the current account balance, on average during a three-year period, the balance is higher (or the deficit is smaller) by 1½ percent of GDP in nontransition GRA-supported programs. PRGF-supported programs continue their underadjustment (relative to program projections), on average by about 2¼ percent of GDP during a three-year period (Table 3.4). Since external debt is normally denominated in foreign currency, debt-projection errors are affected by unanticipated real exchange rate movements.

To quantify the importance of these three sources of errors, Table 3.5 decomposes the difference be-

[47]As discussed in Daseking and others (2004), for example, optimistic growth projections during the early and mid-1990s, partly based on reforms undertaken earlier in the decade, resulted in overly sanguine assessments of public and external debt sustainability.

Table 3.5. Decomposition of Debt-to-GDP Projection Errors

(Accumulated errors at end period; in percent of GDP)

			Error as of End of Period t				Error as of End of Period $t+1$				Error as of End of Period $t+2$					
	Number of Observations	Actual Debt in $t-1$	Growth effect	Exchange rate effect	Adjustment effect	Total effect	Growth effect	Exchange rate effect	Adjustment effect	Total effect	Growth effect	Exchange rate effect	Adjustment effect	Total effect	Projected Debt in $t+2$[1]	Actual Debt in $t+2$[2]
PRGF-supported programs	55	118.0	0.8	–0.4	1.9	2.4	3.0	3.2	3.9	10.2	4.3	7.8	5.7	17.8	105.3	123.2
GRA-supported programs																
Transition[3]	21	41.8	0.2	0.3	–0.1	0.4	0.6	1.2	0.9	2.7	0.7	2.8	2.1	5.6	30.3	36.0
Nontransition[3]	31	53.7	0.7	1.1	–2.0	–0.2	1.2	–1.4	–3.8	–4.0	2.6	–0.5	–3.2	–1.0	47.1	46.0
Capital account crises	5	50.6	5.4	33.1	–7.9	30.7	7.7	29.3	–15.3	21.7	7.5	26.1	–20.5	13.1	52.8	65.9

Sources: IMF, MONA and WEO databases; and IMF staff estimates.

[1]Derived by adding the projected current account balance to the $t-1$ actual debt stock after adjusting for FDI flows. Lack of FDI data in the MONA database results in the use of actual FDI data.

[2]Derived by adding the actual current account balance to the $t-1$ actual debt stock after adjusting for actual FDI flows. May differ from actual WEO data on debt due to changes in coverage and changes in cross-exchange rates of the currencies in which a country's debt is denominated.

[3]Excludes capital account crises.

tween the actual[48] and programmed debt ratio into the part attributable to current account deficits, real exchange rates, or real GDP growth.[49] In PRGF-supported programs, the average initial debt to GDP ratio was 118 percent of GDP and was projected to decline to 105 percent in three years. However, the actual ratio rose to 123 percent of GDP over the three-year period. The divergence over a three-year period between projected and actual face value of external debt thus amounted to almost 18 percent of GDP.[50] Lower-than-projected growth contributed 4¼ percentage points of GDP to this error, larger real exchange rate depreciation contributed a further 8 percentage points, while larger current account deficits than programmed accounted for another 5¾ percentage points.

Among GRA-supported programs, the initial level of external debt averaged 49 percent of GDP and was projected to decline to 41 percent, but in fact declined by less to 44 percent of GDP. The decomposition depends upon the type of country. For transition economies, which saw a significant increase in growth during this period, the projection error was larger (equivalent to 6 percent of GDP; Table 3.5). The error in projecting growth contributes roughly ¾ percentage points to the debt projection error, larger real exchange rate movements account for a further 3 percentage points, and less current account adjustment than anticipated adds another 2 percentage points of GDP. In nontransition GRA programs (excluding capital account crises), the projection error was negligible (1 percentage point of GDP). Lower growth accounted for 2½ percentage points of the error—which is more than offset by greater external adjustment than the program anticipated. In capital account crises the projection error was largest (13 percentage points of GDP). Lower growth and greater real exchange rate depreciation together accounted for the debt ratio being almost 30 percentage points of GDP higher than projected, but over half this increase was offset by greater external adjustment than envisaged and less borrowing.

[48]To derive a consistent external debt series, the current account deficit (net of foreign direct investment) is accumulated starting from the level of external debt in the year preceding the program. The only differences between the level of external debt thus implied and the actual level of external debt should arise from changes in coverage or movements of cross-exchange rates (relative to the U.S. dollar) of the currencies in which countries might be borrowing (generally, yen or euro). "Macroeconomic and Structural Policies: Review of Experience" (Part IV of this occasional paper) reports similar decomposition for public debt dynamics.

[49]Define $\bar{y}^a_{t+k} = \Pi^k_{i=0}(1 + g_{t+i})y^a_{t-1}$ as the actual level of GDP at a constant U.S. dollar value of the GDP deflator, where y^a_{t-1} is the U.S. dollar value of nominal GDP in year t–1, and g is the real GDP growth rate. Likewise, define $\bar{y}^p_{t+k} = \Pi^k_{i=0}(1 + g^p_{t+i})y^a_{t-1}$ as the projected level of GDP at a constant U.S. dollar value of the GDP deflator. Then the projection error in the debt ratio at any horizon k can be written:

$$\frac{d^a_{t+k}}{y^a_{t+k}} - \frac{d^p_{t+k}}{y^p_{t+k}} = \underbrace{\left[\frac{d^a_{t+k}}{y^a_{t+k}} - \frac{d^p_{t+k}}{y^a_{t+k}}\right]}_{\textit{Deficit}} + \underbrace{\left[\frac{d^p_{t+k}}{y^a_{t+k}} - \frac{d^p_{t+k}}{\bar{y}^a_{t+k}}\right] - \left[\frac{d^p_{t+k}}{y^p_{t+k}} - \frac{d^p_{t+k}}{\bar{y}^p_{t+k}}\right]}_{\textit{Real exchange rate}} + \underbrace{\left[\frac{d^p_{t+k}}{\bar{y}^a_{t+k}} - \frac{d^p_{t+k}}{\bar{y}^p_{t+k}}\right]}_{\textit{Real GDP growth}},$$

where the first term represents the effects of larger than expected deficits, the second term is the effect of the real exchange rate (i.e., the U.S. dollar value of the GDP deflator) depreciation, and the third term is the effect of lower real GDP growth. This accounting decomposition does not identify the underlying shocks, driving these deviations from the projections, such as exogenous terms of trade shocks, unpredictable disbursements of foreign aid, or policy slippages.

[50]The increase in the net present value (NPV) of debt will be smaller since the current account adjustment error (which contributes 5.7 percent of GDP to the face value projection error) will affect the NPV by (1 – GE)CAD, where GE is the grant element (equal to the ratio of the NPV to face value) and CAD is the current account deficit.

IV Conclusions

In recent years, the circumstances under which members seek IMF support have evolved considerably, raising the question of whether the process of policy formulation and program design remains appropriate and whether analytical tools remain relevant.

While no single model or analytical framework is universally applicable, policy formulation relies on a variety of models and techniques and employs economic judgment. A key feature of this general approach is its flexibility and adaptability, with program reviews providing an opportunity to reassess policies. In this regard, financial programming provides a convenient approach to tie together projections for individual sectors while ensuring an internally consistent analysis. It also serves as a standardized ex post monitoring tool.

Such adaptability of policies is especially important in capital account crises where unanticipated capital flows may have pervasive macroeconomic consequences. As stressed in the recent theoretical literature, such capital flows can interact with balance sheet exposures, altering not only the magnitude but potentially even the sign of policy multipliers. Balance sheet approaches can shed some light on the possible magnitudes and effects of capital flows, but cannot provide precise predictions, and the data requirements are often formidable.

At short horizons relevant for setting macroeconomic policies and program targets, growth projections are not biased and the errors are relatively small—excluding capital account crises. Over longer horizons, however, programs systematically overestimate growth, especially in low-income countries. Inflation is underestimated both in the year of program approval but also in following years as programmed disinflation targets become more ambitious. Current account projections also exhibit some bias, albeit in opposite directions in GRA- and PRGF-supported programs.[51] In GRA-supported programs, the current account balance improves by more than expected reflecting unanticipated capital outflows. In PRGF-supported programs, by contrast, current account adjustment fall short of expectations and foreign borrowing is higher than envisaged. These results have implications for the accuracy of debt sustainability assessments.

Greater understanding of what drives growth is critical to reduce the systematic bias in growth projections. While there is a substantial empirical literature on factors that could contribute to better growth performance—including macroeconomic stability and certain characteristics of institutions—analytical tools are generally lacking, and such tools as do exist are not always fully used. Cross-country growth regressions can help identify some of the structural areas in which a country lags relative to comparator countries and thus might benefit from reforms, and might serve to discipline medium-term growth projections. At the same time, it is important not to overestimate the growth benefits of specific structural measures—in particular, effects that pertain to short-run growth should be distinguished from those that raise the country's long-term growth potential.

Finally, the diversity of country experiences makes it difficult to formulate strong tests of whether programmed relationships between policies and targets have, at least on average, been correct. With this caveat in mind, it is noteworthy that programs on average project the behavior of the money multiplier as well as the relationship between broad money growth and inflation, and the relationship between government expenditure and output growth. However, programs underestimate the impact on the current account balance of an improvement in the fiscal balance, as well as the positive association between fiscal adjustment and output growth—implicitly assuming that the economy is more closed than it is in reality.

These findings suggest a number of priorities for future work. First, though the current approach of drawing on a variety of models and methods for short-term projections works reasonably well (in that biases in projections, except in regard to the capital account crises, are small), there remains scope for improvement—including through im-

[51] See also "Objectives and Outcomes" (Part II of this occasional paper).

proved statistical data to provide a sounder basis for making projections. Second, both in low- and in middle-income countries, medium-term growth projections—necessary, inter alia, for debt sustainability analysis—need to be improved and disciplined. Third, since in capital account crises the behavioral response of the economy depends on private capital flows, gaining a better understanding of the determinants of such flows could contribute significantly to better program design. Fourth, relatedly, recent theoretical models suggest that balance sheet effects can potentially alter the magnitude and sign of policy multipliers; further development and wider application of the balance sheet approach could help resolve some of the ambiguities that arise during such crises. Finally, national authorities and IMF country teams working collaboratively might explore more systematically the scope for using small econometric models, sharing experiences, and disseminating information on best practices, thus contributing to better designed—and better owned—IMF-supported programs. In a related fashion, a more candid discussion of deviations between program targets and outcomes during program reviews could serve to provide better guidance for the design (and revision) of IMF-supported programs.

Appendix I The Financial Programming Model

"Financial programming" has been used in different contexts and with different meanings. At one extreme, financial programming is an economic model linking the financing of the fiscal deficit to the behavior of foreign exchange reserves (or, under a floating regime, exchange market pressures). This model, first articulated in a series of papers by Polak (1957) and Robichek (1967 and 1971), was developed in a world of fixed (but adjustable) parities, generally limited recourse to domestic bond financing by governments, and little or no mobility of private capital (IMF, 1997). In order to deliver this predicted relationship, the model requires a number of simplifying behavioral assumptions, including exogeneity of growth, no bond financing (at the margin) of the fiscal deficit, and stability of money demand. Even when these assumptions are violated, however, the identities underlying the financial programming framework must hold. At the very least, therefore, the framework provides a convenient consistency check on macroeconomic projections underlying program design. In practice, financial programming is often used as a general approach—helping to inform projections of individual sectors (external, monetary, fiscal) without pinning down precisely every parameter of the program—but, depending upon country circumstances, as more than a mere set of identities that must hold for any set of consistent projections.

This appendix lays out the basic financial programming model and discusses some of its advantages and weaknesses as well as the circumstances in which the financial programming as a general approach is likely to be useful.

Basic Formulation of Financial Programming

Base money (M) consists of domestic credit to the government (DC_G), the private sector (DC_p), or international reserves (R)[52]:

$$\Delta M \equiv \Delta DC_G + \Delta DC_p + \bar{e}\Delta R, \qquad (1)$$

where $\bar{e}$ is a fixed or given exchange rate. The government finances its deficit by borrowing from the central bank, the domestic bond market B_G or (in foreign currency) from the international capital markets B_G^* :

$$Def = \Delta DC_G + \Delta B_G + \bar{e}\Delta B_G^*. \qquad (2)$$

Real output growth is projected, $\Delta y = \Delta \bar{y}$, the inflation target is given, $\pi = \bar{\pi}$, and velocity, v, is predictable, therefore money demand is predictable:

$$\Delta M = \Delta \bar{M} = M(\Delta \bar{y} + \bar{\pi} + \Delta \bar{v}). \qquad (3)$$

Substituting (1) and (3) into (2) yields:

$$Def = \bar{e}\Delta B_G^* + \Delta B_G + (\Delta \bar{M} - \Delta DC_p - \bar{e}\Delta R). \qquad (4)$$

Assuming that the government has, at the margin, no recourse to bond financing $\Delta B_G = 0$, $\Delta B_G^* = 0$, a reserves target, $\Delta R = \Delta \tilde{R}$ at a given exchange rate, $\bar{e}$, and that there is a required minimum expansion of credit to the private sector, $\Delta DC_p = \Delta \overline{DC}_p$, gives a limit on the financeable budget deficit:

$$Def = (\Delta \bar{M} - \Delta \overline{DC}_p - \bar{e}\Delta \tilde{R}). \qquad (5)$$

Modeling Advantage of Financial Programming

As a means of modeling the balance of payments, financial programming offers a number of advantages. It provides a direct link between policies (the fiscal deficit, monetary policy) and the reserves target while requiring only central bank (or banking system) balance sheet data, which should be readily available for both program projections and monitoring. Another advantage is that by exploiting Walras's Law and the assumed stability of money demand it obviates the need to model private capital flows, which is an important advantage inasmuch as existing empirical models of capital flows—based, for instance, on interest parity conditions—tend to perform very poorly.

[52]The model can be applied to the central bank's balance sheet (as done here) or to the banking system aggregates under the assumption of a stable money multiplier.

Table 3.A1. Volatility of Reserve Money Velocity[1]
(In percent a year)

	PRGF-Supported		GRA-Supported		Capital Account Crises	
	σ(t–5, t–1)	σ(t, t+3)	σ(t–5, t–1)	σ(t, t+3)	σ(t–5, t–1)	σ(t, t+3)
Reserve money velocity						
Average	15.0	9.3	10.5	10.2	8.7	14.6
Median	12.2	7.5	8.9	9.1	8.5	12.5

[1]Velocity is defined as reserve money divided by nominal GDP; volatility is measured by standard deviation of velocity growth.

To see the last point, the balance of payments identity can be rewritten:

$$(S_p - I_p) + (S_G - I_g) = CA(\bar{y}, \bar{e}) = -e\Delta B_p^* - e(\Delta B_G^* + \Delta R), \quad (6)$$

which states that, at a given level of economic activity and exchange rate, the current account deficit must be financed by net borrowing by the private sector, ΔB_p^*, or borrowing by the public sector (net of its accumulation of reserves), $\Delta B_G^* - \Delta R$. Using the identity that private saving must take the form of acquiring government bonds, foreign assets, base money (net of credit extended to the private sector) or domestic physical assets:

$$S_p = (\Delta M - \Delta DC_p) + \Delta B_G - e\Delta B_p^* + I_p \quad (7)$$

and substituting (7) into (6) gives:

$$(\Delta M - \Delta DC_p) + \Delta B_G - e\Delta B_p^* - Def = -e\Delta B_p^* - e(\Delta B_G^* - \Delta R) \quad (8)$$

so the term representing private capital flows, $-e\Delta B_p^*$, cancels on both sides of the equation, yielding the familiar financial programming relationship between the fiscal deficit and the accumulation of reserves as shown in (4).

Criticism of Financial Programming

The very simplicity of the financial programming framework, however, is the basis of much of its criticism. Common criticisms center on the theoretical limits to the approach, and on the realism of its underlying assumptions. It is often argued, for instance, that governments typically have at least some scope for bond financing, that real growth is not sufficiently endogenous with respect to the macroeconomic policies (Edwards, 1989; Killick, 1995; and Taylor, 1988), and that money demand is unlikely to be predictable. The model can, in part, accommodate these criticisms. For example, specific projections of the government's ability to borrow internationally or in the domestic bond market are readily accommodated within the framework—although significant reliance on nonbank financing requires a shift in focus to the overall fiscal deficit from controlling the size of the bank-financed fiscal deficit. Likewise, by postulating a link between the provision of credit to the private sector and economic activity, it is possible to endogenize the behavior of output growth, though the framework is not well suited to handling Keynesian effects and is clearly not intended as a model of long-term growth.[53]

The charge that money demand may be unpredictable is potentially more telling, since predictable money demand is the cornerstone of the financial programming approach.[54] Ultimately, however, whether money demand is predictable is an empirical question that needs to be viewed against uncertainties in other economic relationships. Import and export demand functions, for instance, may also be difficult to predict, so that alternative approaches to modeling the

[53]Ghosh (1996) develops a simple empirical model in which output growth depends upon real credit to the private sector, and applies it to the effects of credit expansion (to finance a fiscal deficit) on the dynamics of inflation, wages, the exchange rate, and output.

[54]Empirical studies suggest that, at least in industrial countries, traditional money demand functions began to break down in the late 1970s and 1980s. Notably, in the United States, a deterioration in the link between M2 and GDP over the 1980s led the Federal Reserve to drop M2 as a reliable indicator of monetary policy in 1993. Goldfeld and Sichel (1990) attributed the instability to deregulation and financial innovation and suggested that using broader monetary aggregates might yield more stable results. Indeed, in Germany, financial innovation played a less important role than in other countries contributing to its relatively stable money demand (Issing, 1992 and 1997). More recent studies incorporating financial innovation variables and better econometric tools have yielded somewhat more stable results (e.g., see Lown and others, 1999).

Table 3.A2. Change in Fiscal Balance, Reserve Accumulation, and Change in Reserve Accumulation: Regression Results

Dependent Variable	GRA-Supported				PRGF-Supported			
	Constant	$\Delta GBAL^1$	R^2	Number of observations	Constant	$\Delta GBAL^1$	R^2	Number of observations
ΔRES^1	1.351**	–0.309**	0.121	41	0.929*	0.412*	0.135	23
$\Delta(\Delta RES)^1$	–0.571	–0.440**	0.137	40	–0.263	0.360	0.055	22

[1]*RES* and *GBAL* refer to foreign reserves and general government balance in percent of GDP of the previous year, respectively; Δ indicates a first difference; * significant at 10 percent level, ** significant at 5 percent level, and *** significant at 1 percent level.

balance of payments, and the link to macroeconomic policies, may be equally—or more—unreliable.

Money demand is likely to be highly unpredictable when private capital flows are large and volatile. As noted above, financial programming dispenses with the need to model private capital flows, but this modeling advantage may be somewhat illusory if volatility of private capital flows is manifested elsewhere in the economy. Of particular concern is a situation in which the "tail wags the dog"—that is, capital flows are largely autonomous and represent an independent influence on the balance of payments with the current account balance (and thus the exchange rate and economy activity) driven by capital flows. In this situation, projections of money demand are likely to be unreliable and financial programming as well as other approaches may be of limited ability for modeling the balance of payments and exchange market pressures. It is noteworthy in this respect that the volatility of reserve money velocity rose substantially in capital account crises whereas it fell during the program period in PRGF-supported countries (the trend in other GRA-supported countries is indeterminate); Table 3.A1.[55] Moreover, the link between fiscal balances and reserve accumulation—predicted by financial programming—is stronger among PRGF-supported countries (Table 3.A2).

[55]Ramcharan (2004) argues that volatility of velocity in ESAF/PRGF-supported programs is greater; this refers to the variance across programs rather than the time series volatility of a given country—which is more pertinent to whether the financial programming model should be applied. A separate issue concerns the difference between programmed and actual velocity, which is discussed in "Macroeconomic and Structural Policies: Review of Experience" (see Part IV of this occasional paper).

References

Agénor, Pierre-Richard, and Peter J. Montiel, 1999, *Development Macroeconomics* (Princeton, New Jersey: Princeton University Press).

Aghion, Philippe, Philippe Bacchetta, and Abhijit Banerjee, 2001, "Currency Crises and Monetary Policy with Credit Constraints," *European Economic Review,* Vol. 45, No.7 (June), pp. 1121–50.

Allen, Mark, Christophe B. Rosenberg, Christian Keller, Brad Setser, and Nouriel Roubini, 2002, "A Balance Sheet Approach to Financial Crisis," IMF Working Paper No. 02/210 (Washington: International Monetary Fund).

Baqir, R., R. Ramcharan, and R. Sahay, 2004, "IMF Program Design and Growth: Is Over-Optimism Deliberate? Is it Defensible?" (unpublished; Washington: International Monetary Fund).

Batista, Catia, and Juan Zalduendo, 2004, "Can IMF Medium-Term Growth Projections Be Improved?" IMF Working Paper No. 04/203 (Washington: International Monetary Fund).

Beech, William, Aaron B. Schavey, and Isabel M. Isidro, 1999, "How Reliable Are IMF Economic Forecasts?" Research Paper Center for Data Analysis, No. 99-05 (Washington: Heritage Foundation).

Boughton, James M., 2001, "Different Strokes? Common and Uncommon Responses to Financial Crises," IMF Working Paper No. 01/12 (Washington: International Monetary Fund).

Borensztein, Eduardo, and Atish R. Ghosh, 1989, "Foreign Borrowing and Export Promotion Policies," *IMF Staff Papers*, Vol. 36 (December), pp. 904–33.

Bubula Andrea, and _nci Ötker-Robe, 2002, "The Evolution of Exchange Rate Regimes Since 1990: Evidence from De Facto Policies," IMF Working Paper No. 02/155 (Washington: International Monetary Fund).

———, 2003, "Are Pegged and Intermediate Exchange Rate Regimes More Crisis Prone?" IMF Working Paper No. 03/223 (Washington: International Monetary Fund).

Céspedes, Luis Felipe, Roberto Chang, and Andrés Velasco, 2003, "IS-LM-BP in the Pampas," *IMF Staff Papers*, Vol. 50 (Special Issue), pp. 143–64.

Cohen, Daniel, and Jeffrey Sachs, 1986, "Growth and External Debt Under Risk of Repudiation," *European Economic Review*, Vol. 30 (June), pp. 529–60.

Coorey, Sharmini, Mauro Mecagni, and Erik Offerdal, 1996, "Disinflation in Transition Economies: The Role of Relative Price Adjustment," IMF Working Paper No. 96/138 (Washington: International Monetary Fund).

Daseking, Christina, Atish Ghosh, Timothy Lane, and Alun Thomas, 2004, *Lessons from the Crisis in Argentina,* IMF Occasional Paper No. 236 (Washington: International Monetary Fund).

Dornbusch, Rudiger, 1990, "Policies to Move from Stabilization to Growth," CEPR Discussion Paper No. 456 (London: Centre for Economic Policy Research).

Duttagupta, Rupa, Gilda Fernandez, and Cem Karacadag, 2004, "From Fixed to Float: Operational Aspects of Moving Towards Exchange Rate Flexibility," IMF Working Paper No. 04/126 (Washington: International Monetary Fund).

Easterly, William, 2002, "An Identity Crisis? Testing IMF Financial Programming," Center for Global Development Working Paper No. 9 (Washington).

Edwards, Sebastian, 1989, "What Does the International Monetary Fund Really Do? Reply to Goldstein," *Carnegie-Rochester Conference Series on Public Policy,* Vol. 31 (Autumn), pp. 77–82.

———, 1990, "The International Monetary Fund and the Developing Countries: A Critical Evaluation," NBER Working Paper No. 2909 (Cambridge, Massachusetts: National Bureau of Economic Research).

Eichengreen, Barry, and others, 1998, *Exit Strategies: Policy Options for Countries Seeking Greater Exchange Rate Flexibility*, IMF Occasional Paper No. 168 (Washington: International Monetary Fund).

Eichengreen, Barry, and Ricardo Hausmann, 1999, "Exchange Rates and Financial Fragility," NBER Working Paper No. 7418 (Cambridge, Massachusetts: National Bureau of Economic Research).

Froot, Kenneth A., and Richard H. Thaler, 1990, "Anomalies: Foreign Exchange," *Journal of Economic Perspectives*, Vol. 4 (Summer), pp. 179–92.

Funke, Norbert, 1993, "Timing and Sequencing of Reforms: Competing Views and the Role of Credibility," *Kyklos*, Vol. 46, No. 3, pp. 337–62.

Furman, Jason, and Joseph E. Stiglitz, 1998, "Economic Crises: Evidence and Insights from East Asia, *Brookings Papers on Economic Activity: 2* (Brookings Institution), pp. 1–135.

Gapen, Michael T., Dale F. Gray, Cheng Hoon Lim, and Yingbin Xiao, 2004, "The Contingent Claims Approach to Corporate Vulnerability Analysis: Estimating Default Risk and Economy-Wide Risk Transfer," IMF Working Paper No. 04/121 (Washington: International Monetary Fund).

Goldfeld, S., and D. Sichel, 1990, "The Demand for Money," in *Handbook of Monetary Economics*, ed. by

B. Friedman and F.H. Hahn (Amsterdam; New York: North-Holland).

Ghosh, Atish, 1996, "The Output-Inflation Nexus in Ukraine: Is There a Trade-Off?" IMF Working Paper No. 96/46 (Washington: International Monetary Fund).

———, and Steven Phillips, 1998, "Inflation, Disinflation, and Growth," IMF Working Paper No. 98/68 (Washington: International Monetary Fund).

Ghosh, Atish, Timothy Lane, Marianne Schulze-Ghattas, Ales Bulíř, Javier Hamann, and Alex Mourmouras, 2002, *IMF-Supported Programs in Capital Account Crises,* IMF Occasional Paper No. 210 (Washington: International Monetary Fund).

Heisenberg, W., 1927, "Über den Anschaulichen Inhalt der Quantentheoretischen Kinematik und Mechanik," *Zeitschrift für Physik,* Vol. 43, 172–98. Translated into English by John Archibald Wheeler and Hubert Zurek, in *Quantum Theory and Measurement*, ed. by J.A. Wheeler and H. Zurek (Princeton, New Jersey: Princeton University Press, 1983).

Independent Evaluation Office, 2003, *Fiscal Adjustment in IMF-Supported Programs* (Washington: International Monetary Fund).

International Monetary Fund, 1996, *World Economic Outlook, May,* World Economic and Financial Surveys (Washington).

———, 1997, *The ESAF at Ten Years: Economic Adjustment and Reform in Low-Income Countries,* IMF Occasional Paper No. 156 (Washington).

———, 2002, "Assessing Sustainability;" available at www.imf.org/external/np/pdr/sus/2002/eng/052802.htm.

———, 2003a, "The Balance Sheet Approach and Its Applications at the Fund;" available at www.imf.org/external/np/pdr/bal/2003/eng/063003.htm.

———, 2003b, *World Economic Outlook, April,* World Economic and Financial Surveys (Washington).

———, 2003c, "Sustainability Assessments—Review of Application and Methodological Refinements;" available at www.imf.org/external/np/pdr/sustain/2003/061003.htm.

———, 2004a, "Integrating the Balance Sheet Approach into Fund Operations;" available at www.imf.org/external/np/pdr/bal/204/eng/022304.htm.

———, 2004b, "Debt Sustainability in Low-Income Countries;" available at www.imf.org/external/np/pdr/sustain/2004/020304.pdf.

Issing, Otmar, 1992, "Theoretical and Empirical Foundations of the Deutsche Bundesbank's Monetary Targeting," *Intereconomics*, Vol. 27 (November/December), pp. 289–300.

———, 1997, "Monetary Targeting in Germany: The Stability of Monetary Policy and of the Monetary System," *Journal of Monetary Economics*, Vol. 39 (June), pp. 67–79.

Jager, H., 1994, "Comment on Manuel Guitián: The Role of Monetary Policy in IMF Programs," in *A Framework for Monetary Stability* (Dordrecht; Boston: Kluwer Academic Publishers).

Jeanne, Olivier, and Jeromin Zettelmeyer, 2002, "'Original Sin,' Balance Sheet Crises and the Roles of International Lending," IMF Working Paper No. 02/234 (Washington: International Monetary Fund).

Joshi, B., and A. Ghosh, 2003, "How Good (or Bad) Are Fund Projections?" (unpublished; Washington: International Monetary Fund).

Kaufmann, Daniel, Aart Kraay, and Pablo Zoido-Lobatón, 1999, "Governance Matters," World Bank Policy Research Paper No. 2196 (Washington: World Bank).

Khan, Mohsin S., and Peter Montiel, 1989, "Growth-Oriented Adjustment Programs: A Conceptual Framework," *IMF Staff Papers,* Vol. 36 (June), pp. 279–306.

Killick, Tony, 1995, *IMF Programmes in Developing Countries: Design and Impact*" (London and New York: Routledge).

Krueger, Anne, 1984, "Trade Strategies and Employment in Developing Countries," *Finance & Development,* Vol. 21, No. 4 (June), pp. 23–26.

Lane, Timothy, Atish Ghosh, Javier Hamann, Steven Phillips, Marianne Schulze-Ghattas, and Tsidi Tsikata, 1999, *IMF-Supported Programs in Indonesia, Korea, and Thailand: A Preliminary Assessment,* IMF Occasional Paper No. 178 (Washington: International Monetary Fund).

Lown, C., S. Peristiani, and K. Robinson, 1999, "What Was Behind the M2 Breakdown?" Financial Industry Working Paper No. 99–2 (Dallas: Federal Reserve Bank of Dallas).

Lucas, R., 1976, "Econometric Policy Evaluation: A Critique," *Carnegie-Rochester Conference Series on Public Policy,* Vol. 1.

MacDonald, Ronald, and Mark P. Taylor, 1992, "Exchange Rate Economics: A Survey," *IMF Staff Papers*, Vol. 39 (March), pp. 1–57.

Mauro, Paolo, 1995, "Corruption and Growth," *Quarterly Journal of Economics*, Vol. 110 (August), pp. 681–712.

Michaely, Michael, Demetris Papageorgiou, and Armeane M. Choksi, 1990, *Liberalizing Foreign Trade in Developing Countries: The Lessons of Experience* (Washington: World Bank).

Montiel, Peter, 2003, "Tight Money in a Post-Crisis Defense of the Exchange Rate: What Have We Learned?" *World Bank Research Observer,* Vol. 18, No. 1 (Spring), pp.1–23.

Morgenstern, Oskar, 1950, *On the Accuracy of Economic Observations*" (Princeton, New Jersey: Princeton University Press).

Mussa, Michael, and Miguel A. Savastano, 1999, "The IMF Approach to Economic Stabilization," IMF Working Paper No. 99/104 (Washington: International Monetary Fund).

Musso, Alberto, and Steven Phillips, 2001, "Comparing Projections and Outcomes of IMF-Supported Programs," IMF Working Paper No. 01/45 (Washington: International Monetary Fund).

Nsouli, Saleh M., Mournir R. Rached, and Norbert Funke, 2002, "The Speed of Adjustment and the Sequencing of Economic Reforms: Issues and Guidelines for Policymakers," IMF Working Paper No. 02/132 (Washington: International Monetary Fund).

Polak, J. J., 1957, "Monetary Analysis of Income Formation and Payments Problems," *IMF Staff Papers*, Vol. 6 (November), pp. 1–50.

Ramcharan, R., 2004, "How Well-Designed Are IMF Programs?" (unpublished; Washington: International Monetary Fund).

Reinhart, Carmen M., and Kenneth S., Rogoff, 2004, "The Modern History of Exchange Rate Arrangements: A Reinterpretation," *Quarterly Journal of Economics*, Vol. 119 (February), pp.1–48.

Robichek, E.W., 1967, "Financial Programming Exercises of the International Monetary Fund in Latin America" (unpublished).

———, 1971, "Financial Programming: Stand-By Arrangements and Stabilization Programs" (unpublished; Washington: International Monetary Fund).

Rogoff, Kenneth S., Aasim M. Husain, Ashoka Mody, Robin Brooks, and Nienke Oomes, 2004, *Evolution and Performance of Exchange Rate Regimes*, IMF Occasional Paper No. 229 (Washington: International Monetary Fund).

Sarel, M., 1996, "Nonlinear Effects of Inflation on Economic Growth," *IMF Staff Papers*, Vol 43, No. 1, pp. 199–215.

Senhadji, Abdelhak S., and Mohsin S. Khan, 2000, "Threshold Effects in the Relationship Between Inflation and Growth," IMF Working Paper No. 00/110 (Washington: International Monetary Fund).

Taylor, Lance, 1988, *Varieties of Stabilization Experience* (Oxford: Clarendon Press).

U.S. General Accounting Office, 2003, Report to the Chairman, Committee on Financial Services, and to the Vice-Chairman, Joint Economic Committee, House of Representatives, "International Financial Crises: Challenges Remain in IMF's Ability to Anticipate, Prevent, and Resolve Financial Crises," GAP-03-734 (Washington).

Zalduendo, Juan, 2005, "Pace and Sequencing of Economic Policies," IMF Working Paper No. 05/118 (Washington: International Monetary Fund).

Part IV

Macroeconomic and Structural Policies: Review of Experience

Contents of Part IV

Tables

I Introduction

An IMF-supported program is a package of envisaged policies which, combined with approved financing, is expected to achieve certain economic objectives such as fostering macroeconomic stability and orderly external adjustment, promoting growth and poverty reduction, and reducing vulnerability to future balance of payments problems or financial crises. This paper reviews experience with specific macroeconomic and structural policies intended to achieve these objectives.[1]

In designing their economic program, national authorities have at their disposal a number of instruments, including the exchange rate regime, the monetary stance, fiscal policies, and structural measures. Some of the considerations behind the setting of macroeconomic and structural policies are discussed in "Policy Formulation, Analytical Frameworks, and Program Design" (see Part III of this occasional paper). This paper turns to experience, seeking to answer three broad questions for each policy instrument: Was use of the instrument geared toward achieving program objectives? Were the intended polices carried out? And what was the outcome?

Before turning to a summary of the main findings, four points are worth noting. First, by its very nature, cross-country analysis requires making generalizations—there are always exceptions, however, since individual programs must be tailored to the specific circumstances facing the member. Second, for expositional ease—and to complement the analysis of outcomes in "Objectives and Outcomes" (see Part II of this occasional paper)—the discussion in this paper is organized around the role of each individual policy instrument.[2] But these various policy elements are also intended to work together, and an important consideration in program design is the complementarity of instruments and their appropriate assignment to targets. Third, policy choices and their implementation reflect deep social and institutional determinants of macroeconomic stability that are not modeled here. More generally, caution is required in interpreting the empirical findings owing to possible omitted variable bias and difficulties in establishing counterfactuals.[3] Fourth, during the period under review—1995 to 2000—IMF-supported programs in low-income countries underwent important changes with the shift in 1999/2000 from the ESAF to the PRGF; most of the experience of low-income countries reported in this paper pertains to ESAF-supported programs.

With these points in mind, the main findings based on aggregate, cross-country analysis are as follows. First, up-front devaluations or shifts in the *exchange rate regime* are the exceptions rather than the rule under IMF-supported programs—in less than 20 percent of all programs was the regime changed in the year the program was approved. Most regime shifts involved pegging the exchange rate in transition economies (as they embarked on disinflation programs) or moving to more flexible regimes in nontransition economies (as pegs were abandoned in the face of balance of payments difficulties). Among programs that explicitly targeted disinflation, GRA-supported programs typically used the exchange rate as a nominal anchor, while PRGF-supported programs tended to use money-based stabilizations. But rates of success did not differ markedly, making it difficult

[1]To include both program and postprogram experience, the sample consists of arrangements approved over the period 1995–2000 and supported by the General Resources Account (GRA)—Stand-By Arrangements (SBAs) and Extended Fund Facility (EFF) arrangements—or by concessional facilities—the Enhanced Structural Adjustment Facility (ESAF) prior to 1999/2000 and the Poverty Reduction and Growth Facility (PRGF) since then. For simplicity, the term PRGF is used to refer to both ESAF- and PRGF-supported programs. A list of arrangements can be found in Appendix I of "Objectives and Outcomes" (see Part II of this occasional paper); individual analyses reported below may use subsamples according to data availability.

[2]However, to control for possible omitted variable bias, where relevant, the regressions reported below include the various policy instruments simultaneously.

[3]In particular, the coefficients on policy variables may be misestimated if regressors are correlated with the policy variable (and the dependent variable), but omitted from the regression (see Appendix IV of "Objectives and Outcomes" (Part II of this occasional paper) for a discussion of alternative methodologies for evaluating the effects of programs).

to generalize about which strategy is preferable. Rather, what appears to have been of greater importance in explaining success are the supporting policies—specifically, whether the targeted fiscal adjustment was achieved.

It is also worth examining whether external adjustment came at a lower output cost in countries with more flexible regimes (because of expenditure switching) and whether countries with pegged regimes prior to the program subsequently underwent greater external adjustment as balance sheet mismatches—built up because the guarantee implicit in the peg had encouraged excessive foreign currency exposure in the precrisis period—unwound. While there is evidence that countries with more flexible regimes achieve external adjustment at lower output cost, there is little empirical relationship between pegged regimes and the subsequent adjustment of the current account being greater than programmed.

Second, programs usually target at least some tightening of the *monetary stance*—in order to lower inflation, promote orderly external adjustment, and, especially in capital account crises, to help stem capital outflows. Empirically, the monetary stance is tightened, though usually by not as much as is programmed, leading to higher inflation than projected. Importantly, policies set in the context of IMF-supported programs appear to enjoy greater credibility, leading to higher money demand, and thus lower inflation for a given growth rate of broad money. The empirical evidence does not support the assertion that the monetary stance was set excessively tight in IMF-supported programs leading to lower output growth.[4]

Third, IMF-supported programs also target at least some *fiscal consolidation* to promote external adjustment, underpin macroeconomic stabilization, or put the public finances and debt dynamics on a more sustainable footing. In the event, however, there are typically large slippages in the fiscal adjustment targeted for the first program year, which widen in the following year, mainly because of primary (and, to a lesser degree, interest) expenditure overruns in GRA-supported programs and a combination of primary expenditure overruns and revenue shortfalls in PRGF-supported programs.[5]

The failure to maintain the programmed fiscal consolidation cannot be explained by the planned current account adjustment having been achieved—fiscal consolidation was not sustained even in cases where the external adjustment fell short of expectations. Fiscal slippages undermine disinflation efforts and result in significantly higher public debt ratios than programmed. (Below-the-line operations are, however, the most important source of public debt projection errors.) Fiscal adjustment does contribute to external adjustment—but cannot explain instances in which the country undergoes substantially more external adjustment than anticipated. Empirical evidence does not indicate that fiscal policies in IMF-supported programs have had negative consequences for growth.

Fourth, *structural measures* in IMF-supported programs can be classified according to their primary objectives—bolstering the management of aggregate demand, enhancing the flexibility of the economy and raising efficiency (both of which serve to strengthen a country's growth prospects), and reducing vulnerabilities to future crises. Classifying structural measures into these three categories shows some alignment between structural measures and the broad objectives of economic programs. While it is difficult to establish the impact of individual structural reforms, the evidence suggests that fiscal structural measures have been useful in underpinning fiscal adjustment and that there is a positive correlation between growth-related structural measures in IMF-supported programs and medium-term growth performance.

The paper follows the structure of this summary. Concluding remarks are presented in Section VI.

[4]The Independent Evaluation Office (IEO) comes to a similar conclusion in its assessment of programs in low-income countries (IEO, 2004).

[5]This paper examines performance during the year of program approval and the following year because most programs span more than one calendar year. The average duration of IMF-supported programs in the sample is 17 months for SBAs, and 35 months for programs supported by the EFF as well as by concessional facilities—the ESAF and the PRGF. Further, when an arrangement was approved in the last quarter of the year, for analytical purposes it is treated as having been approved in the subsequent year.

II The Choice of Exchange Rate Regime

Given the primacy of external adjustment and macroeconomic stability in IMF-supported programs, a natural starting point is the exchange rate regime. In particular, a flexible exchange rate can allow for more of the improvement in the current account balance to take place through expenditure switching rather than by monetary and fiscal restraint alone—though, in some circumstances, this can also be achieved through a discrete devaluation under an existing peg.[6] Conversely, when disinflation is a primary objective, the use of the exchange rate as a nominal anchor can help induce policy discipline, engender confidence in the currency, and bring down inflationary expectations and real interest rates. The use of such "exchange-rate-based stabilizations" is not uncontroversial, however (Box 4.1).

This section considers the role of the exchange rate regime in IMF-supported programs—Section III takes up the related but distinct issue of the monetary stance. It first sets the stage by considering the extent to which the exchange rate regime has been used as an explicit tool for achieving program objectives. Next it turns to outcomes, examining three questions: Did use of the exchange rate as a nominal anchor assist in disinflation? Did more flexible exchange rate regimes help achieve external adjustment at a lower cost in terms of output? And did countries with pegged regimes subsequently undergo greater external adjustment as balance sheet mismatches unwound?

Exchange Rate Regimes in IMF-Supported Programs

Table 4.1 reports the distribution of exchange rate regimes in the year prior to (year t–1), and the year of (year t), the approval of the arrangement. PRGF-supported members are split almost equally between pegged and flexible exchange rate regimes, whereas for GRA-supported members a larger proportion (60 percent) had pegged exchange rates.[7] Transitions in the year that the IMF arrangement was approved occur in less than 20 percent of cases.[8] When regime changes occur, these were frequently toward greater flexibility in nontransition GRA-supported countries (as pegs were abandoned[9]) or toward less flexible regimes in transition economies (to assist disinflation efforts).

To examine the determinants of regime choice in IMF-supported programs, Table 4.2 reports the results of estimating an ordered probit, where a higher score on the regime index indicates a more flexible regime. This analysis shows a great deal of persistence in regime choice—that is, consistent with the observation above, the exchange rate

[6]Such up-front devaluations as part of the initial package of policies under the program are rare, however. In the sample (about 130 programs approved during the period 1995–2000), only Mauritania and Ukraine carried out a step devaluation at the beginning of the program.

[7]The results in this section are based on the IMF's official classification of exchange rate regimes, as reported in the *Annual Report on Exchange Arrangements and Exchange Restrictions (AREAER)*. The IMF uses a de facto classification that combines quantitative and qualitative information, including the authorities' stated exchange rate policy. While the IMF changed to a de facto classification in 1999, the data for previous years were obtained from Bubula and Ötker-Robe (2002), who constructed the back series using the same methodology. Using a purely de facto classification (for instance, that proposed by Reinhart and Rogoff, 2004) would lead to a larger proportion of countries being classified as having pegged regimes (perhaps reflecting "fear of floating" (see Calvo and Reinhart, 2002)), which would strengthen the relationship between pegged regimes and better inflation performance reported below. The main conclusions of this section, however, are unaltered.

[8]This proportion is similar to the proportion of countries changing their exchange rate regimes outside the context of an IMF-supported program. These statistics may overstate the proportion of cases where the regime was changed as part of the IMF-supported program since, in some cases, the regime change occurred a few months prior to or a few months following the approval of the IMF arrangement and thus may have not been part of the design of the program. For the purposes of these statistics, any change between the eight categories of exchange rate regime presented in the *AREAER* is counted as a regime shift.

[9]Conventional pegs are more than twice as frequent (37 percent of countries) when the country does not have an IMF-supported program as when it does (15 percent of countries).

Box 4.1. Exchange-Rate-Based Stabilizations

Exchange-rate-based stabilizations (ERBS) are often advocated for countries starting from high and chronic inflation because the nominal exchange rate provides a highly visible anchor for private sector expectations. In particular, in countries with high dollarization and a high pass-through from the exchange rate to prices, the exchange rate can stabilize and coordinate expectations quickly, and may promote policy discipline.[1] An exchange rate anchor could also be attractive to countries with high real interest rates, as an ERBS might reduce them more rapidly than a money-based-stabilization (MBS). Another benefit could be the relative ease of conducting monetary policy, in contrast to MBS, where the appropriate rate of money growth must be determined, often in situations of highly unstable money demand. The transparency of ERBS may also enhance the credibility of the monetary authorities, thus reducing the costs of disinflation.

However, the debate on ERBS is still open. Some authors maintain that the costs of disinflations carried out with an exchange rate anchor are merely postponed. They point to some empirical regularities observed in ERBS (the so-called ERBS syndrome), namely a substantial real exchange rate appreciation and related deterioration in the external accounts, which often leads to a balance of payments crisis, and a boom-bust cycle in GDP, consumption, and investment.[2] ERBS have been linked to financial crises as well.[3] The ability of a predetermined exchange rate regime to impose discipline on other policies, notably fiscal policy, is also disputed.[4] In addition, overvaluation under a pegged exchange rate regime may mask temporarily the extent of public indebtedness.

But other authors challenge empirical regularities that characterize the ERBS syndrome. For example, some authors do not find evidence that output dynam-

Table A. Successful Stabilization Episodes

	Episodes	Successful[1] Criterion 1	Successful[1] Criterion 2
Total number of episodes	51	20	34
Of which successful stabilizations (in percent)		39	67
Exchange-rate-based stabilizations	13	5	9
Of which successful stabilizations (in percent)		38	69

Source: Hamann (2001).

[1]Criterion 1 defines success as inflation at t+2 and t+3 is no higher than during stabilization year. Criterion 2 defines success as inflation at t+2 and t+3 is no higher than three-fourths of the inflation rate prevailing the year before stabilization.

[1]See Calvo and Végh (1999) and Hamann (2001) for surveys of the literature on ERBS.

[2]See for example Kiguel and Liviatan (1992), Végh (1992), and Calvo and Végh (1994).

[3]See Sobolev (2000).

[4]Hamann (2001) does not find evidence of increased fiscal discipline of ERBS.

regime is seldom changed as part of an IMF-supported program. The exchange rate regime (whether or not it is changed at the time of program approval) can be explained by various explanatory variables for nontransition country programs. Specifically, in GRA-supported nontransition programs, a pegged (or less flexible) regime is more likely the larger the programmed decline in inflation. Moreover, though the programmed change in the current account balance is not statistically significant, a flexible regime is more likely the greater the estimated overvaluation of the real exchange rate. Other significant determinants are foreign exchange reserves (a higher level of reserves makes a peg more likely) and the output gap (a smaller gap makes a peg more likely). Overall, the probit explains 90 percent of the observations correctly. By contrast, in a similar analysis for PRGF-supported nontransition countries, only the lagged regime variable has the correct sign and is statistically significant—suggesting greater inertia in the choice of exchange rate regime for these countries.[10] For transition economies, the fit of the equation is much worse, and only the lagged regime and the estimated degree of overvaluation are statistically significant.

[10]Among PRGF-supported countries, members of the CFA zone maintain a pegged regime for long-standing institutional reasons. For non-CFA zone members, there may be hesitation in adopting a peg even in the context of an attempt at disinflation because the institutions and policy discipline necessary to maintain the peg may be lacking.

Table B. Disinflation Attempts Under Alternative Exchange Rate Regimes

(Initial inflation above 50 percent a year, at least 20 percentage point decline)

	Pegged	Intermediate	Float
Proportion of cases with inflation below post-disinflation level in:			
Year t+1	53.1	41.0	51.4
Year t+2	43.8	35.9	40.0
Year t+3	43.8	25.6	28.6

Source: Ghosh, Gulde, and Wolf (2003).

ics differ based on the anchor used in the stabilization. Others find expansionary effects on output of ERBS from high inflation.[5] Similarly, the claim that ERBS have a higher percentage of failures has been questioned (see Tables A and B).[6] In fact, these differences in findings may reflect the small samples used in some studies: for example, Calvo and Végh (1999) examined 5 episodes of MBS compared to 12 ERBS. However, in studies where a large number of episodes are studied (typically identified by rules), the evidence of the ERBS syndrome is much weaker, if extant at all.[7]

[5]Fischer, Sahay, and Végh (2002).

[6]See Easterly (1996); Ghosh, Gulde, and Wolf (2002); Hamann (2001); Hamann and Prati (2002); and Santaella and Vela (1996).

[7]Fischer, Sahay, and Végh (2002) and Hamann (2001).

Schadler and others (1995) in the 1994 Conditionality Review studied 16 countries (out of a total sample of 36) that adopted a monetary anchor—defined as either a money supply rule (1 country) or a predetermined exchange rate path (15 countries). They concluded that, while there is no substitute for tight financial policies and wage restraint, exchange rate anchors appeared to have sped up disinflation and helped keep inflation low. At the same time, they pointed to significant costs in terms of competitiveness, export growth, and possibly short-term output growth associated with the disinflation gains. Finally, they viewed the adoption of some nominal anchor as indispensable in reducing high or intermediate inflation, but underscored the key role of supporting policies.

Finally, when the exchange rate regime chosen for disinflation differs from the regime considered more suitable for the country from a longer-run perspective, issues of exit arise. For example, as discussed in *Lessons from the Crisis in Argentina* (Daseking and others, 2004), the currency board arrangement adopted by Argentina in 1991 was instrumental in bringing down inflation after decades of high inflation, but given extensive dollarization of the economy and turbulence in international capital markets, it was difficult to find an opportunity to exit the regime gracefully even as it became apparent that a lack of competitiveness was impeding growth and that fiscal policy necessary to sustain the peg was not forthcoming. The IMF-supported program in Turkey (1999) preannounced an explicit exit strategy (and timetable) for exiting the quasi-currency board arrangement adopted at the outset of the stabilization program. The preannouncement does not appear to have undermined credibility of the regime, though in the event it collapsed for other reasons prior to the planned exit date.

Experience

A number of findings can be highlighted in terms of macroeconomic performance and exchange rate regime, though of course the regime choice may itself be endogenous to macroeconomic performance.[11] Inflation for the full sample is lower under pegged exchange rates and inflation declines rapidly over the program period under both pegged and flexible regimes, though remaining higher in countries with flexible regimes (see Table 4.1). The evidence on growth is less clear. Pegged regimes experienced modest variations in real growth while countries with flexible regimes saw an acceleration in real growth. For countries that switched regimes, pegging the exchange rate is associated with better inflation performance, though the sample of such countries is small and the results mostly driven by the experience of the transition economies. The growth experience of countries switching regimes is mixed: transition economies saw a sharp acceleration in growth under their exchange rate pegs (albeit after an initial collapse in output and a sharp depreciation of the real exchange rate), while non-transition economies that switched to flexible

[11]Ghosh, Gulde, and Wolf (2003) find that the association between low inflation and pegged exchange rate regimes survives the inclusion of other explanatory variables and a battery of robustness tests including possible endogeneity of the exchange rate regime. The association between the exchange rate regime and growth, however, breaks down once endogeneity of the regime is taken into account.

Table 4.1. Macroeconomic Performance Under Alternative Exchange Rate Regimes

	Pegged[1]			Flexible[1]			Countries That Moved to	
	$t-1$	t	$t+1$	$t-1$	t	$t+1$	Flexible regimes	Pegged regimes
Proportion of observations								
Full sample	54.3	56.6	57.4	45.7	43.4	42.6	8.5	10.9
GRA-supported nontransition economies	62.8	60.5	58.1	37.2	39.5	41.9	16.3	9.3
PRGF-supported nontransition economies	52.1	50.0	47.9	47.9	50.0	52.1	4.2	4.2
Transition economies	47.4	60.5	60.5	52.6	39.5	31.6	5.3	21.1
	Average for Countries That Did Not Switch Regimes[2]						Change Between Years $t-1$ and $t+1$ for Countries That Switched Regimes to: Flexible regimes	Change Between Years $t-1$ and $t+1$ for Countries That Switched Regimes to: Pegged regimes
Inflation (in percent a year)[3]								
Full sample	12.1	8.4	6.6	19.9	15.3	12.2	1.7	–27.5
GRA-supported nontransition economies	7.1	6.9	5.5	14.8	14.7	13.5	1.1	1.8
PRGF-supported nontransition economies	8.0	6.3	5.4	10.3	10.0	9.5	–8.4	–9.6
Transition economies	24.1	13.3	9.7	42.5	25.7	16.0	13.9	–42.9
Real GDP growth (in percent a year)								
Full sample	3.2	3.5	3.1	2.2	3.3	4.3	–0.4	3.9
GRA-supported nontransition economies	3.2	3.9	2.5	1.5	1.3	3.3	–1.0	–3.6
PRGF-supported nontransition economies	5.1	4.2	3.4	4.9	3.8	4.0	2.0	–0.1
Transition economies	0.4	2.1	3.5	–2.0	4.5	5.7	–0.9	6.8

Sources: IMF, *Annual Report on Exchange Arrangements and Exchange Restrictions (AREAER)* and *World Economic Outlook;* and IMF staff calculations.

[1]Exchange rate regimes as classified by the *AREAER.* "Pegged regimes" include exchange arrangements with no separate legal tender, currency boards, other conventional pegs, pegs with horizontal bands, crawling pegs, and crawling bands; "flexible regimes" include managed and independently floating regimes.

[2]Classified by regime prevailing in year of program approval *(t).*

[3]To reduce the influence of outliers, the inflation rate is mapped into the interval (–100, 100) percent.

regimes fared better than those that switched to pegged regimes.

Disinflation Attempts

Most GRA-supported programs that started from high (above 20 percent a year) inflation rates and that targeted substantial disinflation used an exchange rate anchor. In 80 percent of the cases, the target was achieved, and in two-thirds inflation remained low up to three years later (Table 4.3 and Figure 4.1). For GRA-supported programs starting with relatively low inflation rates, about half of the disinflation attempts were based on flexible regimes and these programs had higher rates of success than similar disinflations under pegged regimes. In PRGF-supported programs, by contrast, disinflation attempts starting from high inflation did not use the exchange rate as a nominal anchor. Success rates have been similar to GRA-supported programs: in about 80 percent of cases the initial disinflation was achieved, and in three-quarters inflation remained low up to three years later (Table 4.3, Figure 4.2).

While individual country circumstances—for instance, initial credibility of newly (re)established central banks in transition economies—may suggest a particular (exchange-rate-based versus money-based) disinflation strategy, the contrasting findings for disinflation attempts under GRA- and PRGF-supported programs do not allow for unequivocal conclusions about which strategy is more likely to succeed. Rather, a distinguishing feature between successful and failed stabilization efforts appears to be whether supporting policies were in place. Although the proximate reason that inflation targets are missed and disinflation attempts fail is

Table 4.2. Choice of Exchange Rate Regime: Results of Ordered Probit[1,2]

	Dependent Variable: Exchange Rate Regime in Year of Program Approval *(t)*		
	Nontransition GRA	Nontransition PRGF	Transition
Explanatory variables			
Exchange rate regime in year *t*–1	3.56***	1.21***	0.81***
Programmed change in inflation	0.31**	0.00	–0.01
Programmed change in the current account balance	–0.22	0.01	0.06
Output gap at *t*–1[3]	0.30**	–0.01	–0.01
Deviation of the real exchange rate from a long-term trend at *t*–1[4]	0.22***	0.01	0.06***
Level of reserves in months of imports at *t*–1	–0.15*	–0.08	0.15
Dummy for CFA countries	. . .	–1.33	. . .
Pseudo-R^2	0.74	0.67	0.32
No. of observations	41	42	36
Observations correctly predicted (in percent)	90	90	44

Sources: IMF, *AREAER*, *International Financial Statistics*, and Information Notice System, MONA, and WEO databases; and IMF staff estimates.

[1]A higher score indicates more flexible regimes on the eight-category scale of the *AREAER*. The categories are (1) no separate legal tender; (2) currency boards; (3) other conventional pegs; (4) pegged arrangements with horizontal bands; (5) crawling pegs; (6) crawling bands; (7) managed floats; and (8) independent floats.

[2]Significant at: *** 1 percent, ** 5 percent, and * 10 percent levels.

[3]Positive value indicates output below trend. Trend GDP is obtained from a Hodrick-Prescott filter.

[4]Positive value indicates overvaluation. The trend real exchange rate is obtained from a Hodrick-Prescott filter.

often monetary overruns—as discussed in Section III—it is also worth considering some of the underlying causes of failures. To this end, Table 4.4 correlates success at disinflations—under both pegged and more flexible regimes—to fiscal performance under the IMF-supported program. From the table, fiscal slippage is significantly greater in cases where disinflation was unsuccessful. Indeed, whereas the fiscal balance was marginally better than programmed in cases that succeeded in disinflation, it fell short by 2.3 percent of GDP in cases that failed—a difference that is statistically significant. Countries that succeeded in achieving and maintaining low inflation also managed to achieve their fiscal targets, compared to a fiscal slippage of 1.5 percent of GDP among those programs that failed to maintain low inflation.

When the exchange rate is not pegged, the country needs some other monetary framework to conduct monetary policy (Box 4.2). In IMF-supported programs, countries with no exchange rate peg, used either a monetary target, or an inflation target, or had no explicit nominal anchor.[12] Countries with monetary targeting aimed at more ambitious disinflations and achieved greater reductions in inflation than countries that had no explicit nominal anchor (Table 4.5).[13] Even in those cases where the projected decline in inflation was smaller under monetary targeting than in countries without an explicit nominal anchor (GRA-supported programs in nontransition economies and PRGF-supported programs in transition economies), the actual decline in inflation was greater under monetary targeting. Only two countries in the sample had an inflation-targeting framework in the year the arrangement was approved. These countries sought to maintain inflation at about 5 percent; in the event, inflation turned out to be 6¼ percent a year.

External Adjustment

Besides the inflation objective, the exchange rate regime may be important for external adjustment. Flexible exchange rate regimes should allow for more of the adjustment to take place through expenditure switching rather than by demand restraint alone, implying a smaller output cost of a given improvement in the current account balance. To examine this hypothesis, the change in real GDP growth (between

[12]In most cases where no explicit monetary anchor was in place, a ceiling on net domestic assets (NDA) and a floor on net international reserves (NIR) were targeted.

[13]The 1994 Conditionality Review (Schadler and others, 1995) drew a similar conclusion.

Table 4.3. Success Rates for Disinflation Attempts Under Alternative Exchange Rate Regimes

	All		Nontransition		Transition	
	Pegged[1]	Flexible[1]	Pegged[1]	Flexible[1]	Pegged[1]	Flexible[1]
I. GRA-supported programs						
1. Low-inflation countries[2]	5	4	4	3	1	1
Success[3]	1	3	1	2	0	1
Of which: Success II[4]	0	3	0	2	0	1
Failure	4	1	3	1	1	0
2. Moderate-inflation countries[5]	12	1	5	1	7	0
Success[3]	8	1	3	1	5	0
Of which: Success II[4]	7	1	3	1	4	0
Failure	4	0	2	0	2	0
3. High-inflation countries[6]	9	2	1	1	8	1
Success[3]	9	2	1	1	8	1
Of which: Success II[4]	7	1	0	0	7	1
Failure	0	0	0	0	0	0
II. PRGF-supported programs						
1. Low-inflation countries[2]	8	9	8	7	0	2
Success[3]	5	3	5	2	0	1
Of which: Success II[4]	3	1	3	1	0	0
Failure	3	6	3	5	0	1
2. Moderate-inflation countries[5]	0	8	0	5	0	3
Success[3]	0	6	0	3	0	3
Of which: Success II[4]	0	5	0	2	0	3
Failure	0	2	0	2	0	0
3. High-inflation countries[6]	0	4	0	2	0	2
Success[3]	0	4	0	2	0	2
Of which: Success II[4]	0	4	0	2	0	2
Failure	0	0	0	0	0	0

Sources: IMF, *AREAER* and MONA and WEO databases; and IMF staff estimates.

[1]Exchange rate regime at *t*+1.

[2]Low-inflation cases refer to end-of-period inflation of less than 20 percent and programmed change in inflation between *t*–1 and *t*+1 of less than –5 percent.

[3]Success is defined as actual disinflation performance at least meeting the programmed disinflation target (i.e., 5 percent, 10 percent, and 20 percent).

[4]Success II refers to the cases within Success in which disinflation is maintained, as measured by the difference between the average of end-period inflation in *t*+2 and *t*+3 and inflation in *t*–1 at least meeting the programmed disinflation target (i.e., 5 percent, 10 percent, and 20 percent).

[5]Moderate-inflation cases refer to end-of-period inflation between 20 percent and 50 percent and programmed change in inflation between *t*–1 and *t*+1 of less than –10 percent.

[6]High-inflation cases refer to end-of-period inflation greater than 50 percent and programmed change in inflation between *t*–1 and *t*+1 of less than –20 percent.

years *t*–1 and *t*+1) is regressed on the change in the current account balance, where the latter is instrumented by the projected change (Table 4.6). A given improvement in the current account balance is associated with lower output growth under fixed exchange rate regimes (significantly so for GRA-supported programs in nontransition economies[14]), but the corresponding coefficient under floating regimes is not significantly different from zero. The hypothesis of equality of coefficients under fixed and flexible regimes is strongly rejected, suggesting that, for these countries, more flexible regimes facilitated external adjustment.

A second hypothesis regarding the relationship between the exchange rate regime and external adjustment is that countries with pegged regimes are more susceptible to capital account shocks because the exchange rate guarantee implicit in the peg encourages unhedged foreign-currency-denominated borrowing by the private sector.[15] Although a number of capital

[14]However, in contrast, for PRGF-supported programs in nontransition economies, the equation does not show any statistically significant correlations.

[15]A common argument is that the de jure or de facto exchange rate pegs in the Asian crisis countries provided an implicit exchange rate guarantee, encouraging unhedged foreign borrowing.

Figure 4.1. Inflation and Growth in GRA-Supported Programs Under Alternative Disinflation Strategies[1,2,3]
(In percent; 1995–2000)

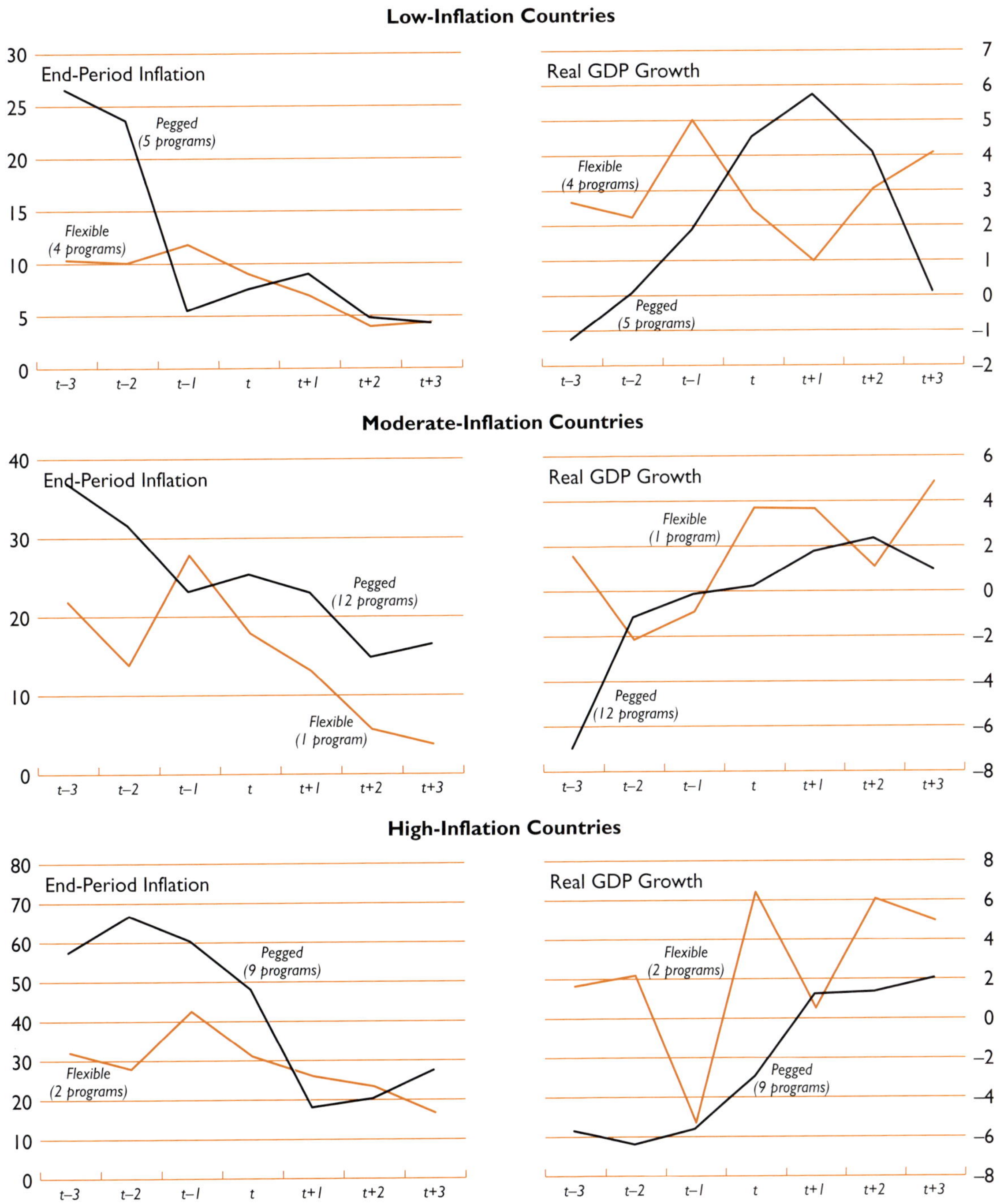

Sources: IMF, MONA and WEO databases; and IMF staff estimates.
[1]Inflation rates are transformed to be mapped into the interval (–100,100) percent.
[2]Exchange rate regime at *t*+1.
[3]Definitions of low-, moderate-, and high-inflation are given in Table 4.3.

Figure 4.2. Inflation and Growth in PRGF-Supported Programs Under Alternative Disinflation Strategies[1,2,3]
(In percent; 1995–2000)

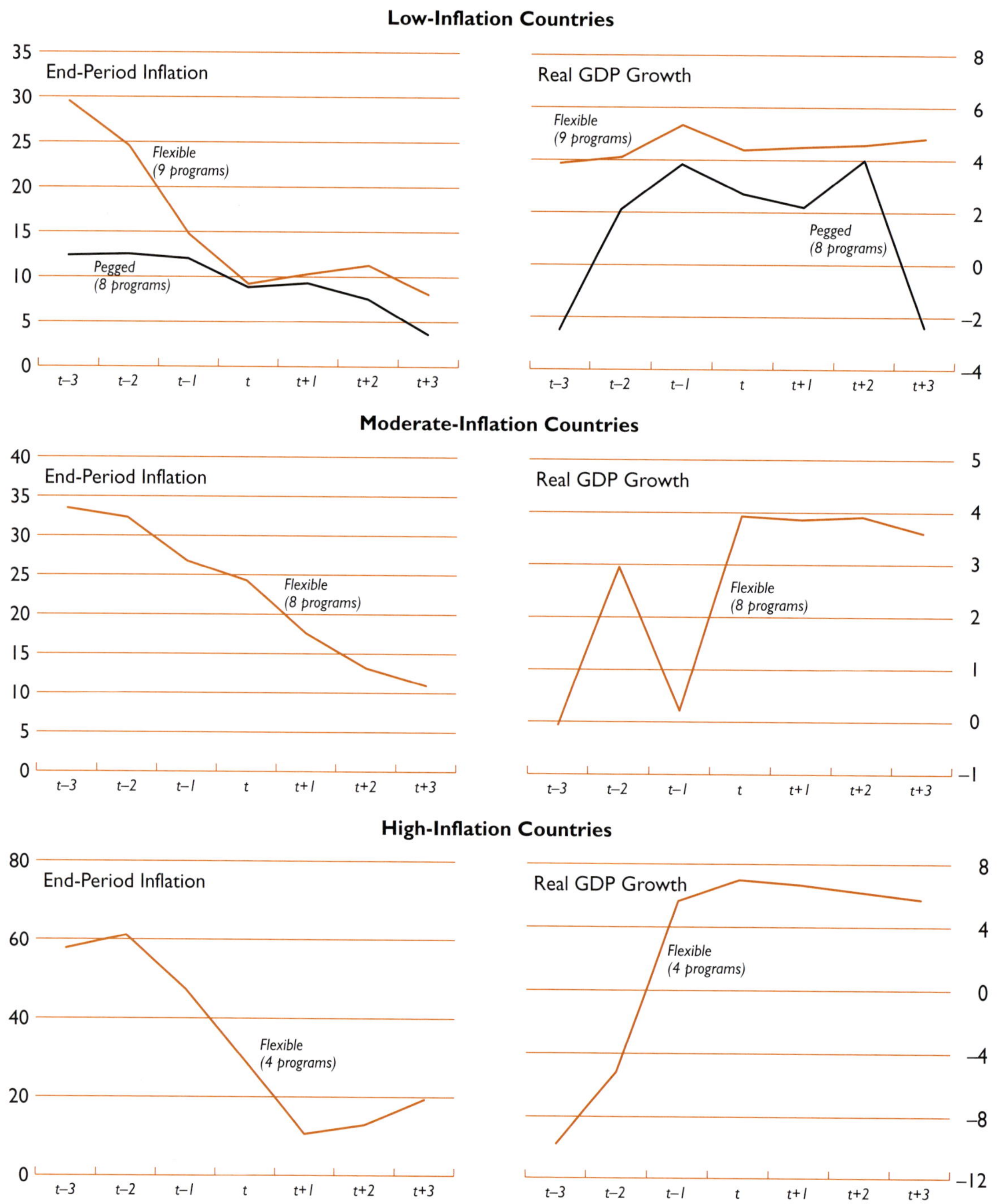

Sources: IMF, MONA and WEO databases; and IMF staff estimates.
[1]Inflation rates are transformed to be mapped into the interval (–100,100) percent.
[2]Exchange rate regime at *t+1*.
[3]Definitions of low-, moderate-, and high-inflation are given in Table 4.3.

Table 4.4. Fiscal Adjustment and Success Rates for Disinflation Attempts

	Projection Error: Actual – Projected[1]					
	Full sample		GRA-supported		PRGF-supported	
	Fiscal balance[2]	Inflation[2]	Fiscal balance[2]	Inflation[2]	Fiscal balance[2]	Inflation[2]
1. Disinflation attempts[3]	–0.83	4.42	–0.75	5.98	–0.91	2.76
(Number of observations)	58	58	30	30	28	28
Success[4]	0.05	0.31	0.12	2.01	–0.03	–1.60
(Number of observations)	36	36	19	19	17	17
Of which:						
Success II[5]	0.10	0.80	0.39	2.14	–0.34	–1.20
(Number of observations)	30	30	18	18	12	12
Failure II	–1.46	–4.02	–4.81	–0.25	0.22	–5.91
Failure	–2.26	11.16	–2.26	12.82	–2.26	9.49
(Number of observations)	22	22	11	11	11	11
2. Nondisinflation programs	–0.50	0.62	–0.88	1.04	–0.09	0.16
(Number of observations)	54	54	28	28	26	26
3. Failure + Nondisinflation	–1.01	3.67	–1.27	4.37	–0.73	2.94
(Number of observations)	76	76	39	39	37	37
t-statistics for:[6]						
H_0: Success = Failure	3.62***	–4.02***	2.13*	–2.39**	3.37***	–3.71***
H_0: Success II = Failure II	0.92	1.72	. . .	. . .	–1.60	1.40

Sources: IMF, MONA and WEO databases; and IMF staff estimates.

[1]Average of projection errors for years t and $t+1$.

[2]Fiscal balance refers to the change in fiscal balance in percent of actual GDP; inflation is end of period, in percent a year.

[3]Disinflation attempts refer to programs that envisaged disinflation between years $t-1$ and $t+1$ of (1) over 5 percent when initial inflation in $t-1$ is less than 20 percent, or; (2) over 10 percent, when initial inflation is between 20 percent and 50 percent, or (3) over 20 percent, when initial inflation is higher than 50 percent.

[4]Success is defined as actual disinflation performance between years $t-1$ and $t+1$ at least meeting the disinflation target (i.e., 5 percent, 10 percent, and 20 percent).

[5]Success II refers to the cases within Success in which disinflation is maintained, as measured by the difference between average inflation for $t+2$ and $t+3$ and inflation at $t-1$ at least meeting the disinflation target (i.e., 5 percent, 10 percent, and 20 percent).

[6]Two-sided t-test for differences in mean. Significant at 10 percent *, 5 percent **, and 1 percent *** levels.

Box 4.2. Monetary Regimes When the Exchange Rate Is Not Pegged

When the country does not peg its exchange rate (thereby subordinating its monetary policy to maintaining the peg), it must have some other nominal anchor and monetary regime. Of countries without pegged regimes in the year of program approval, other monetary frameworks prevailed in 70 percent of the cases. In most cases, only a ceiling on net domestic assets (NDA) and a floor on net international reserves (NIR) were specified in a program context.[1] A further 27 percent targeted monetary aggregates (e.g., reserve, base money, or a broader monetary aggregate such as M2), and only 4 percent had an inflation-targeting framework.

Countries that had only an NDA ceiling and an NIR floor as part of the program conditionality and no explicit monetary framework, arguably lacked a nominal anchor as the NDA/NIR configuration in IMF-supported programs is intended primarily to monitor progress toward external viability and safeguard IMF resources—not to act as a nominal anchor for inflation expectations or monetary policy.[2]

Predictable money demand is required for aggregates to serve as a useful nominal anchor. Partly because of unstable money demand functions, central banks in several emerging market countries have shifted to inflation targeting. Indeed, in the sample, inflation targeting became more prevalent subsequent to the year in which the arrangement was approved, with several emerging market countries adopting inflation targeting within three years of the approval of the IMF arrangement. In part, this may be because inflation targeting needs institutional and technical requirements—such as central bank operational autonomy, effective monetary policy instruments, a system of accountability for the central bank, and reliable models to forecast inflation and the impact of monetary policy actions on inflation—to make it an effective monetary framework.[3] Some countries adopted inflation targeting "lite" before formally adopting this framework.[4] (In some programs, some of the changes required to establish a formal inflation-targeting framework are part of the measures included under the program). The time pattern of adopting inflation-targeting frameworks suggests that such frameworks have been considered useful for reducing inflation from moderate or relatively low levels, rather than disinflating from high inflation (see figure).

No PRGF-supported country in the sample adopted inflation targeting.

End-Period Inflation in Inflation-Targeting Countries, 1995–2000[1]

(In percent a year)

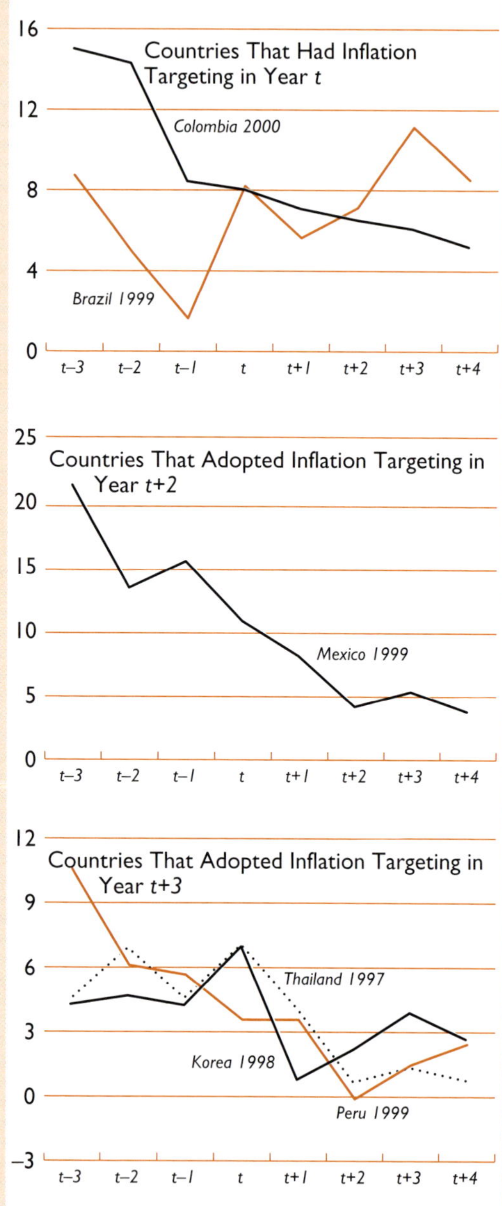

Sources: IMF, WEO database; and IMF staff estimates.

[1]Inflation rates are transformed to be mapped into the interval (–100,100) percent.

---

[1]Due to data availability, these statistics on nominal anchors are based on a smaller sample (78 arrangements) compared to the sample used in the rest of the paper: only the most recent arrangement for each country is considered in the same 1995–2000 period. The monetary regimes are classified following the IMF's *AREAER* into five categories: (1) exchange rate anchor; (2) monetary aggregate target; (3) inflation-targeting framework; (4) IMF-supported or other monetary program; and (5) other.

[2]The IMF's focus on NDA originated from the Polak model with a fixed exchange rate regime, where the overall money supply is endogenous and only its composition is under the authorities' control. Even under a flexible exchange rate arrangement, limits on NDA can: (1) prevent sterilized intervention in the presence of capital outflows; (2) allow an accommodation of money growth if capital outflows are quickly reversed; and (3) act as a disciplining device on fiscal policy. However, NDA limits do not control the overall monetary expansion when the latter is generated by foreign inflows, and hence may not provide a nominal anchor.

[3]Truman (2003) and Schaechter, Stone, and Zelmer (2000).

[4]See Stone (2003).

Table 4.5. Inflation Performance Under Alternative Monetary Regimes[1,2]

	Number of Countries in Year t	Inflation in Year $t-1$	Change in Inflation Between Year $t-1$ and Year $t+1$	
		Actual (Percent)	Programmed (Percentage points)	Actual (Percentage points)
Full sample	41	17.3	–11.3	–7.9
Of which for programs with				
Inflation targeting	2	5.0	–0.3	1.3
Monetary targeting	11	20.6	–14.8	–11.4
No explicit nominal anchor[3]	28	16.9	–10.8	–7.2
GRA-supported nontransition economies	11	8.1	–3.0	–0.7
Of which for programs with				
Inflation targeting	2	5.0	–0.3	1.3
Monetary targeting	3	5.6	–2.4	–2.7
No explicit nominal anchor[3]	6	10.3	–4.2	–0.3
PRGF-supported nontransition economies	19	9.5	–5.2	–3.2
Of which for programs with				
Inflation targeting	0	—	—	—
Monetary targeting	6	13.8	–9.0	–5.2
No explicit nominal anchor[3]	13	7.5	–3.4	–2.2
Transition economies	11	40.0	–30.4	–23.4
GRA-supported transition economies	4	50.1	–39.2	–24.9
Of which for programs with				
Inflation targeting	0	—	—	—
Monetary targeting	1	95.7	–82.6	–61.2
No explicit nominal anchor[3]	3	34.9	–24.7	–12.8
PRGF-supported transition economies	7	34.1	–25.3	–22.5
Of which for programs with				
Inflation targeting	0	—	—	—
Monetary targeting	1	30.8	–19.3	–25.2
No explicit nominal anchor[3]	6	34.7	–26.3	–22.1

Sources: IMF, *AREAER* and MONA and WEO databases; and IMF staff estimates.

[1]The monetary regime classification is based on the regime prevailing in year of program approval *(t)*. The sample used for this exercise is smaller than in the rest of the paper due to data availability. Only the last arrangement of each country is considered.

[2]Inflation is end of period. To reduce the influence of outliers, the inflation rate was transformed to be mapped into the interval (–100,100) percent.

[3]No explicit nominal anchor was in place, except—in most cases—for a ceiling on net domestic assets (NDA) of the central bank and a floor on net international reserves (NIR) under the IMF-supported program.

account crisis countries had de jure or de facto pegs prior to the crisis and much larger capital outflows than projected at the time the arrangement was approved, this does not hold more generally. In fact, countries with more flexible regimes were more likely subsequently to undergo greater external adjustment than programmed (Table 4.7).[16]

[16]In "Objectives and Outcomes" (see Part II of this occasional paper) two metrics were employed to assess external adjustment: the comparison with the projected current account balance, and the comparison with the debt-stabilizing balance (when the initial level of external debt is below 40 percent of GDP). There is no statistically significant difference between (subsequent) external adjustment under pegged and flexible regimes using the latter criterion.

Summary

Empirically, countries are no more likely to alter their exchange rate regime at the outset of an IMF-supported program than otherwise. Successful disinflations have been undertaken both under pegged and under flexible exchange rate regimes, suggesting that the consistency of macroeconomic policies, and the fiscal adjustment achieved, may be of greater importance than the choice of the nominal anchor. At the same time, some nominal anchor seems needed for disinflation. The exchange rate regime also has implications for external adjustment—in some cases, countries with more flexible regimes achieved a given improvement in the current account at a lower output cost.

Table 4.6. External Adjustment and Growth Under Alternative Exchange Rate Regimes: Regression Results[1]

Dependent Variable: Change in Output Growth[2]	All programs	Nontransition GRA-Supported: All	Nontransition GRA-Supported: Excluding capital account crises	Nontransition PRGF-Supported	Transition Economies
I. Fixed exchange rate regime[3]					
Constant	0.427	0.686	0.423	–1.780	3.732**
Change in terms of trade growth[2]	0.065*	0.122*	0.117*	0.011	0.085
Change in current account balance[2, 4]	–0.686***	–0.860**	–0.879**	–0.361	–0.181
R^2	0.154	0.307	0.363	0.045	0.035
Number of observations	71	26	24	24	21
II. Flexible exchange rate regime[3]					
Constant	1.899**	0.950	1.358	–0.463	4.558**
Change in terms of trade growth[2]	0.086	0.136*	0.172**	–0.033	0.267***
Change in current account balance[2, 4]	–0.134	0.375	0.507	0.480	–0.490
R^2	0.081	0.299	0.480	0.057	0.406
Number of observations	53	15	11	23	15
t-statistics for equality:[5]					
Constant	1.439*	0.189	0.576	1.089	0.441
Change in current account balance	1.643*	2.747***	2.763***	1.201	–0.738

Sources: IMF, MONA and WEO databases; and IMF staff estimates.

[1]* significant at 10 percent, ** significant at 5 percent, and *** significant at 1 percent levels.

[2]Changes between year *t*–1 and *t*+1; the current account balance (net of official transfers) is in percent of GDP at *t*–1; all regressors except for the constant term were transformed to be mapped into an interval (–100,100) percent to reduce the influence of outliers.

[3]Exchange rate regimes are classified by *AREAER;* "fixed regimes" include no separate legal tender, currency board arrangement, other conventional pegs, pegs with horizontal bands, crawling pegs, and crawling bands; "flexible regimes" include managed and independent floats.

[4]Instrumented by programmed change in the current account balance and the change in actual growth of the terms of trade.

[5]*t*-statistics for the hypothesis of equality of coefficients between fixed and flexible regime.

Table 4.7. Exchange Rate Regime and External Adjustment[1]

	Year *t*–1: Pegged[2]	Year *t*–1: Flexible[2]	Year *t*: Pegged[2]	Year *t*: Flexible[2]
GRA-supported nontransition economies	25	18	26	17
Of which proportion with current account balance (in percent)				
Above programmed current account balance	32.0	77.8**	34.6	76.5**
Above debt-stabilizing balance and initial debt below 40 percent of GDP	24.0	5.6	19.2	11.8
GRA-supported transition economies	17	13	23	7
Of which proportion with current account balance (in percent)				
Above programmed current account balance	5.9	30.8	13.0	28.6
Above debt-stabilizing balance and initial debt below 40 percent of GDP	35.3	15.4	26.1	28.6

Sources: IMF, *AREAER* and MONA and WEO databases; and IMF staff estimates.

[1]The difference in proportions under pegged and flexible regimes is tested. Significant at the 1 percent ***, 5 percent **, and 10 percent * levels.

[2]Exchange rate regimes as classified by *AREAER;* "pegged regimes" include exchange arrangements with no separate legal tender, currency boards, other conventional pegs, pegs with horizontal bands, crawling pegs, and crawling bands; "flexible regimes" include managed and independent floats.

III Monetary Policy

Beyond the exchange rate (and, under flexible exchange rates, the monetary) regime, the authorities must also specify the monetary stance under their IMF-supported economic programs. This section therefore discusses the monetary stance in terms of the behavior of broad money. Since the monetary authorities typically control (or have influence over) narrow aggregates, a first question concerns the mapping between narrow and broad money—that is, behavior of the money multiplier. It turns out that this relationship is generally stable and well predicted in programs, making it appropriate to consider the monetary stance in terms of broad money aggregates (Box 4.3). This section therefore considers broad money growth rates and velocity targeted in IMF-supported programs and their relationship to program objectives. It then examines the impact of monetary policy on inflation and growth. In particular, does a tighter monetary stance contribute to lower inflation? Do overruns of broad money growth account for cases where program inflation targets were missed; and does the composition of this overrun (between net domestic assets and net foreign assets) matter for inflation performance? Was the monetary stance associated with lower output growth?

Programmed Monetary Stance

Across various IMF-supported programs, broad money growth rates are targeted to decline, as are inflation rates (Table 4.8). The higher the initial inflation rate and rate of monetary expansion, the greater the targeted deceleration. For countries whose initial inflation was below 20 percent a year, the targeted deceleration was modest—from 12 percent in the year prior to program approval to 10 percent in the year following program approval. For countries whose initial inflation exceeds 50 percent a year, the deceleration is more marked, declining to annual rates of 13 percent in the year following program approval.[17]

Nominal money growth provides one gauge of the intended monetary stance, but it does take account of the increase in money demand associated with either real growth or inflation projected under the program.[18] A simple metric is the expected change in money velocity—with an increase relative to the historical trend indicating that a tighter monetary stance was envisaged (though a decrease need not indicate a monetary loosening if inflation is expected to decline).[19] By this metric, programs in high-inflation countries sought significant monetary tightening, especially in the GRA sample (see Table 4.8).

To examine more systematically the determinants of the programmed monetary stance (as captured by program velocity), Table 4.9 reports the results of a regression of the programmed change in broad money velocity. Higher initial inflation and a larger targeted improvement in the current account balance should call for a tighter monetary stance (an increase in programmed velocity), while a larger output gap,

[17]To reduce the influence of high-inflation outliers, all figures are transformed to map into the interval (–100, 100) percent prior to taking averages.

[18]An alternative gauge of monetary policy is given by the behavior of interest rates. Problems of availability and comparability of data however make it less useful in cross-country comparisons.

[19]Define a benchmark growth in broad money $\Delta\hat{m}$ as the growth rate implied by program expectations of inflation and real GDP growth and the expected behavior of velocity: $\Delta\hat{m} = \pi^p - \Delta y^p - \Delta\hat{v}$. One way to capture the expected behavior of velocity is to use the country's trend velocity growth: $\Delta\hat{v} = \Delta\bar{v}$. Similarly, the programmed increase in broad money growth can be written $\Delta m^p = \pi^p + \Delta y^p - \Delta v^p$. Subtracting, yields: $\Delta m^p - \Delta\hat{m} = \Delta\bar{v} - \Delta v^p$ so that $\Delta v^p > \Delta\bar{v}$ implies that broad money growth envisaged under the program is lower than would be implied by trend velocity (and program expectations of inflation and growth). As such, it can be interpreted as a programmed tightening of the monetary stance. One possibility, however, is that velocity itself depends upon expected inflation. In that case, the appropriate benchmark is not the trend change in velocity but the expected change in velocity, $\Delta\hat{v}$, taking account of possible remonetization. Although it is difficult to establish how much remonetization should occur, since programs typically target disinflation, this should at least imply $\Delta\hat{v} \leq \Delta\bar{v}$. Therefore, if programmed velocity is *higher* than the historical trend, then this necessarily implies a tighter programmed monetary stance: $\Delta v^p > \Delta\bar{v} \Rightarrow \Delta v^p > \Delta\hat{v} \Leftrightarrow \Delta m^p < \Delta\hat{m}$. (To the extent that velocity rises relative to trend in the year prior to approval of the arrangement, however, this measure may overstate the degree of tightening.) On the other hand, if programmed velocity is *lower* than the historical trend, then this need not indicate a monetary loosening since it is possible that $\Delta v^p < \Delta\bar{v}$ but $\Delta v^p > \Delta\hat{v}$.

Box 4.3. Relationship Between Program and Actual Money Multiplier

The text discusses the programmed monetary stance—and its impact on key macroeconomic targets—in terms of the behavior of broad money (and the velocity of broad money). Since national authorities typically control (or have more direct influence over) narrower monetary aggregates, this raises questions about the stability of the money multiplier, and whether errors in projecting the money multiplier are an important source of program slippages.

The table below seeks to examine the behavior of money multiplier—defined as the ratio of broad money to reserve money—in IMF-supported programs that were arranged during 1995–2000. The actual money multiplier has remained remarkably stable around its historical average across all types of programs (top panel): the null hypothesis of a constant multiplier cannot be rejected by the data. In addition, according to the regression results (bottom panel), program multiplier appears to be a good predictor of the actual multiplier (none of the reported F-statistics are statistically significant), accounting for more than 80 percent of cross-country variation. As such, the link between narrow and broad money aggregates is relatively stable and predictable.

Money Multiplier: Program Versus Actual[1]

	Average (t–5:t–1)	Year t–1	Year t	Year t+1	H_0: Constant Multiplier[2]
1. Actual money multiplier (mm^A)					
Nontransition GRA-supported	6.22	6.33	6.43	6.29	0.01
Nontransition PRGF-supported	2.41	2.49	2.49	2.54	0.20
Transition economies	2.37	2.39	2.37	2.37	0.03
	b_0	b_1	R^2	H_0: b_0 = 0 and b_1 = 1[2]	
2. Regression results: $mm^A = b_0 + b_1 \cdot mm^P$[3]					
Year t					
GRA-supported	–0.133	0.994***	0.894	1.145	
PRGF-supported	0.412	0.801***	0.811	2.538	
Transition economies	–0.161	1.048***	0.847	2.101	
Pooled (year t and t+1)					
GRA-supported	0.038	0.932***	0.838	1.391	
PRGF-supported	0.291	0.891***	0.808	0.870	
Transition economies	–0.083	1.029***	0.844	0.098	

Sources: IMF, *International Financial Statistics* and MONA and WEO databases; and IMF staff calculations.
[1]Money multiplier is defined as the ratio of broad money to reserve money; year t refers to the year of program approval; significant at * 10 percent, ** 5 percent, and *** 1 percent levels.
[2]F-statistics are reported.
[3]mm^A and mm^P refer to actual and program multiplier, respectively. Due to limited data availability, the sample of GRA- and PRGF-supported programs includes both transition and nontransition country programs.

a flexible exchange rate, or a higher expected rate of remonetization of the economy (proxied by the targeted decline in inflation) would, ceteris paribus, argue for a looser stance. For GRA-supported programs, all variables have the expected signs and are statistically significant. Overall, the regression explains some 60 percent of the variation in velocity in GRA-supported nontransition programs. Among PRGF-supported programs and programs in transition economies, the most important determinants are the lagged inflation rate and the expected inflation decline, while the exchange rate regime is not statistically significant; nonetheless, the regression explains some 50 percent of the variation in transition economies but only about 35 percent of the variation in PRGF-supported programs.

Experience

Inflation

IMF-supported programs generally succeed in reducing inflation—though by not as much as targeted. Slippages in the year of program approval

Table 4.8. Programmed Money Growth, Velocity, and Inflation
(In percent)

	Broad Money Growth[1]			Velocity Growth[2]			Inflation[1]		
	t–1	*t*	*t*+1	*t*–1	*t*	*t*+1	*t*–1	*t*	*t*+1
1. Full sample	19.5	14.5	11.3	6.4	5.3	0.4	17.2	12.2	6.1
Inflation at *t*–1 < 20%	12.0	10.3	10.7	5.0	–0.7	–0.5	6.9	6.4	4.5
20% < inflation at *t*–1 < 50%	19.7	16.7	13.0	2.3	6.0	4.4	23.9	16.5	8.8
Inflation at *t*–1 > 50%	52.6	30.8	12.7	18.6	31.7	–0.3	55.8	33.9	10.3
2. GRA-supported	22.6	16.9	11.8	11.3	9.2	1.1	20.9	15.9	7.0
Nontransition	12.4	11.0	10.7	14.1	3.5	2.0	10.2	9.7	5.5
Transition	36.9	25.0	16.3	7.3	16.9	–2.2	36.0	24.8	9.5
Inflation at *t*–1 < 20%	12.5	10.9	11.3	10.9	–1.2	0.4	6.8	7.6	4.9
20% < inflation at *t*–1 < 50%	18.2	17.3	14.4	3.2	6.5	6.6	23.4	18.7	10.1
Inflation at *t*–1 > 50%	54.7	33.0	11.1	21.2	42.1	–2.5	58.2	38.2	10.7
3. PRGF-supported	15.4	11.6	10.8	–0.1	0.2	–0.2	12.3	7.2	4.9
Nontransition	12.7	10.3	10.0	–0.2	0.3	0.0	9.2	5.8	4.3
Transition	31.6	18.8	16.0	0.4	0.1	–1.6	31.1	15.4	8.7
Inflation at *t*–1 < 20%	11.4	9.7	10.2	–0.8	–0.2	–1.1	7.0	5.2	4.2
20% < inflation at *t*–1 < 50%	22.1	15.7	11.9	0.9	5.1	2.6	24.7	13.0	6.8
Inflation at *t*–1 > 50%	44.7	22.6	15.8	6.8	–4.7	3.9	46.7	17.9	9.1

Sources: IMF, MONA and WEO databases; and IMF staff estimates.
[1]Money growth and inflation are end-period figures and transformed to be mapped into (–100,100) percent.
[2]For nontransition economies, programmed velocity growth for year *t* and *t*+1 is relative to trend velocity growth as measured by the five-year historical average; velocity is defined as nominal GDP divided by (period-average) stock of broad money.

Table 4.9. Programmed Monetary Stance: Regression Results[1]

	Dependent Variable: Monetary Stance[2]		
Regressor[3]	Nontransition GRA-supported	Nontransition PRGF-supported	Transition economies
Initial inflation	0.937***	1.011***	1.207***
Initial output gap[4]	–1.102***	0.428	–1.693***
Change in current account balance	0.763*	0.731*	1.264
Change in inflation	0.545***	1.802***	1.361**
Flexible exchange regime	–2.142***	0.352	–1.219
Constant	2.245	–3.969	–13.619
R^2	0.609	0.340	0.522
Number of observations	38	43	36

Sources: IMF, MONA and WEO databases; and IMF staff estimates.
[1]Significant at *** 1 percent, ** 5 percent, and * 10 percent levels.
[2]Monetary stance is measured as programmed velocity growth in year *t* relative to trend velocity growth (as measured by the five-year historical average).
[3]The current account balance (net of official transfers) is in percent of GDP; inflation was transformed to be mapped into an interval (–100,100) percent to reduce the influence of outliers.
[4]Output gap is defined as a percentage deviation of real GDP from its Hodrick-Prescott filtered trend; positive value implies current output below trend.

Table 4.10. Programmed and Actual Inflation, Money Growth, and NDA Contribution

	Actual Inflation[2]		Projection Error[1]					
			Inflation		Broad money growth		NDA contribution[3]	
	t	*t*+1	*t*	*t*+1	*t*	*t*+1	*t*	*t*+1
1. Full sample	13.3	9.4	1.1	3.6	2.9	2.9	22.3	7.5
Inflation at *t*–1 < 20%	6.47	5.57	2.1	–0.2	6.4	4.5	29.5	4.6
20% < inflation at *t*–1 < 50%	22.1	18.7	5.5	10.5	4.6	13.1	2.0	14.8
Inflation at *t*–1 > 50%	34.9	17.5	1.0	6.8	5.4	9.4	–32.7	29.0
2. GRA-supported	17.6	11.1	1.6	4.5	4.0	5.8	24.5	9.9
Nontransition	11.0	8.5	1.3	3.6	3.4	3.4	33.6	12.1
Transition	27.2	14.8	2.1	5.9	4.8	14.8	2.1	–6.4
Inflation at *t*–1 < 20%	7.3	5.3	–0.3	0.9	3.3	1.0	35.8	12.8
20% < inflation at *t*–1 < 50%	24.4	22.4	5.7	12.3	4.1	24.8	4.8	–21.0
Inflation at *t*–1 > 50%	41.9	19.0	3.7	8.0	6.3	11.3	–32.7	31.4
3. PRGF-supported	7.7	7.2	0.5	2.7	1.6	0.4	19.7	5.6
Nontransition	7.6	6.8	1.8	2.7	1.1	1.7	17.2	8.8
Transition	8.2	9.8	–7.3	2.8	4.5	–7.4	36.3	–8.1
Inflation at *t*–1 < 20%	5.7	5.8	0.5	1.8	0.9	–1.0	22.8	–2.5
20% < inflation at *t*–1 < 50%	18.3	12.6	5.2	7.5	5.3	5.4	–1.5	32.7
Inflation at *t*–1 > 50%	8.8	12.1	–9.1	3.1	1.9	5.6	...	26.5

Sources: IMF, MONA and WEO databases; and IMF staff estimates.

[1]Projection errors are calculated as actual minus program values after transformation.

[2]Transformed to be mapped into (–100,100) percent.

[3]NDA contribution is defined as $\Delta NDA/\Delta M$, where Δ indicates level difference.

were generally modest, about 1½ percent a year across GRA-supported programs and ½ percent a year in PRGF-supported programs, though as much as 5 percent per year for countries whose starting inflation rates were between 20 percent and 50 percent a year. In addition, for the following year, inflation was, on average, higher than programmed by about 4½ percent a year in GRA-supported programs and 2½ percent a year in PRGF-supported programs (Table 4.10). The decline in inflation was driven in part by lower money growth rates. Moreover, a given growth rate of the money supply in the context of an IMF-supported program is associated with lower inflation, possibly because greater credibility in the authorities' policies engenders confidence in the currency and thus raises money demand (Box 4.4). In GRA-supported programs, this effect is both economically and statistically significant—ceteris paribus, inflation is 10 percentage points lower (in the year following program approval) under an IMF-supported program than it would be under similar money growth rates but without a program. The effect is weaker and not statistically significant among PRGF-supported countries.

While lower money growth contributed to the disinflation achieved, money growth tended to be higher than programmed—by about 4 percent in the year of program approval and 6 percent the following year in GRA-supported countries, and 1.6 percent and 0.4 percent, respectively, in PRGF-supported countries. Again, among countries starting with high inflation rates, the slippages are considerably greater—as much as 25 percent in the year following program approval in GRA-supported countries (Table 4.10). Table 4.11 seeks to explain some of the factors behind the slippage in broad money growth. In part, higher broad money growth reflects the effect of depreciation of the nominal exchange rate on foreign currency deposits—the only variable statistically significant for the sample of transition economies. Beyond this effect, among nontransition economies, fiscal slippages are correlated with money growth slippages, while the performance of output growth appears to have little explanatory power (except for GRA-supported programs in year *t*+1). Finally, a larger programmed decline in inflation is associated with larger money growth slippages, presumably reflecting the difficulty of achieving ambitious disinflations. Overall, the regressions have greater difficulty in explaining slippages during the first program year, accounting for only 9 percent to 25 percent of the variation, but somewhat greater

Box 4.4. Does IMF Support Engender Confidence in Disinflation Efforts?

Beyond the effects of slower money growth on inflation, if IMF support enhances the credibility of the authorities' policies then this should be reflected in greater confidence in the currency and higher money demand. Higher money demand, in turn, should result in lower inflation for a *given* growth rate of money. To test this hypothesis, it is useful to consider a standard money demand function:

$$m - p = \alpha y - v, \qquad (1)$$

where m is broad money, p the consumer price index, y is real GDP, and v is (residual) velocity. Inverting and taking first differences yields:

$$\pi = \Delta m - \alpha \Delta y + \Delta v, \qquad (2)$$

where the behavior of velocity is assumed to reflect the additional confidence that IMF support might impart.

Equation (2) is estimated for both low- and middle-income countries that had an IMF-supported program at some point during the period 1990–2000 and whose inflation is above 10 percent a year.

The results in the table for upper- and lower-middle-income countries suggest that, while IMF support has little immediate effect on confidence and inflation (in part because inflation in the current year may be largely determined), it has an economically and statistically significant impact by the following year; ceteris paribus, lowering inflation by as much as 10 percentage points.

The confidence effects of IMF support in low-income countries are much weaker (ceteris paribus, lowering inflation by 3 percentage points) and not statistically significant. Although broad money growth is highly significant in both regressions, the residual standard error is 15 percent a year in the low-income country regression compared to 7 percent a year in the middle-income country regression.

Inflation and Money Growth Under IMF-Supported Programs: Regression Results[1]

	Regressor[2]						
Dependent variable: π[2]	Constant	*prog*	$prog_{-1}$	Δm	Δy	R^2	Number of Observations
Middle-income countries	0.07*	–0.02	–0.10***	1.00***	–1.25	0.63	222
Low-income countires	0.09*	–0.02	–0.03	0.91***	–1.27	0.71	205

Source: IMF staff estimates.

[1]*** significant at 1 percent, ** significant at 5 percent, and * significant at 10 percent levels.

[2]π, Δm, and Δy represent inflation, broad money growth, and real GDP growth, respectively; *prog* is a dummy variable indicating an IMF-supported program; Δm and Δy are instrumented with their own lags; annual dummies are also included in the regression (not reported).

success in accounting for slippages in the subsequent year.

In turn, Figure 4.3 correlates the slippage in broad money growth to the higher-than-programmed inflation rates. The relationship is statistically significant and—for the subsample in which money growth was higher than programmed—accounts for 30–60 percent of the variation of inflation projection error. The inflationary impact of monetary overruns naturally depends on whether there was a concomitant increase in money demand. A common hypothesis, in this regard, is that monetary expansions that reflect higher net foreign assets correspond to capital inflows responding to higher money demand, and should thus have a smaller inflationary impact; conversely, monetary overruns that reflect larger NDA growth than programmed should have a larger inflationary impact. Empirically, however, the source of the monetary overrun makes no difference to the inflationary impact (Table 4.12). This underscores the finding above that a NDA/NIR framework is not well suited to controlling inflation, which generally requires a more explicit nominal anchor. It also underscores the need to sterilize capital inflows or large donor support if the inflation target is to be achieved.[20]

Output Growth

While controlling inflation is usually the primary goal of monetary policy in IMF-supported programs, the monetary stance may also affect other macroeconomic variables—for instance, output growth. One concern is that tight monetary policies in IMF-supported programs may have deleterious effects on activity and output growth. In fact, the empirical evi-

[20]The appropriate response to large donor inflows will be examined in the forthcoming review of PRGF-supported programs.

Table 4.11. Determinants of Broad Money Growth: Regression Results[1]

Dependent Variable: Δm^{ER}[2]	Regressor[2]					R^2	Number of Observations
	Constant	Δexr^{ER}	$\Delta fbal^{ER}$	Δy^{ER}	$\Delta \pi^{P}$		
All programs							
Year t	2.729***	0.152	–0.315	0.198	0.037	0.032	117
Year t+1	–1.554	0.345***	0.274	0.341	–0.929***	0.501	65
Year t and t+1 (pooled)	2.020**	0.301***	–0.032	0.357	–0.076	0.096	182
Fixed[3]	1.824	–0.087	–0.402	0.258	–0.034	0.026	98
Flexible[3]	2.466*	0.421***	0.596	0.470	–0.042	0.260	84
Nontransition GRA-supported[4]							
Year t	2.344	–0.145	–0.277	0.169	–0.401	0.089	33
Year t+1	0.240	0.013	–1.360**	0.766*	–0.708***	0.603	22
Year t and t+1 (pooled)	1.662	–0.147	–0.809*	0.440	–0.597***	0.261	55
Fixed[3]	1.620	–0.489***	–1.144**	0.111	–0.704***	0.503	36
Flexible[3]	1.129	0.263*	0.713	0.713	0.094	0.277	19
Nontransition PRGF-supported							
Year t	–0.295	0.829***	–1.099**	0.182	–0.159	0.246	45
Year t+1	–4.274***	0.537***	0.333	0.244	–2.346***	0.514	31
Year t and t+1 (pooled)	–1.046	0.685***	–0.520	0.458	–0.300	0.214	76
Fixed[3]	–2.725	0.589**	–0.569	0.501	–0.216	0.152	37
Flexible[3]	0.799	0.696***	–0.358	0.166	–0.257	0.252	39
Transition economies							
Year t	5.109**	0.769*	–0.399	0.899	0.084	0.152	33
Year t+1	–6.384	0.401	2.141	0.730	–0.935	0.715	11
Year t and t+1 (pooled)	2.992	0.580***	0.455	0.209	0.020	0.261	44
Fixed[3]	3.635	0.366	0.169	0.321	0.078	0.055	23
Flexible[3]	2.825	0.524*	0.996	–0.181	–0.096	0.378	21

Sources: IMF, MONA and WEO databases; and IMF staff estimates.

[1]*** significant at 1 percent, ** significant at 5 percent, and * significant at 10 percent levels.

[2]Δm^{ER}, Δy^{ER}, Δexr^{ER} and $\Delta fbal^{ER}$ represent projection error in broad money growth, real GDP growth, percentage change in the nominal exchange rate (national currency per U.S. dollar) and fiscal balance in percent of GDP, respectively; $\Delta \pi^{P}$ refers to programmed change in inflation; projection errors are calculated as actual minus program values after transformation that maps underlying variables into an interval (–100,100) percent.

[3]Exchange rate regimes are classified by *AREAER*; "fixed regimes" include no separate legal tender, currency board arrangement, other conventional pegs, pegs with horizontal bands, crawling pegs, and crawling bands; "flexible regimes" include managed and independent floats.

[4]Excludes capital account crisis programs.

dence does not support the hypothesis that monetary policy has been tightened excessively in IMF-supported programs leading to lower output growth.[21] Table 4.13 (top panel) reports the results of a regression of output growth on the monetary stance, where the latter is instrumented by its programmed value.[22] Only for the transition economies sample is the coefficient significant, and even in this case, the effect is numerically small: a 1 percentage point increase in velocity growth is associated with less than one-tenth of a percentage point decline in the output growth rate. Moreover, an unexpectedly tight monetary stance cannot explain growth projection errors.

External Adjustment

A further reason for monetary restraint in IMF-supported programs is to promote external adjustment.[23] Table 4.13 (bottom panel) examines the

[21]The IEO came to a similar conclusion based on a smaller sample of PRGF-supported programs.

[22]For this exercise, the monetary policy stance is measured by velocity (with an increase indicating a tighter stance), instrumented by the programmed velocity. These regressions also include the overall fiscal balance (instrumented by its program projection) to control for possible omitted variable bias. The role of fiscal policy is discussed in Section IV, below.

[23]Monetary policy also has an important role to play—particularly in capital account crises—in stemming capital outflows and achieving a more orderly external adjustment. Empirical evidence on the impact of higher interest rates on capital flows is discussed in *IMF-Supported Programs in Capital Account Crises* (see Ghosh and others, 2002).

Figure 4.3. Projection Errors in Inflation and Money Growth[1]

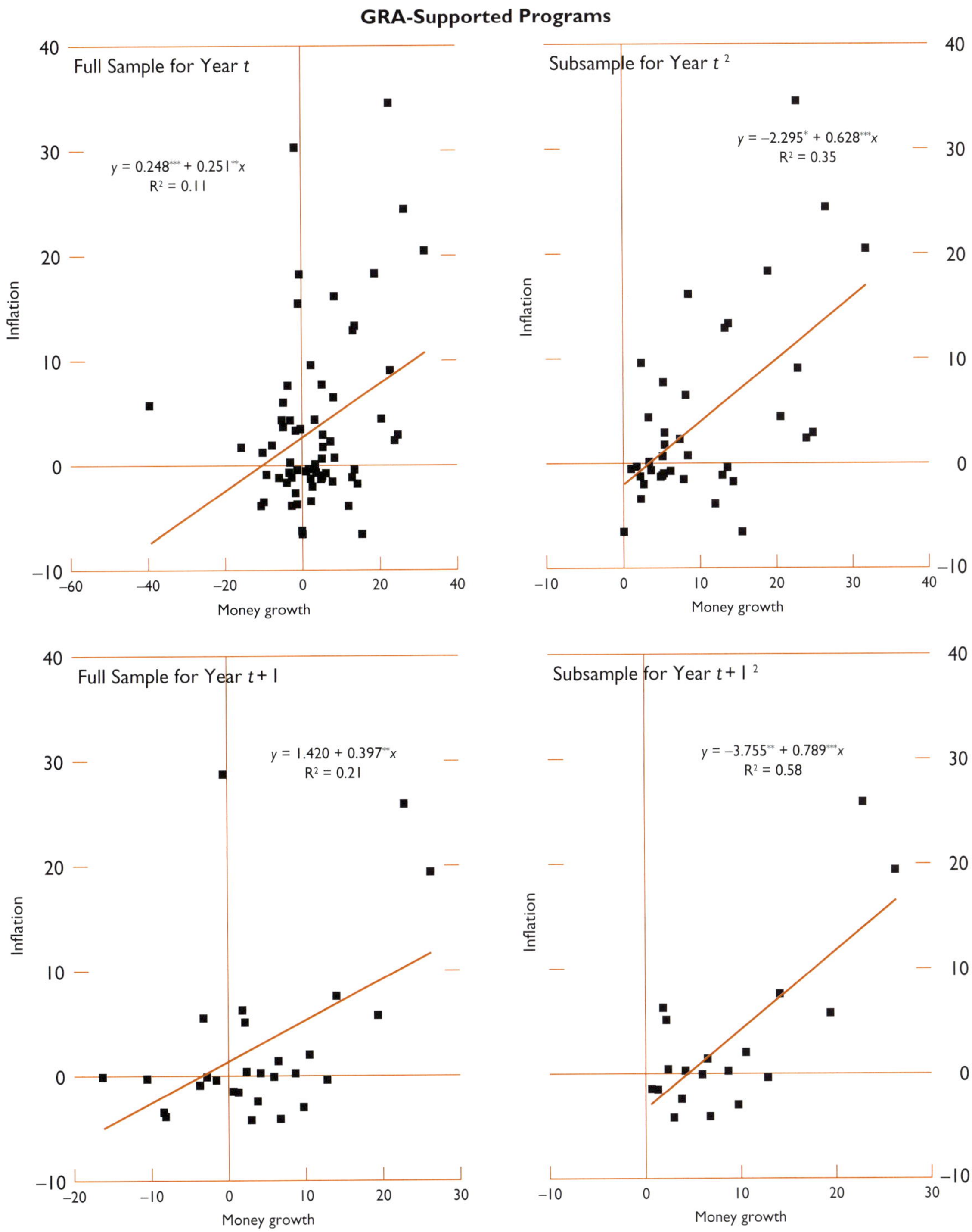

Figure 4.3 (*concluded*)

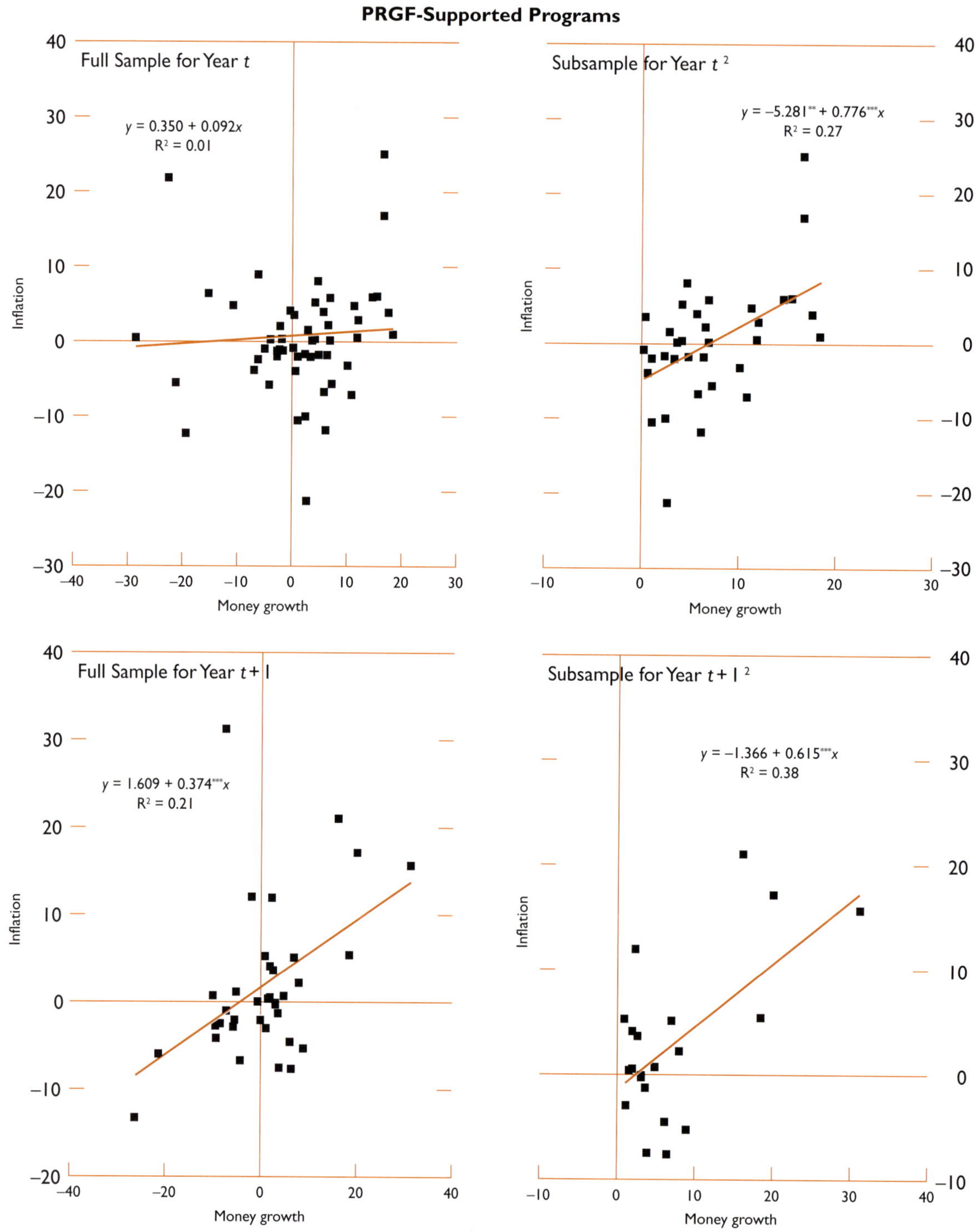

Sources: IMF, MONA and WEO databases; and IMF staff estimates.
[1] Projection errors are defined as actual minus projection; *significant at 10 percent, **significant at 5 percent, and ***significant at 1 percent levels.
[2] Subsample includes observations with positive projection error in money growth only.

Table 4.12. Projection Errors in Inflation and Money Growth: Regression Results[1]

Dependent Variable: $INF^{ER\,2}$	Regressor[2]								Number of
	Constant	MG^{ER}	$D50$	$D90$	$D50 \cdot MG^{ER}$	$D90 \cdot MG^{ER}$	$NDAMG$	R^2	Observations
				A. Regression with no dummy					
1. Full sample									
GRA-supported									
Year t	2.106*	0.228**	—	—	—	—	—	0.153	62
Year t+1	0.121	0.335**	—	—	—	—	—	0.406	28
Year t and t+1 (pooled)	1.481	0.253***	—	—	—	—	—	0.219	90
Fixed[3]	0.958	0.167*	—	—	—	—	—	0.185	59
Flexible[3]	1.851	0.383***	—	—	—	—	—	0.316	31
PRGF-supported									
Year t	0.205	0.065	—	—	—	—	—	0.074	53
Year t+1	–0.708	0.295***	—	—	—	—	—	0.459	36
Year t and t+1 (pooled)	–0.068	0.164**	—	—	—	—	—	0.223	89
Fixed[3]	1.662*	–0.097	—	—	—	—	—	0.462	36
Flexible[3]	–2.191*	0.400***	—	—	—	—	—	0.322	53
2. Subsample: $MG^{ER} > 0$ only									
GRA-supported									
Year t	–2.644*	0.604***	—	—	—	—	—	0.360	37
Year t+1	–3.464**	0.685***	—	—	—	—	—	0.641	19
Year t and t+1 (pooled)	–2.931**	0.625***	—	—	—	—	—	0.437	56
Fixed[3]	–2.450*	0.504***	—	—	—	—	—	0.418	39
Flexible[3]	–3.121	0.732***	—	—	—	—	—	0.441	17
PRGF-supported									
Year t	–6.221***	0.844***	—	—	—	—	—	0.338	34
Year t+1	–6.663***	1.153***	—	—	—	—	—	0.871	20
Year t and t+1 (pooled)	–7.151***	1.073***	—	—	—	—	—	0.707	54
Fixed[3]	–2.664*	0.573***	—	—	—	—	—	0.685	22
Flexible[3]	–8.627***	1.238***	—	—	—	—	—	0.763	32
				B. Regression including NDA dummy					
1. $D50$ ($\Delta NDA/\Delta M > 50\%$)									
Year t	0.212	0.168*	0.056	—	0.065	—	—	0.205	64
Year t+1	0.560	0.364***	–2.212	—	–0.061	—	—	0.474	38
Year t and t+1 (pooled)	0.398	0.236**	–0.666	—	0.037	—	—	0.314	102
Fixed[3]	0.127	0.169*	–0.850	—	–0.074	—	—	0.485	54
Flexible[3]	0.189	0.295*	–0.729	—	0.145	—	—	0.283	48

Table 4.12 *(concluded)*

Dependent Variable: INF^{ER} [2]	Regressor[2]							R^2	Number of Observations
	Constant	MG^{ER}	*D50*	*D90*	$D50 \cdot MG^{ER}$	$D90 \cdot MG^{ER}$	*NDAMG*		
2. *D90* (ΔNDA/ΔM > 90%)									
Year *t*	0.824	0.261*	—	–1.136	—	–0.194	—	0.234	64
Year *t*+1	0.343	0.298**	—	–1.969	—	0.099	—	0.468	38
Year *t* and *t*+1 (pooled)	0.617	0.268***	—	–1.548	—	–0.025	—	0.323	102
Fixed[3]	–0.043	0.101	—	–1.110	—	0.161	—	0.490	54
Flexible[3]	0.460	0.464***	—	–1.806	—	–0.211	—	0.310	48
C. Regression including *NDA* contribution to money growth									
Year *t*	0.245	0.203*	—	—	—	—	0.003	0.203	64
Year *t*+1	–0.151	0.355***	—	—	—	—	–0.018	0.459	38
Year *t* and *t*+1 (pooled)	0.098	0.260***	—	—	—	—	–0.006	0.313	102
Fixed[3]	–0.150	0.164**	—	—	—	—	–0.054	0.501	54
Flexible[3]	–0.210	0.371***	—	—	—	—	0.001	0.276	48

Sources: IMF, MONA and WEO databases; and IMF staff estimates.

[1]All regressions include as a control variable projection error in fiscal balance; significant at * 10 percent, ** 5 percent, and *** 1 percent levels.

[2]INF^{ER} and MG^{ER} refer to projection errors in inflation (end-period) and broad money growth, respectively; *D50* and *D90* are dummy variables that equal 1 if Δ*NDA*/*DM* > 50 percent and Δ*NDA*/*DM* > 90 percent, respectively, and 0 otherwise; *NDAMG* represents the contribution of *NDA* to broad money growth.

[3]Exchange rate regimes are classified by *AREAER*; "fixed regimes" include no separate legal tender, currency board arrangement, other conventional pegs, pegs with horizontal bands, crawling pegs, and crawling bands; "flexible regimes" include managed and independent floats.

Table 4.13. Monetary Stance, Growth, and External Adjustment: Regression Results[1]

	Regressor[2]						
	Constant	Δv[3]	Δv_{-1}	Δy_{-1}	ΔCA_{-1}	R^2	Number of Observations
			I. Dependent variable: Δy[2]				
A. Contenporaneous effect:							
Nontransition GRA-supported							
Year *t*	2.048	0.047	—	0.138	—	0.056	38
Year *t*+1	1.268	0.135	—	0.263	—	0.167	22
Year *t* and *t*+1 (pooled)	2.300***	–0.111	—	0.077	—	0.072	60
Fixed[4]	3.209***	–0.093	—	0.315*	—	0.217	38
Flexible[4]	0.848	–0.238	—	–0.417	—	0.186	22
Nontransition PRGF-supported							
Year *t*	0.806	–0.040	—	–0.125	—	0.065	45
Year *t*+1	1.976	–0.120	—	0.500	—	0.252	31
Year *t* and *t*+1 (pooled)	2.560***	0.024	—	0.313***	—	0.130	76
Fixed[4]	2.784**	–0.021	—	0.224	—	0.084	37
Flexible[4]	2.175**	0.091	—	0.379***	—	0.223	39
Transition economies							
Year *t*	0.425	0.067**	—	–0.189	—	0.254	35
Year *t*+1	0.642	0.002	—	–0.302	—	0.240	11
Year *t* and *t*+1 (pooled)	1.765*	–0.037	—	0.498***	—	0.337	46
Fixed[4]	–0.031	–0.069**	—	0.431***	—	0.508	24
Flexible[4]	4.016**	0.012	—	0.488**	—	0.263	22
B. Lagged effect:							
Nontransition GRA-supported							
Year *t*+1	2.326*	—	–0.029	0.161	—	0.039	38
Nontransition PRGF-supported							
Year *t*+1	1.021	—	0.036	0.455**	—	0.182	46
Transition economies							
Year *t*+1	3.500***	—	0.048***	0.651***	—	0.619	30
			II. Dependent variable: ΔCA[2]				
A. Contenporaneous effect:							
Nontransition GRA-supported							
Year *t*	2.425	0.036	—	—	–0.125	0.057	38
Year *t*+1	1.496	0.080	—	—	–0.340*	0.249	22
Year *t* and *t*+1 (pooled)	2.251***	0.041	—	—	–0.251*	0.154	60
Fixed[4]	0.046	0.146**	—	—	–0.385***	0.254	38
Flexible[4]	5.024***	–0.002	—	—	–0.023	0.295	22
Nontransition PRGF-supported							
Year *t*	0.505	–0.041	—	—	–0.209*	0.101	45
Year *t*+1	3.582	–0.107	—	—	–0.369*	0.207	31
Year *t* and *t*+1 (pooled)	1.209*	–0.059	—	—	–0.281**	0.114	76
Fixed[4]	1.941*	–0.115	—	—	–0.432*	0.221	37
Flexible[4]	–0.180	0.035	—	—	–0.229	0.079	39
Transition economies							
Year *t*	0.991	0.065***	—	—	–0.221*	0.282	35
Year *t*+1	0.241	–0.002	—	—	–0.928***	0.705	11
Year *t* and *t*+1 (pooled)	1.084	0.052**	—	—	–0.357***	0.339	46
Fixed[4]	0.642	0.033	—	—	–0.304**	0.551	24
Flexible[4]	1.676	0.075	—	—	–0.387*	0.297	22
B. Lagged effect:							
Nontransition GRA-supported							
Year *t*+1	1.198	—	–0.005	—	–0.344***	0.233	38
Nontransition PRGF-supported							
Year *t*+1	2.805	—	–0.004	—	–0.431*	0.162	46
Transition economies							
Year *t*+1	0.102	—	0.034	—	–0.502*	0.186	30

Sources: IMF, MONA and WEO databases; and IMF staff estimates.

[1]All regressions include as a control the change in fiscal balance (instrumented by programmed change); significant at * 10 percent, ** 5 percent, and *** 1 percent levels.

[2]Δv, Δy, and ΔCA represent velocity growth relative to trend velocity growth (as measured by the five-year historical average prior to year *t*), real GDP growth, and change in the current account balance (net of official transfers) in percent of GDP at *t*–1, respectively; all underlying variables are transformed to be mapped into an interval (–100,100) percent prior to taking differences; velocity is defined as nominal GDP divided by (period average) stock of broad money with an increase, ceteris paribus, indicating a tighter monetary stance.

[3]Velocity growth (Δv) was instrumented by its own lag and programmed velocity growth (relative to trend velocity growth).

[4]Exchange rate regimes are classified by *AREAER;* "fixed regimes" include no separate legal tender, currency board arrangement, other conventional pegs, pegs with horizontal bands, crawling pegs, and crawling bands; "flexible regimes" include managed and independent floats.

impact of a tighter monetary stance on external adjustment. The results are broadly similar to those for output growth. Except for the transition economies sample, almost no coefficient is statistically significant—suggesting a limited role for monetary policy in targeting current account adjustment.

Summary

IMF-supported programs normally target and achieve a deceleration of broad money growth and a tightening of the monetary stance. Stabilization efforts undertaken in the context of IMF-supported programs appear to enjoy greater credibility such that, in GRA-supported programs, inflation is lower for a given rate of money growth; a similar impact in PRGF-supported programs was not found. Overruns in broad money growth—whether reflecting unanticipated NDA or NFA expansion—are associated with slippages in inflation performance relative to program targets. The high correlation between monetary aggregates and inflation reaffirms the importance of nominal anchors for controlling inflation.

Monetary policy appears to have played a limited role in regard to external adjustment and real activity. This suggests that, in terms of instrument assignment, monetary policy should be geared mainly toward inflation control, while fiscal and exchange rate policies take center stage in achieving the necessary external adjustment.

IV Fiscal Policy

Fiscal adjustment often forms a key element of IMF-supported programs for a variety of reasons, including the need to foster orderly external adjustment, to underpin disinflation and macroeconomic stabilization, to put public debt dynamics on a more sustainable footing, or to raise economic efficiency. This section takes up the role of fiscal adjustment in IMF-supported programs. It first examines the fiscal adjustment envisaged in IMF-supported programs and its relation to program objectives. Next, it turns to experience, reviewing first the record on adjustment and the reasons for slippages and then considering the implications for public debt dynamics, external adjustment, and growth.

While the focus here is on aggregate fiscal adjustment, the role of fiscal policy in IMF-supported programs typically goes much beyond fiscal consolidation. Indeed, other important objectives of fiscal policy changes in IMF-supported programs include improving governance, protecting social welfare, and reducing poverty. Often, this is to be achieved by lowering the interest bill, reducing tax distortions, and freeing resources for priority primary expenditures, especially those targeted to vulnerable groups. Over the short run, this may require reducing the overall deficit, but with the goal of permitting higher primary expenditures once the stabilization gains have been consolidated. In low-income countries, expenditure on poverty-reducing activities may be raised by increasing the resource envelope (through donor support or domestic resource mobilization) and by reorienting expenditures from nonpriority areas; indeed, more recent programs in low-income countries, supported by PRGF arrangements, have tended to target somewhat less fiscal adjustment than previous programs supported by SAF/ESAF arrangements (which generally had to contend with worse initial macroeconomic conditions) as well as laying greater emphasis on supporting poverty-reducing expenditures (Box 4.5).[24]

Programmed Fiscal Adjustment

The initial fiscal positions, programmed adjustment, and outcomes across IMF-supported programs are summarized in Table 4.14. On average, the initial fiscal positions (inclusive of grants) were substantially better than those prevailing at the time of the previous Conditionality Review (Box 4.6). Programs targeted improvements in the overall balance during the first program year ranging from 0.2 percent of GDP in PRGF-supported programs to about 1½ to 2 percent of GDP in nontransition and transition GRA-supported programs, and a further improvement in the following year ranging from 0.2 percent to 0.9 percent of GDP. In capital account crisis programs, the overall balance was projected to deteriorate by 1.2 percent of GDP during the first program year (from a deficit of 3.3 percent of GDP in the year prior to the program),[25] but the projections also assumed substantial fiscal consolidation (3.2 percent of GDP) in the following year.

Of the targeted improvement of 2.2 percent of GDP in the overall balance over two years in GRA-supported nontransition programs, 1.6 percent of GDP represents a higher primary balance, consisting of higher revenues (0.9 percent of GDP) and lower primary expenditures (0.5 percent of GDP). In PRGF-supported programs, around one-half of the narrowing of 0.9 percent of GDP in the overall deficit represents a higher primary balance (0.5 percent of GDP), consisting of higher revenues (0.3 percent of GDP) and lower primary expenditures (0.2 percent of GDP). Regarding expenditure subcomponents, although a lack of consistent data makes any systematic treatment difficult, it is noteworthy that PRGF-supported programs in particular strive to protect capital expenditure, which is programmed to

[24]Since the sample here is arrangements approved over the period 1995–2000, the results reported for PRGF-supported programs actually refers mostly to ESAF-supported programs.

[25]These figures pertain to targets specified in the original program. As discussed in Box 2.2 of "Objectives and Outcomes" (Part II of this occasional paper), in a number of capital account crises, especially in East Asia, the initial fiscal targets were revised as it became apparent that activity was turning out significantly weaker than expected.

Box 4.5. Fiscal Adjustment Under PRGF-Supported Programs

Two of the key features of the Poverty Reduction and Growth Facility (PRGF) are fiscal flexibility and budgets that are more pro-poor and pro-growth. Fiscal flexibility implies that fiscal targets should accommodate higher public spending in support of a country's poverty reduction strategy as long as macroeconomic stability is not threatened. Pro-poor budgeting implies that government spending should be oriented toward poverty-reducing activities and outlays that foster the development of human and physical capital.

PRGF-supported programs, on average, have targeted an increase in the budget deficit and government expenditures in the first year of these programs (see table). With external financing, grants, and revenues increasing, countries were targeted to increase their outlays by about 0.5 percent of GDP. In this way, PRGF programs have sought to combine both macroeconomic stability with a higher envelope for government spending. In later years of the program—where data on external support were less certain—spending increases were not necessarily envisaged. Earlier assessments of PRGF program design have also confirmed the fiscal flexibility of these arrangements.[1]

PRGF countries have been successful in increasing poverty-reducing spending (see figure). Such spending increased by 1.4 percent of GDP in 2002 with respect to the pre-PRGF year. Budgets are also becoming more pro-poor, as the share of these outlays in government spending increased by more than 2 percentage points over the same period. Poverty-reducing spending is projected to increase further during 2003–04 both as a share of GDP as well as total government spending.

[1]See Gupta and others (2002).

Poverty-Reducing Spending in PRGF Countries[1]

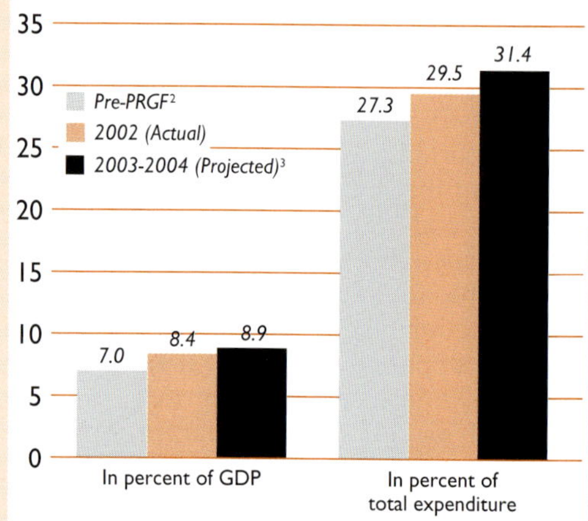

Sources: Country authorities; and IMF staff estimates.
[1]Based on a sample of 30 countries.
[2]In most cases refers to 1999.
[3]Average projected expenditure for 2003 and 2004.

Targeted Fiscal Adjustment in PRGF-Supported Programs, 1999–2003[1]
(Averages, in percent of GDP)

	Pre-PRGF Level	Program Targets (Change from pre-PRGF year) Year 1	Year 2	Year 3
Fiscal balance, including grants	–4.9	0.7	1.2	1.6
Fiscal balance, excluding grants	–8.4	–0.2	0.6	1.5
Total revenues, excluding grants	18.5	0.4	0.9	1.6
Total expenditures and net lending	26.9	0.5	0.2	–0.1
Grants	3.6	0.8	0.7	0.1
Net external financing[2]	6.4	0.7	0.8	–0.3

Source: Independent Evaluation Office (2004).
[1]Based on a sample of 41 PRGF-supported programs. However, due to missing observations, some of the averages are based on fewer observations than others.
[2]The sum of grants and net external borrowing in the government accounts.

Table 4.14. Initial Conditions and Programmed and Actual Fiscal Adjustment
(In percent of GDP)

	Level								Changes					
	Program			Outturn			Outturn – program[1]		Program		Outturn		Outturn – program[1]	
	t–1	*t*	*t*+1	*t*–1	*t*	*t*+1	*t*	*t*+1	*t*	*t*+1	*t*	*t*+1	*t*	*t*+1
EFF/SBA—nontransition economies														
Fiscal balance	–3.2	–1.9	–1.0	–3.0	–2.5	–4.2	–0.6	–3.2***	1.3	0.9	0.5	–1.7	–0.8	–2.5
Primary balance	1.2	2.9	2.8	1.7	1.9	0.2	–0.9	–2.6***	1.6	–0.1	0.2	–1.7	–1.4	–1.7**
Total expenditure	27.4	27.3	26.2	27.8	28.1	29.6	0.8	3.4***	–0.1	–1.1	0.3	1.5	0.5	2.6***
Interest payments	4.5	4.8	3.8	4.8	4.4	4.4	–0.4	0.7	0.3	–1.0	–0.4	0.1	–0.7	1.1
Revenues	24.3	25.4	25.2	24.8	25.6	25.4	0.2	0.2	1.1	–0.3	0.8	–0.2	–0.4*	0.0
EFF/SBA—economies in transition														
Fiscal balance	–3.6	–1.7	–1.5	–4.3	–2.4	–1.8	–0.7	–0.3	1.9	0.2	1.9	0.6	0.0	0.4
Primary balance	0.6	1.7	2.0	–0.3	0.7	1.0	–1.0	–1.0	1.1	0.3	1.0	0.2	–0.1	0.0
Total expenditure	38.3	36.2	34.1	38.5	36.8	36.6	0.6	2.6	–2.1	–2.1	–1.7	–0.2	0.5	1.9
Interest payments	4.2	3.4	3.4	4.0	3.1	2.8	–0.3	–0.6	–0.7	–0.1	–0.9	–0.4	–0.1	–0.3
Revenues	34.8	34.5	32.6	34.3	34.4	34.8	0.0	2.3	–0.3	–1.9	0.2	0.4	0.5	2.3*
Capital account crisis countries														
Fiscal balance	–3.3	–4.5	–1.3	–3.9	–4.0	–4.9	0.4	–3.7	–1.2	3.2	–0.2	–0.9	1.0*	–4.1*
Primary balance	1.4	1.5	2.5	2.6	0.2	–0.4	–1.3	–3.0	0.1	1.0	–2.4	–0.7	–2.5*	–1.7**
Total expenditure	21.5	23.4	19.7	26.2	26.8	28.8	3.4	9.1**	1.9	–3.8	0.6	2.0	–1.3	5.8***
Interest payments	4.7	6.0	3.8	6.5	4.3	4.5	–1.7	0.7*	1.3	–2.2	–2.2	0.2	–3.5	2.4
Revenues	18.2	19.0	18.4	22.3	22.7	23.9	3.8*	5.5*	0.7	–0.6	0.4	1.1	–0.3	1.7
SAF/ESAF/PRGF														
Fiscal balance	–4.1	–3.9	–3.2	–3.7	–3.7	–4.7	0.2	–1.5***	0.2	0.7	–0.1	–0.9	–0.3	–1.7
Primary balance	–0.4	–0.4	0.1	–0.1	–0.5	–1.5	–0.1	–1.6***	0.0	0.5	–0.4	–1.1	–0.4*	–1.6
Total expenditure	26.7	26.9	26.1	26.0	26.3	27.0	–0.6	0.9	0.2	–0.8	0.3	0.7	0.1	1.5**
Interest payments	3.7	3.6	3.3	3.5	3.3	3.1	–0.3*	–0.2	–0.1	–0.2	–0.2	–0.2	–0.1	0.1
Revenues	22.6	23.0	22.9	22.4	22.6	22.3	–0.4	–0.6	0.4	–0.1	0.2	–0.3	–0.1	–0.2

Sources: IMF, MONA database; and IMF staff calculations.
[1]Statistically significant differences are at the 1 percent (***), 5 percent (**), and 10 percent (*) levels.

increase (as a share of GDP) throughout the program period.

Beyond these averages, to what extent does the targeted fiscal adjustment reflect program objectives? The targeted fiscal adjustment (between years *t*–1 and *t*+1) depends positively (and, generally, significantly) on the initial level of expenditure, the size of the initial fiscal deficit, and on the programmed improvement in the current account balance; the resulting R^2 of the regressions are high, ranging from 0.5 to 0.75 (Table 4.15).[26, 27]

Regression results for the primary fiscal balance are broadly similar, except that in the GRA sample, a larger output gap is associated with a smaller adjustment effort in nontransition economies.[28] In sum, the targeted fiscal adjustment appears to be quite closely

[26]Other variables that might influence the programmed fiscal adjustment are public debt and either the preprogram inflation rate or the targeted reduction in inflation. Specifications (not shown in Table 4.15) that included these variables did not yield significant coefficients however, and—in the case of public debt—entailed dropping a large number of observations due to the lack of data availability.

[27]The results here are given in terms of overall fiscal balance adjustment. Qualitatively, the results are similar when the primary balance is used in the regressions, albeit with generally lower statistical significance because fewer observations are available.

[28]In the transition economies, by contrast, a larger gap is associated with a larger adjustment effort, though this most likely reflects the difficulties of estimating meaningful output gaps in a period in which potential output growth was changing rapidly.

Box 4.6. Fiscal Adjustment Then and Now: Conditionality and ESAF Reviews

The last comprehensive review of fiscal adjustment in IMF-supported programs took place in 1994.[1] For low-income countries, an ESAF review was conducted in 1997.[2] A comparison between their findings and the findings in this paper provide an interesting snapshot of how things have changed over the last decade. Although there are some methodological incompatibilities between the papers, including a rather small sample utilized in the 1994 conditionality review (covering programs spanning only a three-year period, from 1988 to 1991), a longer sample utilized in the 1997 ESAF review (covering the period 1985–95), and occasionally different analytical categories in terms of program types, some interesting patterns nevertheless emerge.

The average program in the previous studies faced an overall fiscal deficit of 8.2 percent of GDP (versus 3.7 percent of GDP in the current study) and a primary deficit of 2.2 percent of GDP (compared to a surplus of 0.3 percent). For SAF/ESAF programs, when the 1985–95 sample is split, the deficit is similarly found to have fallen from 9.1 percent of GDP for the average program in the period 1981–85, to 5.6 percent of GDP in the period 1991–95. Prolonged users of IMF resources in the 1994 Conditionality Review, as in this paper, tended to face more favorable initial conditions than new users. Transition economies faced lower fiscal deficits then, but much larger public sectors, which programs aimed to reduce. Over time, it is striking how successful adjustment has been in achieving the desired reduction in the size of the public sectors of transition economies.

Adjustment in programs included in the previous studies sought to improve the overall fiscal balance by 3.4 percent of GDP (compared to 1.5 percent of GDP between years $t-1$ and $t+1$ in the current study), and the primary balance by 3.3 percent of GDP (compared to 1.0 percent of GDP). In the 1997 ESAF sample, the average programmed improvement in the primary balance was 3.0 percent of GDP. Then as now, there was a pattern that new users had larger planned adjustments than more frequent users of IMF resources. Transition economies also had larger planned fiscal adjustments then, but the difference is smaller than for other program types.

Comparing program/forecast errors across studies is difficult because of the wide variation across program types and some incompatibility in the definitions. The error for all countries is now lower in the year of program approval (an underperformance of 0.4 percent of GDP in the overall balance) but higher overall because of a much larger error in year $t+1$ (1.6 percent of GDP). For transition economies there was an overperformance of 1.3 percent of GDP then (compared to 0.4 percent of GDP in the current study). From the 1997 ESAF review the stylized fact is that about half of the targeted improvement was achieved. For these countries the error is now relatively small in the year of program approval (0.3 percent of GDP) but much larger in the following year (1.7 percent of GDP).

There has been significant improvement in the fiscal situation facing countries over time, and it has therefore been possible for programmed fiscal adjustment to become less ambitious for countries. On the other hand, difficulties in attaining fiscal targets appear to have persisted over time, with no clear trend toward a reduction in the program/forecast errors—though there has been some improvement with year of program approval but a widening of the slippage in the subsequent year.

[1]Schadler and others (1995) and IEO (2004).

[2]Abed and others (1998).

aligned to program objectives.[29] Moreover, consistent with the greater fiscal flexibility of IMF-supported programs in low-income countries, the targeted fiscal adjustment in these programs is 1.3 percent of GDP less than the adjustment targeted in GRA-supported programs.

Experience

Fiscal Adjustment

In GRA-supported programs in nontransition economies, fiscal adjustment falls short of program targets by 0.8 percent of GDP in the first program year and by 2.5 percent of GDP in the following year (Table 4.14)—though there are some cases in which fiscal adjustment was greater than projected (Box 4.7). In the first program year, these slippages are mainly on account of higher primary expenditures (1.2 percent of GDP) and lower revenues (0.4 percent of GDP). Interestingly, in the following year, both primary and interest expenditures are higher than programmed, perhaps because slippages during the first program year result in a resurgence of interest rates at which the government borrows. Another possibility may be the resumption of orderly debt service—the precise timing of which may be difficult to capture in program projections.

In capital account crises, fiscal adjustment exceeds the target by 1 percent of GDP in the first program year, though mainly because lower interest payments

[29]The Independent Evaluation Office Report on *Fiscal Adjustment in IMF-Supported Programs* (IEO, 2003) likewise finds that programmed fiscal adjustment is tailored to the country's specific circumstances.

Table 4.15. Programmed Fiscal Adjustment: Regression Results[1]

	Full Sample		GRA-Supported		PRGF-Supported		Nontransition		Transition	
	Coefficient	*t*-statistics	Coefficient	*t*-statistics	Coefficient	*t*-statistics	Coefficient	*t*-statistics	Coefficient	*t*-statistics
Based on overall fiscal balance										
Constant	–0.736	–1.06	–1.587	–1.91*	–1.898	–2.45**	–1.258	–1.93*	–1.827	–1.33
Transition dummy	–0.200	–0.37	–0.438	–0.77	0.230	0.28	. . .	. . .	. . .	. . .
Lagged expenditure	0.030	1.75*	0.044	1.86*	0.044	1.68*	0.057	3.11***	0.025	0.98
ESAF/PRGF dummy	–1.327	–3.09***	. . .	. . .	. . .	. . .	–1.091	–2.51**	–2.117	–1.74*
Lagged fiscal balance	–0.459	–7.16***	–0.686	–9.70***	–0.295	–3.59***	–0.342	–5.45***	–0.902	–9.79***
Programmed change in current account balance	0.162	2.92***	0.111	1.85*	0.232	2.82***	0.146	2.36**	0.124	1.68*
Output gap[2]	0.009	0.20	–0.005	–0.15	0.076	1.58	0.042	0.53	–0.021	–0.67
Flexible exchange rate dummy	0.155	0.37	0.404	0.76	0.582	1.07	0.452	1.08	–1.250	–1.25
F-statistic, p-value	10.795	0.000	13.966	0.000	3.789	0.001	8.148	0.000	6.517	0.000
Number of observations, R^2	125	0.54	70	0.73	55	0.49	88	0.54	37	0.74
Based on primary fiscal balance										
Constant	–0.143	–0.14	1.354	0.83	–2.677	–3.13***	–0.770	–1.07	0.040	0.02
Transition dummy	0.020	0.02	0.024	0.02	1.123	0.82	. . .	. . .	. . .	. . .
Lagged expenditure	0.020	0.55	0.026	0.49	0.028	0.91	0.048	1.72*	–0.001	–0.03
ESAF/PRGF dummy	–1.002	–1.90*	. . .	. . .	. . .	. . .	–1.130	–2.70***	5.162	3.50***
Lagged fiscal balance	–0.258	–2.79***	–0.171	–1.31	–0.302	–3.67***	–0.241	–2.98***	–0.027	–0.25
Programmed change in current account balance	0.152	1.96**	0.139	1.07	0.191	2.52**	0.200	2.64***	0.070	0.34
Output gap[2]	0.109	1.55	0.169	2.28**	0.060	0.80	–0.256	–1.77*	0.310	5.80***
Flexible exchange rate dummy	0.273	0.56	–0.590	–0.57	0.358	0.60	0.672	1.50	–4.950	–3.63***
F-statistic, p-value	3.088	0.002	1.050	0.434	4.614	0.001	6.091	0.000	2.634	0.182
Number of observations, R^2	74	0.35	36	0.30	38	0.63	59	0.56	15	0.87

Sources: IMF, MONA and WEO databases; and IMF staff estimates.

[1]Dependent variable is fiscal balance in year $t+1$ minus fiscal balance in year $t-1$; annual dummies included in regression (not reported). Regression estimated using heteroscedasticity-robust estimator of the covariance matrix.

[2]Positive gap implies current output below Hodrick-Prescott trend.

Box 4.7. Fiscal Overadjustors

While attention is usually focused on countries that achieve less than their targeted fiscal adjustment, in about one-third of programs in the sample, fiscal adjustment was greater than targeted—primarily in the transition economies and some low-income countries (see table). Not surprisingly, growth tended to be stronger than expected in these programs (at least for the GRA sample; in the PRGF sample, the pattern is less clear-cut). In the GRA sample, among fiscal overadjustors there was a somewhat larger proportion of cases where the current account balance was weaker than programmed. In the PRGF sample, reflecting a tighter link between fiscal and external adjustment, countries with stronger fiscal balances than targeted also had stronger external positions than programmed.

When examining expenditure and revenue component contributions separately, it is found that expenditure tends to be the dominant component for all program types of underadjustment, and for most instances of overadjustment. In some cases, it is even the case that expenditure more than reverses an opposite effect from revenues, so that revenue shortfalls are more than made up by expenditure overperformance (and vice versa for underperformers).

Selected Characteristics of Fiscal Overadjustors

(In percent of GDP unless otherwise noted)

	All Programs			SAF/ESAF/PRGF			SBA/EFF		
	All	Transition	Non-transition	All	Transition	Non-transition	All	Transition	Non-transition
Overadjustors									
Number of programs	41	14	27	21	2	19	20	12	8
Percent of category	32.5	37.8	30.3	37.5	25.0	39.6	28.6	41.4	19.5
Average fiscal balance forecast error	1.6	2.4	1.3	1.4	1.5	1.4	1.9	2.6	0.9
Underadjustors									
Number of programs	85	23	62	35	6	29	50	17	33
Percent of category	67.5	62.2	69.7	62.5	75.0	60.4	71.4	58.6	80.5
Average fiscal balance forecast error	–3.4	–3.3	–3.4	–3.2	–2.9	–3.2	–3.6	–3.4	–3.6
Overadjustors, of which									
Growth higher than program									
Percent of category	57.5	61.5	55.6	42.9	50.0	42.1	73.7	63.6	87.5
Average fiscal balance forecast error	2.2	3.5	1.5	2.0	2.2	1.9	2.3	3.7	1.0
Growth lower than program									
Percent of category	42.5	38.5	44.4	57.1	50.0	57.9	26.3	36.4	12.5
Average fiscal balance forecast error	1.0	1.2	1.0	1.0	0.7	1.0	1.0	1.3	0.0
Overadjustors, of which									
Current account higher than program									
Percent of category	53.7	42.9	59.3	66.7	100.0	63.2	40.0	33.3	50.0
Average fiscal balance forecast error	1.7	2.2	1.5	1.6	1.5	1.6	1.8	2.5	1.1
Current account lower than program									
Percent of category	46.3	57.1	40.7	33.3	0.0	36.8	60.0	66.7	50.0
Average fiscal balance forecast error	1.6	2.6	0.9	1.0	—	1.0	1.9	2.6	0.6

Sources: IMF, MONA and WEO databases; and IMF staff estimates.

offset higher primary expenditures. Fiscal adjustment falls short of the target by 4.1 percent of GDP in the second year because of much higher expenditures (both primary and interest). In low-income countries, slippages in the overall balance amount to 2 percent of GDP over a two-year period, reflecting almost entirely higher primary expenditures (1.6 percent of GDP) and lower revenues (0.3 percent of GDP). The

Table 4.16. Determinants of Fiscal Adjustment: Regression Results[1]

	Full Sample		GRA-Supported		PRGF-Supported	
	Coefficient	*t*-statistics	Coefficient	*t*-statistics	Coefficient	*t*-statistics
Constant	–0.330	–0.42	–0.222	–0.204	0.646	0.641
ESAF/PRGF dummy	1.030	1.16	. . .	. . .	. . .	. . .
Growth projection error[2]	0.155	2.67***	0.100	1.10	0.148	1.90*
Current account balance projection error[3]	–0.010	–1.32	–0.178	–1.56	–0.060	–0.71
Primarily revenue adjustment dummy	–1.621	–1.86*	–0.622	–0.41	–2.564	–1.69*
Transition economy dummy	1.890	1.84*	1.405	1.22	2.900	1.73*
Terms of trade, change at *t*	–0.314	–0.07	–3.453	–0.38	0.354	0.10
Terms of trade, change at *t*+1	4.220	1.00	12.542	1.79*	3.559	0.83
Large-adjustment dummy (top quartile)	–2.620	–2.75***	–3.347	–2.65***	–2.812	–3.25***
F-statistic, p-value	3.777	0.001	2.341	0.041	2.142	0.068
Number of observations, R^2	80	0.31	41	0.37	39	0.35

Sources: IMF, MONA and WEO databases; and IMF staff estimates.

[1]Dependent variable: Actual program change in fiscal balance between years *t*–1 and *t*+1. Annual dummies included in regression (output not shown). Regression estimated using heteroscedasticity-robust estimator of the covariance matrix. Significant at * 10 percent, ** 5 percent, and *** 1 percent levels.

[2]Projection error: actual minus program real GDP growth rate.

[3]Projection error: actual minus program current account balance (in percent of GDP).

revenue impact of programmed trade liberalization is often difficult to judge ex ante, and may have contributed to revenue slippages.

What accounts for these fiscal outturns? While individual outturns are the result of many complex factors including country-specific circumstances, in general, the fiscal balance is more likely to fall short of the program target in cases where: growth was weaker than expected; the adjustment was based primarily on improvements in revenue;[30] or the targeted adjustment was especially large[31]—perhaps because of the social and political costs of undertaking such adjustment (Table 4.16).[32] These findings seem consistent with the literature.[33] The finding on large adjustment mirrors the finding in the IEO report on fiscal adjustment (IEO, 2003). A less convincing finding (whose interpretation is discussed below) is that greater external adjustment than programmed is associated with weaker fiscal adjustment, though the coefficient is not statistically significant. Both the magnitude and statistical significance of the results are generally stronger for the PRGF sample, with the exception of external adjustment variable, which is larger (albeit only marginally significant) in the GRA-sample.

Inasmuch as fiscal adjustment is intended to promote external adjustment, and the current account improves by more than programmed, sustained fiscal adjustment may be viewed as less pressing. The positive correlation between greater current account adjustment and lower fiscal adjustment (both relative to the program) for GRA-supported countries, noted above, is suggestive of this policy behavior. To examine this possibility more closely, fiscal and external adjustment achieved (compared to the programmed adjustment) are separated into overperformers and underperformers in Table 4.17. The 31 GRA-supported programs in nontransition economies where fiscal adjustment was below the program target are

[30]Defined as cases in which more than one-half of the programmed improvement in the fiscal balance reflects improved revenues.

[31]Defined as the top quartile of programs ranked by the programmed adjustment.

[32]When interpreting these results it is important to bear in mind the possible endogeneity of the regressors, particularly the projection errors for the current account balance and real GDP growth. The results reported below (Table 4.19) using instrumental variable estimation suggest that (actual) fiscal adjustment contributes to current account adjustment, which would imply a positive bias to the coefficient on the programmed current account balance reported in Table 4.16; the results in Table 4.19 suggest that fiscal adjustment has very little effect on growth. An alternative specification is to estimate a probit of cases where fiscal adjustment fell short of the program target, regardless of the magnitude of the slippage. Although the main findings are similar, those results are somewhat stronger in both the GRA- and PRGF-samples, with about 80 percent of the observations correctly classified.

[33]A recent paper that indeed finds that expenditure cuts increase the probability of successful fiscal adjustment (albeit for the short term) is Baldacci and others (2004). They also find that political economy variables capturing social cohesion as well as IMF-supported programs contribute to a higher probability of successful fiscal adjustment.

Table 4.17. External Adjustment and Fiscal Adjustment in IMF-Supported Programs

Fiscal Adjustment Year *t*, *t*+1	Current Account Balance (*t*) Above programmed	Below programmed	Total
Nontransition economies			
GRA-supported			
Fiscal, above programmed	7	5	12
Fiscal, below programmed	15	16	31
Total	22	21	43
PRGF-supported			
Fiscal, above programmed	8	14	22
Fiscal, below programmed	10	16	26
Total	18	30	48
Transition economies			
GRA-supported			
Fiscal, above programmed	2	6	8
Fiscal, below programmed	3	19	22
Total	5	25	30
PRGF-supported			
Fiscal, above programmed	0	2	2
Fiscal, below programmed	2	4	6
Total	2	6	8
All	47	82	129

Sources: IMF, MONA and WEO databases; and IMF staff estimates.

split almost evenly between cases where the current account balance in the first program year was stronger than programmed (15 cases) and those where it had been weaker than programmed (16 cases).[34] Of the 26 PRGF-supported programs where fiscal adjustment was below target, in 10 external adjustment in the first program year had been greater than programmed and in 16 it had been weaker than programmed. Similar patterns are evident for the transition economies. As such, whether the external objective was fulfilled does not explain fiscal adjustment falling short of program targets.

Public Debt Dynamics

Beyond the direct effects on the overall balance, fiscal policy—and slippages relative to program targets—has implications for other macroeconomic variables, such as inflation. Fiscal performance also has implications for public debt dynamics. Since consistent time series on public debt (especially on the domestic component) are generally lacking, Table 4.18 focuses on the experience of 24 emerging market countries, decomposing the error in the debt projection into the part attributable to lower real output growth than expected, to lower inflation than expected, and to a higher overall deficit than programmed.[35] The residual difference represents below-the-line operations (realization of contingent liabilities and privatization receipts) as well as exchange rate movements on the foreign-currency-denominated part of public debt that are not offset by inflation.

From the Table 4.18, IMF-supported programs on average targeted a reduction in public debt from 70 percent of GDP to 51 percent of GDP at the end of three years; in the event, the debt ratio rose slightly instead. Of the 20 percentage points of GDP difference between outcome and target, 3 percentage points was due to lower real output growth, which was more than offset by higher than projected inflation, while slippages in the overall fiscal deficit contributed 4 per-

[34]This distribution is not statistically significantly different from the distribution of cases where fiscal adjustment was more than had been programmed (12 cases, total); 7 out of 12 cases had above-programmed external adjustment and 5 out of 12 cases had below-programmed external adjustment.

[35]As noted in the IEO report on fiscal adjustment (IEO, 2003) and the 2003 *World Economic Outlook* chapter on public debt (IMF, 2003), consistent time series on public debt (including the domestic component) are often lacking. A recent paper (Christensen, 2004) reports data on domestic debt for a set of 27 sub-Saharan African economies, but issues of coverage and the lack of consistent series on above-the-line fiscal accounts preclude its use here.

Table 4.18. Initial Conditions and Evolution of Public Debt in Emerging Market Countries Under IMF-Supported Programs
(In percent of GDP)

	Stock of Public Debt				Error, of which			
	Actual $t-1$	Program $t+2$	Actual $t+2$	Error	Growth effect	Inflation effect	Deficit effect	Below-the-line cumulative
Full sample								
Average	70.0	51.2	71.4	20.2	3.1	–4.3	4.4	17.1
Averages for								
First quartile	29.2	21.9	50.7	28.8	3.1	–3.6	7.0	22.3
Second quartile	50.9	42.7	61.6	18.9	4.7	–5.1	4.9	14.5
Third quartile	85.1	61.8	74.5	12.7	3.1	–4.8	3.6	10.9
Fourth quartile	116.9	79.8	99.9	20.1	1.4	–3.6	1.8	20.6
Total observations	54	54	54	54	54	54	54	54
Standard deviation	36.8	28.2	29.3	11.4	8.7	12.7	5.5	25.2
Standard error of the mean	5.0	3.9	4.0	1.6	1.2	1.7	0.8	3.5
Selected cases								
Average	50.0	40.9	74.1	33.3	6.0	–8.1	8.4	27.0
Argentina, 1998	38.1	34.3	45.0	10.7	4.8	3.4	6.8	–4.2
Brazil, 1999	41.7	46.6	52.6	6.0	–0.5	–6.4	8.9	4.0
Indonesia, 1998	23.7	16.7	91.8	75.0	4.7	–9.1	4.8	74.7
Indonesia, 2000	91.8	81.6	80.7	–1.0	3.4	–14.5	–1.8	12.0
Mexico, 1995	35.8	22.7	51.2	28.5	3.0	–10.9	9.7	26.7
Mexico, 1999	54.9	36.9	48.0	11.1	–5.5	7.6	9.5	–0.5
Philippines, 1994	95.1	72.7	75.4	2.7	–7.9	2.9	–0.8	8.6
Philippines, 1998	83.2	60.7	99.0	38.3	31.0	–30.0	9.6	27.7
Thailand, 1997	14.5	9.5	55.6	46.1	1.7	1.6	16.8	26.0
Turkey, 1999	43.7	57.9	95.0	37.1	29.9	–40.7	9.3	38.6
Total observations	10	10	10	10	10	10	10	10

Sources: IMF, MONA, WEO, and Research Department databases; and IMF staff estimates.

Note. Programmed data are forward estimates based on fiscal balance programmed flows and program assumptions on GDP growth. The timing of the end-point data is $t+2$ or latest available. The error is defined as actual minus programmed in $t+2$ or the latest available year. Quartiles defined on the basis of $t-1$ actual debt stocks.

centage points of GDP. By far the largest source of this difference was below-the-line effects, amounting to just over 17 percentage points (or 85 percent of the deviation). In some individual cases (Table 4.18, bottom panel), these effects reflected the fiscal costs of banking crises (Turkey, 30 percent of GDP; Indonesia, 55 percent of GDP; Thailand, 45 percent of GDP; and Mexico, 20 percent of GDP) and the impact of real exchange rate depreciations in the aftermath of currency crises.

External Adjustment

As noted above, an important reason for fiscal adjustment in IMF-supported programs is to promote orderly external adjustment. Table 4.19 examines the impact of fiscal policy on the current account balance, estimating some simple fiscal multipliers using program projections to instrument for possible endogeneity of the fiscal balance. The multipliers suggest that a 1 percent of GDP improvement in the fiscal balance is associated with a 0.83–1.65 percent of GDP improvement in the current account balance.

As documented in "Objectives and Outcomes" (Part II of this occasional paper), in some GRA-supported programs (particularly in capital account crises) external adjustment was greater than programmed, raising the question of whether this was the result of fiscal tightening. Empirically, however, there is almost no relationship: the correlation between fiscal adjustment and the error in projecting the current account balance is insignificant and the regression R^2 is less than 1 percent. Thus, excessively tight fiscal policy does not appear to have caused greater external adjustment than projected (Figure 4.4).

Table 4.19. Estimated Impact of Fiscal Adjustment on Growth and Current Account Balance[1]

	PRGF			GRA		
	1	2	3	4	5	6
Output growth and fiscal balance						
Dependent variable						
Change in the GDP growth rate						
Regressors[2]						
Change in the fiscal balance[3]	1.56**	0.17	0.13	0.28	0.33	0.14
Growth lagged		–0.88***	–0.93***		–0.76***	–0.70***
Fiscal balance lagged[4]		0.11	0.02		0.33	0.31
Broad money growth[3]			0.10			–0.12**
Terms of trade			–0.03			0.15***
Intercept	0.39	2.95***	1.52	–0.90	0.31	1.68
Number of observations[5]	108	108	88	118	118	83
R squared	0.10	0.58	0.66	0.10	0.48	0.56
Current account and fiscal balance						
Dependent variable						
Change in the current account balance as a percent of GDP						
Regressors[2]						
Change in the fiscal balance[3]	1.69**	1.52*	1.24	0.83***	0.93**	0.91**
Current account lagged		–0.17**	–0.14**		–0.30***	–0.32***
Fiscal balance lagged[4]		0.27**	0.30**		0.07	–0.05
Broad money growth[3]			–0.12			0.09*
Terms of trade			0.06			0.17***
Intercept	–0.70	–1.30	0.84	1.12	1.07	–0.03
Number of observations[5]	108	108	88	118	118	83
R squared	0.09	0.16	0.23	0.15	0.26	0.57

Sources: IMF, MONA database; and IMF staff estimates.

Note. * significant at 10 percent level, ** significant at 5 percent level, and *** significant at 1 percent level.

[1]Fixed effect regressions. OLS regressions provide similar results.

[2]Econometric estimations include year dummies and dummies for type of program (i.e., transition economy and capital account crises).

[3]Instrumented using MONA projections.

[4]Based on MONA database.

[5]Balanced panel data set for period *t* and period *t*+1 except for equations 3 and 6. Equations 3 and 6 are estimated for available data.

These apparently contradictory findings—that fiscal consolidation promotes external adjustment but cannot explain cases where the improvement in the current account balance was much sharper than expected—can be reconciled by recognizing that different forces may be at play in different situations. In particular, the current account may reflect the effects of lower aggregate demand (driven, in part, by fiscal tightening) or a sharp reduction in available external financing (most notably in capital account crises). In the latter case, the appropriate fiscal policy response depends on whether the loss of confidence and capital outflows stem from perceived fragilities in the public finances (in which case fiscal tightening, or at least a credible commitment to a path of future primary surpluses, would be required) or in private sector balance sheets, in which case the appropriate fiscal policy response depends on whether the effects of the capital outflows on the economy are in the nature of a supply-side or a demand-side shock.[36]

[36]Arithmetically, for a given capital outflow, the higher the public sector saving-investment balance, the smaller the private sector's balance needs to be, but this does not necessarily imply a lower burden of adjustment on the private sector in terms of consumption and investment. If the effects of capital outflows are in the nature of a supply-side shock (for example, the associated exchange rate depreciation raises the price of imported intermediate inputs or leads to widespread bankruptcies because of the private sector's foreign exchange exposure), then a higher public sector balance indeed reduces the adjustment burden on the private sector. By contrast, if capital outflows represent (or exacerbate) a demand-side shock, and if Keynesian effects are important so that a fiscal loosening has an expansionary effect on activity, then allowing the public sector balance to deteriorate could help achieve the requisite external adjustment with a smaller decline of output and of private consumption and investment. For a fuller discussion, see *IMF-Supported Programs in Capital Account Crises* (Ghosh and others, 2002).

Figure 4.4. Fiscal Adjustment and Projection Errors in Current Account and Growth[1]

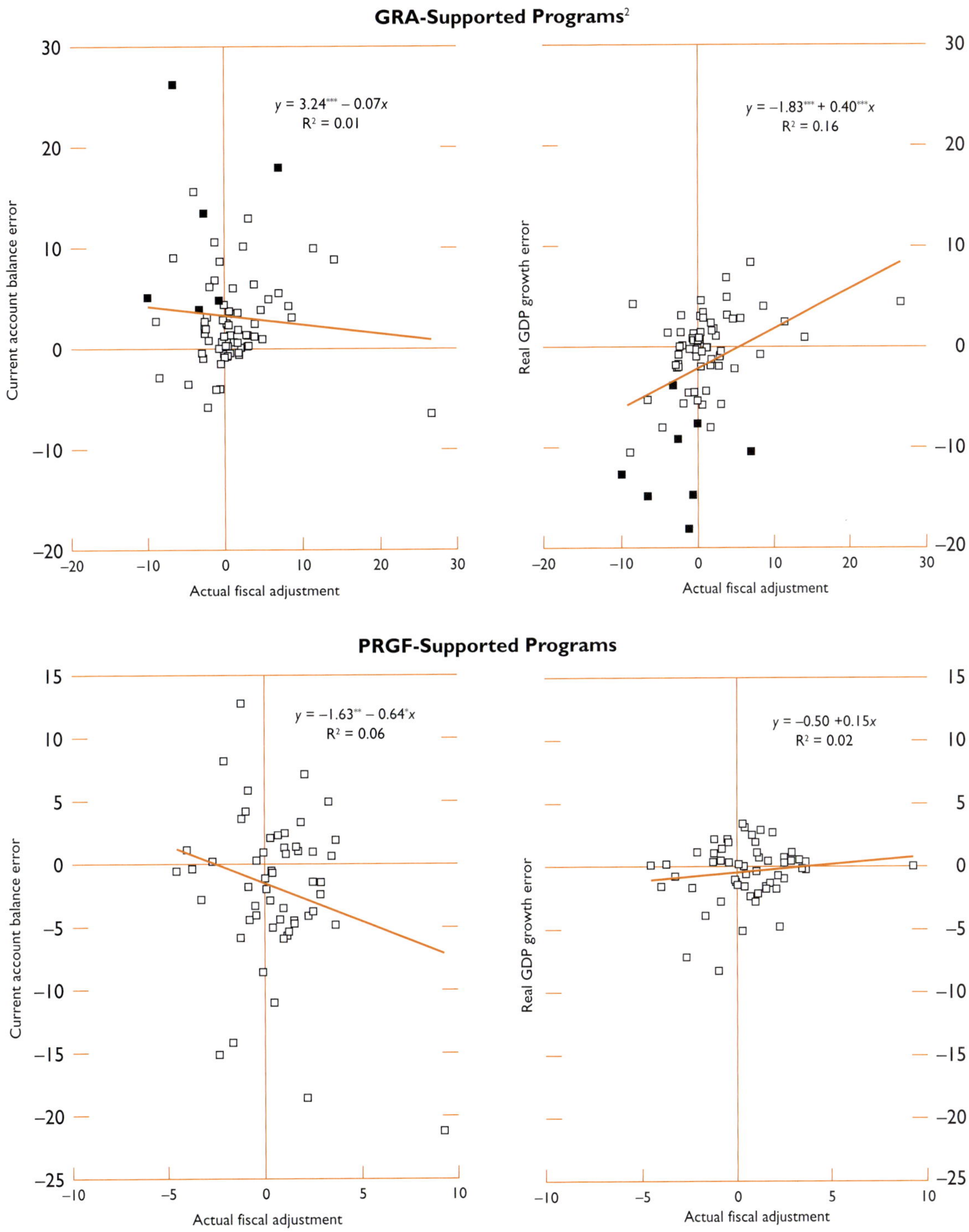

Sources: IMF, MONA and WEO databases; and IMF staff estimates.
[1]Projection errors are defined as actual minus projection; *significant at 10 percent, **significant at 5 percent, and ***significant at 1 percent levels.
[2]Solid squares represent capital account crisis countries.

Output Growth

Finally, an important consideration in setting fiscal policy—and targeting fiscal adjustment under the program—is the possible impact on output growth. Estimated fiscal multipliers (using program projections to instrument for possible endogeneity of the fiscal balance) are reported in Table 4.19.[37] In particular, in the PRGF sample, a higher fiscal surplus (or smaller deficit) is associated with higher output growth, though the coefficient becomes insignificant once lagged real GDP growth is included in the regression. In the GRA sample, the lagged effects of a larger fiscal surplus (or smaller deficit) is associated with higher growth, though the coefficient again becomes insignificant when other controls are included in the regression. While caution is required in interpreting these findings since there is always the possibility of omitted variable bias, it is noteworthy that none of the reported regressions suggest a negative effect on growth of a larger fiscal surplus (or a smaller deficit)—possibly because of "crowding in" effects of lower interest rates and greater availability of finance to the private sector, confidence effects, and flexibility of prices and wages in countries typically seeking IMF support makes Keynesian effects relatively unimportant.[38] Consistent with this, fiscal adjustment does not explain cases in which growth turned out to be weaker than projected (Figure 4.4).

Summary

IMF-supported programs target fiscal adjustment according to the size of the initial deficit, the level of public expenditure, the targeted improvement in the current account balance, and the estimated output gap. On average, fiscal adjustment falls short of that targeted for both the first program year and the following year, with adverse consequences for macroeconomic stabilization and for public debt dynamics. Fiscal adjustment contributes to external adjustment but cannot explain cases where current account adjustment was greater than programmed. In terms of instrument assignment, this suggests that fiscal policy in IMF-supported programs should be directed primarily at tackling external adjustment.

[37]Although there is an extensive literature on this topic (with various findings), most of it does not focus on countries that have IMF-supported programs. Hemming and others (2002) provide a literature review, which generally asserts that there are significant Keynesian effects between fiscal balances and output, though these results pertain mostly to industrial economies. Consistent with the results reported in this paper, Gupta and others (2002), find instead that strong fiscal consolidation is associated with higher growth in a sample of low-income countries. One explanation may be that fiscal consolidation stimulates growth in countries with weak institutions by a reduction in rent-seeking and the scope for corruption, raising overall productivity and growth.

[38]Some specifications (not reported), for instance using two lags of the fiscal balance, yield a negative coefficient (i.e., a larger fiscal balance is associated with lower growth), but even in these regressions the implied Keynesian effects are small: a 1 percent of GDP improvement in the overall balance would be associated with 0.3 percentage points lower growth two years later. Similarly, using government expenditures rather than the overall balance does not suggest a substantial role for stimulative fiscal policy. Inclusion of other control variables, such as the real effective exchange rate, does not affect the results. Segmenting observations by exchange rate regime suggest a stronger positive impact of fiscal adjustment on growth among countries with flexible regimes.

V Structural Reforms

Since the mid-1980s, structural policies have played an important role in IMF-supported programs.[39] These structural measures are intended to complement and buttress macroeconomic policies, raising the likelihood that program objectives will be attained. This section examines whether structural measures included in IMF-supported programs have been geared toward, and have contributed to, achieving program objectives.[40] To this end, this section first proposes a simple classification of structural measures according to their primary economic objective—underpinning stabilization efforts, increasing economic flexibility and efficiency, and addressing vulnerabilities.[41] It then reviews the structural content of programs to see how various measures, thus classified, have been aligned to the broad objectives of different types of IMF-supported programs. Next, while recognizing the inherent difficulties in establishing the impact of individual structural measures, the section considers experience with two of the most common goals of structural measures in IMF-supported programs: underpinning fiscal adjustment and promoting sustained output growth. This analysis is based on the outcomes observed in the first three years following the approval of each arrangement.

[39] "Structural Conditionality in Fund-Supported Programs" (see IMF, 2001) documents the increase in the structural content of IMF-supported programs over the period 1987–99. In 2000–02, the IMF undertook a broad review of structural conditionality in IMF-supported programs, culminating in the 2002 Conditionality Guidelines. A review of the 2002 Conditionality Guidelines, which examines the application of the revised guidelines, has recently been completed (IMF, 2005).

[40] Recognition that balance of payments problems may reflect structural weaknesses was part of the rationale for the IMF Executive Board decision to create the Extended Fund Facility (EFF) in 1974. The decision notes that structural policies are required in "an economy experiencing serious payments imbalance relating to structural maladjustments . . . or . . . characterized by slow growth and . . . weak balance of payments" (Decision No. 4377-74/114).

[41] The classification into these three categories is carried out by mapping the eight categories in the MONA database into the three groups specified. The MONA classification is prepared by country teams at the time of approval and following each review. The alignment between structural measures and policy objectives is examined in the Review of the Conditionality Guidelines (IMF, 2005).

Structural Content of IMF-Supported Programs

Structural reforms in IMF-supported programs range from measures that are very specific to the particular circumstances of the country or the macroeconomic instruments being employed—such as establishing the legal and institutional framework of a currency board arrangement—to those that are more common across programs such as the introduction of a value-added tax to raise revenues. To examine the alignment of structural reforms to program objectives requires classifying these disparate measures. While any classification system inevitably involves an element of arbitrariness—some measures may fit more than one group,[42] while others are difficult to assign to any category—it is useful to divide reforms into three categories or groups according to their intended goals.[43] These groups are as follows:

- *Measures that underpin a medium-term framework for demand management and for addressing flow imbalances.* These policies are designed to underpin stabilization efforts and to enhance the functioning of fiscal, monetary, and exchange rate policies. For example, reducing fiscal imbalances may require underlying reforms to expenditure and revenue in order to be sus-

[42] For instance, changes to the tax structure may be important to bolster macroeconomic stabilization (category 1, below) but also for increasing economic efficiency (category 2). Likewise, reforms in specific sectors such as agriculture may reduce the cost of untargeted subsidies, but may also have important efficiency and growth benefits as well as raising incomes of farmers by dismantling distortionary state marketing boards.

[43] IMF-supported programs have increasingly included measures geared toward institution building, which are usually included in the "economic efficiency" category. Indeed, the share of conditions that are related to institution building has risen from about 3 percent of all annual conditions in 1995 to more than 10 percent by 2000 (especially in transition economies and PRGF-supported programs), though these figures probably understate the proportion of measures related to institution building as many might be classified elsewhere within the MONA database; for example, measures to improve budget control and expenditure management also aim at improving a country's institutional framework.

tained and remain credible. Structural policies in the fiscal area include measures that improve the tax structure—including widening the tax base—and tax administration, as well as policies that strengthen public expenditure management. Deepening financial markets and expanding the menu of instruments available to the monetary authorities can provide for a more stable environment for conducting monetary policy. Finally, other policies aim at strengthening exchange systems; for example, measures that strengthen foreign exchange markets.

- *Measures that enhance economic flexibility and efficiency.* These measures often have a combination of objectives, making it difficult to distinguish precisely their flexibility and efficiency goals. Nevertheless, among the flexibility goals are all measures that increase the ability of the economy to adapt to new conditions. Usual examples are trade reforms and policies that affect resource allocation across sectors, such as pricing policies of factor markets (labor and capital) and the institutional features of these markets. They also include pricing policies that transcend individual sectors, such as energy prices. In contrast, the private sector efficiency component refers to impediments to investment and growth and reforms that affect individual sectors, such as pricing policies and marketing arrangements in agricultural markets and institutional changes that affect corporate sector behavior. Privatization of state enterprises and utilities also fall into this category, though often these measures have other objectives as well, including use of privatization receipts for stabilization efforts or to strengthen balance sheets.[44] Finally, the public sector efficiency component relates to measures that improve the delivery of public services or redefine the role of the state in the economy.
- *Measures that address economic vulnerabilities, including stock or balance sheet mismatches.* These policies may be directed at tackling unsustainable public or external debt dynamics, reducing the vulnerability of domestic balance sheets to sharp swings in the exchange rate or interest rates, as well as structural weaknesses in the financial sector—particularly those that may result in contingent liabilities of the public sector. Strengthening prudential regulations and financial sector supervisory capabilities form an important element of this category.[45]

As discussed in "Objectives and Outcomes" (Part II of this occasional paper), most IMF-supported programs can be usefully classified as "classic" (current account) adjustment, poverty-reducing and growth-enhancing programs, or capital account crises. In a classic adjustment program, structural policies are expected to center primarily on the first of the above categories, but reforms that increase efficiency and reduce vulnerabilities can also be important.[46] The emphasis of structural reforms in PRGF-supported programs is on efficiency measures that improve potential output growth, including measures to enhance human capital, health, and education. However, medium-term demand management measures are also necessary for various reasons, including the role played by macroeconomic stability in strengthening growth and the challenges faced by these countries in mobilizing tax revenues and strengthening expenditure control.[47] Transition economies, reflecting the numerous systemic transformation challenges faced by these countries, are a hybrid of these two types of programs; efficiency and growth-oriented measures are critical, though demand management and financial sector reforms are also needed. Capital account crisis programs have more clearly defined reform needs. Specifically, reforms that reduce stock vulnerabilities take center stage among these countries, partly driven by the urgency in improving confidence in the economy. In crises where the capital outflows are primarily from the private sector, this means financial and corporate sector reforms. By contrast, where markets are responding to concerns about public debt sustainability,

[44]Many goals are sought through privatization. For example, the sale of utility companies is proposed when services are poor and an infusion of capital is needed—the purpose is to improve services and modernize the capital infrastructure. In some cases, this is also an opportunity through which to attract foreign investment. Privatization receipts may also play a fiscal role. Privatization of utilities should be assessed carefully so as to avoid transforming a public monopoly into a private monopoly. In contrast, privatization of state firms in other sectors (from wineries to steel mills) are sought either to redefine the role of the state or to stem the fiscal implications of loss-making state firms. In particular, IMF conditionality is justified when loss-making state firms compromise the sustainability of the fiscal position.

[45]Typically, reforms in the financial sector are divided between measures aimed at strengthening the central bank, such as measures to increase its independence, and measures aimed at strengthening the financial sector more generally. The latter focuses on strengthening banking supervision and dealing with problem banks.

[46]Within GRA-supported programs, therefore, those supported by EFF arrangements are more likely to have structural measures oriented toward enhancing economic flexibility and efficiency than those supported by stand-by arrangements.

[47]Between classic adjustment and PRGF-supported programs, the former might be expected to have a slight bias toward demand management measures, and the latter toward efficiency and growth-enhancing measures. Programs in transition economies are likely to straddle these two groups, since achieving macroeconomic stability and adjustment was a critical objective of these programs as was longer-term structural transformation of the economy.

Figure 4.5. Distribution of Structural Conditionality in IMF-Supported Programs

(In percent of total number of conditions per program year; average 1995–2000)

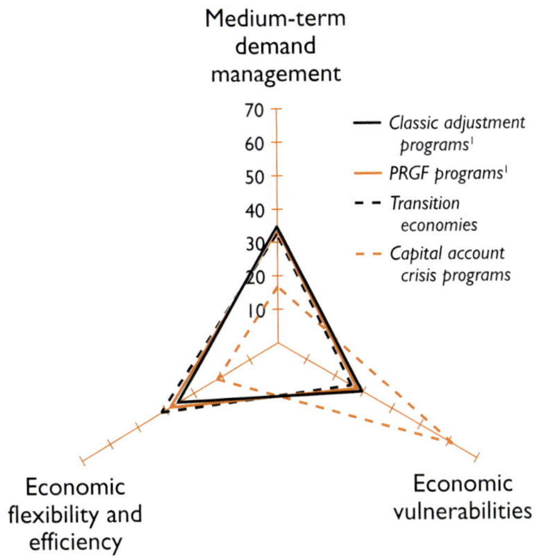

Type of Conditions[2]

(In percent of total conditions per program year; 1995–2000)

	Medium-term demand management	Economic vulnerabilities	Economic flexibility and efficiency
GRA-supported[2]	0.35	0.30	0.35
Transition economies	0.32	0.26	0.41*
PRGF-supported[2]	0.34	0.28	0.38
Capital account crisis programs	0.17***	0.61***	0.22***

Sources: IMF, MONA database; and IMF staff estimates.

[1]Excludes transition economics.

[2]For each type of condition, the null hypothesis of no difference from GRA-supported programs is tested; *significant at 10 percent level and ***significant at 1 percent level.

measures that improve the viability of public finances are required, even if they only have an impact over the medium term. Although the source of the balance sheet imbalances has a bearing on the design of reforms and may reveal structural weaknesses throughout the economy (from weak demand management to efficiency bottlenecks for private sector growth), the core reform efforts of these programs are directed toward addressing balance sheet weaknesses.

How well aligned are structural measures to the broad objectives of the various types of IMF-supported programs in practice? The distribution of structural measures (classified into the three categories described above) is reported in Figure 4.5 for GRA-supported programs (excluding programs in transition economies and capital account crises), transition economy programs, capital account crises, and PRGF-supported programs in low-income countries (again, excluding transition economies). The distribution mirrors, at least to some extent, the expected distribution by type of IMF-supported programs. In particular, measures in GRA-supported programs in nontransition economies are split between macroeconomic management (35 percent) and efficiency and growth-related measures (35 percent), and those aimed at reducing vulnerabilities (30 percent). Relative to this benchmark, programs in transition economies are somewhat more oriented toward

Table 4.20. Structural Measures and Fiscal Adjustment: Regression Results[1]

	Dependent Variables: Actual Adjustment in[2]					
	Fiscal balance		Government revenue		Government expenditure	
	All programs	Nonstopped programs[3]	All programs	Nonstopped programs[3]	All programs	Nonstopped programs[3]
Regressors						
Number of fiscal measures related to the[4]						
Fiscal balance[5]	0.11*	0.14*				
Revenues			0.16**	0.32***		
Expenditures					0.00	0.02
Dummy variables						
Stopped program[3]	–0.27	—	–0.13	—	–0.05	—
PRGF program	–0.05	–0.69	0.05	–0.08	0.18	0.20
Transition economy	0.71*	0.31	–0.37	–0.54	1.40***	1.29***
Capital account crisis	0.45	–0.09	0.80	0.46	0.08	0.39
Intercept	–0.14	0.28	–0.17	–0.17	–0.32	–0.18
Number of observations/programs	100	67	100	67	100	67
R^2	0.11	0.12	0.08	0.16	0.15	0.23
F-statistic[6]	1.9*	1.6	1.3	2.2*	2.8**	3.7***

Sources: IMF, MONA database; and IMF staff estimates.

Note. * significant at 10 percent level, ** significant at 5 percent level, and *** significant at 1 percent level.

[1]Regressions based on a dataset of programs approved during the period 1995–2000 for which data on fiscal balance, revenues, and expenditures are available.

[2]Average adjustment in years *t*, *t*+1, and *t*+2, where *t* is the year the program is approved.

[3]A stopped program is defined as a program that terminates earlier than was originally anticipated.

[4]The number of fiscal measures is normalized by the duration of the program.

[5]Structural measures that affect the fiscal balance includes revenue and expenditure reforms.

[6]F-statistic for null hypothesis that all explanatory variables (other than the constant) are jointly equal to zero.

growth-enhancing measures (41 percent, a difference that is statistically significant from the nontransition GRA sample). PRGF-supported programs likewise show a somewhat greater preponderance of growth enhancing measures (38 percent, though this difference with GRA-supported programs is not statistically significant). The largest, and statistically significant, difference lies between capital account crisis programs, with their much greater emphasis on reducing sources of vulnerability—60 percent of measures (versus 17 percent on macroeconomic management and 22 percent on growth-related measures), and all other program groups.

Experience

The inherent problems of quantifying structural policies make it difficult to establish links between specific structural reforms and macroeconomic outcomes. With this limitation in mind, this section takes up two of the most common goals of structural measures in IMF-supported programs—underpinning fiscal adjustment and enhancing economic efficiency and output growth—with a view to shedding some light on whether, or to what extent, structural policies have been useful in attaining these objectives. Given the lack of better alternatives, the analysis is limited to the effects of the number of conditions on the objectives these structural measures seek to accomplish. The analysis also distinguishes between stopped and nonstopped programs in an attempt to identify implementation issues.

Fiscal Adjustment

Part of the impetus for structural reforms in IMF-supported programs was the observation in the early 1980s that fiscal adjustment efforts were often not sustained. To examine whether structural measures help underpin fiscal adjustment, program conditions related to fiscal measures were classified according to their intended effects on revenues and expenditures. The three categories related to tax and expenditure measures in the MONA database, are reclassified into two core revenue categories (tax policy and tax administration), two core expenditure categories (expenditure control and expenditure management),

Table 4.21. Structural Measures and Growth: Regression Results[1]

	Dependent Variables: Average Change in Real GDP Growth Rates in the First Three Years Following Program Approval[2]			
	All programs		Nonstopped programs[3]	
Regressors				
Number of growth-related structural measures[4]	0.08**	0.07**	0.12*	0.10*
Dummy variables				
Stopped program[3]	–0.04	0.06	—	—
PRGF program	–0.30	–0.26	–0.53	–0.38
Transition economy	1.77***	0.93**	1.38**	0.98*
Capital account crisis	0.52	0.52	0.77	0.71
Macroeconomic variables				
Average change in the fiscal balance	—	0.28**	—	0.25*
Average change in the inflation rate	—	–0.08***	—	–0.04
Intercept	–0.24	–0.38	–0.19	–0.30
Number of observations/programs	100	100	63	63
R^2	0.30	0.40	0.27	0.32
F-statistic[5]	8.2***	8.7***	5.4***	4.4***

Sources: IMF, MONA database; and IMF staff estimates.

Note. * significant at 10 percent level, ** significant at 5 percent level, and *** significant at 1 percent level.

[1]Regressions based on a dataset of programs approved during the period 1995–2000.

[2]Average growth in years *t*, *t*+1, and *t*+2, where *t* is the year the program is approved.

[3]A stopped program is defined as a program that terminates earlier than was originally anticipated.

[4]The number of growth-related structural measures is normalized by the duration of the program.

[5]F-statistic for null hypothesis that all explanatory variables (other than the constant) are jointly equal to zero.

and a number of ancillary revenue and expenditure categories.[48] The ancillary group includes measures related to fiscal transparency, debt-related measures, civil service reform, and measures targeting a country's social security system.

Table 4.20 reports the results of regressions of fiscal adjustment—over the three-year period that begins with the approval of each arrangement—in the overall balance, and of adjustment in revenues and expenditures separately, on the corresponding structural measures. The results suggest that structural measures are related with better fiscal performance, particularly in regard to core revenue measures on revenue adjustment and to core revenue and core expenditure measures on the overall fiscal adjustment. Core expenditure measures do not, however, appear to have a correlation with expenditure reduction—except perhaps among transition economies where the country-type dummy is positive and highly significant. Not surprisingly, among arrangements that did not go off-track, the impact of these measures on fiscal adjustment is stronger.[49] In addition, the numerous ancillary fiscal measures that characterize IMF-supported programs (see previous paragraph) are not found to have a correlation with overall balance, revenue, or expenditure adjustment and are not included in the regressions reported in the table.

Output Growth

Both in PRGF-supported programs and, to a lesser degree, in classic adjustment programs, structural reforms may be undertaken to enhance economic efficiency and long-term growth performance, raising the question of the effectiveness of such reforms. Typical reforms include measures aimed at liberalizing the trade regime as well as changes in pricing and marketing policies. Table 4.21 reports the results

[48]The three categories reclassified are the "tax and expenditures" category of the MONA database, a category referenced as "other measures," that also includes fiscal measures, and a category related to trade measures as many of those measures aim at improving the collection of customs taxes.

[49]The results presented are derived using a balanced panel of 100 programs approved in the period 1995–2000 and for which fiscal data (projected and actual) is available for three years after program approval. Data used include fiscal revenues, fiscal expenditures, and the fiscal balance. An unbalanced panel based on available data provides broadly similar results.

of a regression of the average change in real GDP growth (between years $t-1$ and $t+2$) on growth-related structural measures. Growth, of course, may depend on a number of other factors. To purge the effects of variables that are unlikely to vary significantly over a two- to three-year horizon—such as the stocks of human and physical capital—the dependent variable is specified as the change in real GDP growth. To proxy for macroeconomic variables that are likely to change at higher frequency, both the change in the fiscal balance and the change in the inflation rate are included in the regression as additional explanatory variables.

From the table, growth-related structural measures are positively and significantly related to better growth performance, especially in programs in which there are no stoppages. At the same time, the effects are not large: from the estimates, each additional measure is associated with 0.1 percentage point higher real GDP growth. Of course, it bears emphasizing that these results should only be viewed as indicative, given the possibility of omitted variables, endogeneity of program participation, and the inherent difficulties of quantifying structural measures. Moreover, it is plausible that the real relationship is nonlinear, possibly as a result of threshold effects, with diminishing returns to the number of structural measures. These more complicated relationships, however, would not be captured by the simple linear regression reported here.

Summary

Structural policies have played an increasingly important role in IMF-supported programs, complementing macroeconomic policies by underpinning stabilization efforts and orderly adjustment, enhancing efficiency and growth, and reducing vulnerabilities to future crises. There is broad alignment between the nature of structural reforms included in IMF-supported programs and the objectives of the program. Thus, classic adjustment programs tend to focus on medium-term demand management issues, PRGF-supported programs include growth and efficiency measures (as is also the case for transition economies), and capital account crisis programs aim at addressing vulnerabilities. Turning to experience, within the inherent limitations of quantitative analysis of the effects of structural reforms, the evidence suggests that structural measures included in IMF-supported programs might have had some positive effects on achieving sustained fiscal adjustment and output growth.

VI Conclusions

IMF-supported programs are intended to address specific economic problems such as fostering macroeconomic stability and orderly external adjustment, promoting growth and poverty reduction, and reducing vulnerability to future balance of payments problems or financial crises. In formulating their economic programs, national authorities have at their disposal a number of instruments, including the country's exchange rate regime, the monetary stance, fiscal policies, and structural reforms.

Although there is some alignment between the choice of exchange rate regime and program objectives, countries are no more likely to alter their exchange rate regime at the outset of an IMF-supported program than otherwise, perhaps because of concerns about the difficulty of achieving a graceful exit if the regime is less well suited for the country over the longer term. At the same time, successful disinflations have been achieved both under pegged and under flexible regimes—the key underlying factor determining success at disinflation being whether the requisite fiscal adjustment is undertaken. National authorities also typically tighten the monetary stance in IMF-supported programs to restore macroeconomic stability and reduce inflation, and IMF support appears to impart greater credibility to the authorities' policies thus assisting in the disinflation effort.

Fiscal policy often forms a key element of IMF-supported programs in order to underpin stabilization efforts and to foster orderly external adjustment. Programs target fiscal adjustment according to the size of the initial deficit, the level of public expenditure, and the targeted improvement in the current account balance—ceteris paribus, targeted adjustment is smaller when there is a large output gap and in PRGF-supported programs. On average, fiscal adjustment falls short of program targets, undermining disinflation efforts and leading to worse public debt dynamics than programmed—though the most important factor explaining debt projection errors is below-the-line operations, including the costs of financial sector restructuring. Fiscal adjustment contributes to external adjustment, but there is no evidence that fiscal tightening resulted in cases of greater current account adjustment than programmed or in lower output growth.

Structural measures are intended to buttress stabilization efforts, reduce vulnerabilities and balance sheet mismatches, and enhance economic flexibility and efficiency. Structural measures in IMF-supported programs are broadly aligned to the overall objectives of the program—thus, for instance, capital account crisis programs have a proportionately larger share of measures aimed at reducing vulnerabilities, including in the financial sector; while other programs mirror the alignment expected from the program objectives, these are not always statistically significant. Fiscal structural measures are related to better fiscal performance, particularly in regard to revenue measures. Finally, there is at least some evidence that structural measures oriented toward improving economic flexibility and efficiency are correlated with better output growth performance.

Overall, the findings of this paper suggest that the setting of macroeconomic and structural policies in IMF-supported programs are generally well aligned to program objectives. By the same token, however, this also means that any slippages in policy implementation (especially in fiscal policy) are likely to be reflected in program targets being missed.

References

Abed, George, and others, 1998, *Fiscal Reforms in Low-Income Countries,* IMF Occasional Paper No. 160 (Washington: International Monetary Fund).

Baldacci, E., and others, 2004, "Front-Loaded or Back-Loaded Fiscal Adjustments: What Works in Emerging Market Economies," IMF Working Paper No. 04/157 (Washington: International Monetary Fund).

Bubula, Andrea, and Inci Ötker-Robe, 2002, "The Evolution of Exchange Rate Regimes Since 1990: Evidence from De Facto Policies," IMF Working Paper No. 02/155 (Washington: International Monetary Fund).

Calvo, Guillermo, and Carmen Reinhart, 2002, "Fear of Floating," *Quarterly Journal of Economics,* Vol. 117 (May), pp. 379–408.

Calvo, Guillermo, and Carlos Végh, 1994, "Inflation Stabilization and Nominal Anchors," *Contemporary Economic Policy,* Vol. 12 (April), pp. 35–45.

———, 1999, "Inflation Stabilization and BOP Crises in Developing Countries," NBER Working Paper No. 6925 (Cambridge, Massachusetts: National Bureau of Economic Research).

Christensen, Jakob E., 2004, "Domestic Debt Markets in Sub-Saharan Africa," IMF Working Paper No. 04/46 (Washington: International Monetary Fund).

Daseking, Christina, Atish R. Ghosh, Alun J. Thomas, and Timothy D. Lane, 2004, *Lessons from the Crisis in Argentina,* IMF Occasional Paper No. 236 (Washington: International Monetary Fund).

Easterly, William R., 1996, "When Is Stabilization Expansionary? Evidence from High Inflation," *Economic Policy,* No. 21, pp. 67–107.

Fischer, Stanley, Ratna Sahay, and Carlos Végh, 2002, "Modern Hyper- and High Inflations," IMF Working Paper No. 02/197 (Washington: International Monetary Fund).

Ghosh, Atish, Timothy Lane, Marianne Schulze-Ghattas, Aleš Bulíř, Javier Hamann, and Alex Mourmouras, 2002, *IMF-Supported Programs in Capital Account Crises,* IMF Occasional Paper No. 210 (Washington: International Monetary Fund).

Ghosh, Atish, Anne-Marie Gulde, and Holger C. Wolf, 2002, *Exchange Rate Regimes: Choices and Consequences* (Cambridge, Massachusetts: MIT PRess).

Gupta, Sanjeev, Mark Plant, Benedict Clements, Thomas Dorsey, Emanuele Baldacci, Gabriela Inchauste, Shamsuddin Tareq, and Nita Thacker, 2002, *Is the PRGF Living Up to Expectations? An Assessment of Program Design,* IMF Occasional Paper No. 216 (Washington: International Monetary Fund).

Hamann, Javier, 1999, "Exchange-Rate-Based Stabilization: A Critical Look at the Stylized Facts," IMF Working Paper No. 99/132 (Washington: International Monetary Fund).

———, 2001, "Exchange Rate-Based Inflation Stabilization," *IMF Research Bulletin,* Vol. 2, No. 3 (September).

———, and Alessandro Prati, 2002, "Why Do Many Disinflations Fail? The Importance of Luck, Timing, and Political Institutions," IMF Working Paper No. 02/228 (Washington: International Monetary Fund).

Hemming, Richard, Michael S. Kell, and Selma Mahfouz, 2002, "The Effectiveness of Fiscal Policy in Stimulating Economic Activity—A Review of the Literature," IMF Working Paper No. 02/208 (Washington: International Monetary Fund).

Independent Evaluation Office, 2003, *Fiscal Adjustment in IMF-Supported Programs* (Washington: International Monetary Fund).

———, 2004, *Evaluation of the IMF's Role in Poverty Reduction Strategy Papers and the Poverty Reduction and Growth Facility* (Washington: International Monetary Fund).

International Monetary Fund, 2001, "Structural Conditionality in Fund-Supported Programs;" available at www.imf.org/external/np/pdr/cond/2001/eng/struct/index.htm.

———, 2003, *World Economic Outlook, September,* World Economic and Financial Surveys (Washington).

———, 2005, "Review of the 2002 Conditionality Guidelines;" available at www.imf.org/External/np/pp/eng/2005/030305.htm.

Kiguel, Miguel, and Nissan Liviatan, 1992, "The Business Cycle Associated with Exchange Rate-Based Stabilizations," *World Bank Economic Review,* Vol. 6 (May), pp. 279–305.

Reinhart, Carmen, and Kenneth Rogoff, 2004, "The Modern History of Exchange Rate Arrangements: A Reinterpretation," *Quarterly Journal of Economics,* Vol. 119 (February), pp. 1–48.

Santaella, Julio, and Abraham Vela, 1996, "The 1987 Mexican Disinflation Program: An Exchange-Rate-Based Stabilization?" IMF Working Paper No. 96/24 (Washington: International Monetary Fund).

Schadler, Susan, Adam Bennett, Maria Carkovic, Louis Dicks-Mireaux, Mauro Mecagni, James H.J. Morsink, and Miguel Savastano, 1995, *IMF Conditionality: Experience Under Stand-By and Extended Arrangements, Part I: Key Issues and Findings*, IMF

Occasional Paper No. 128, and *Part II: Background Papers,* IMF Occasional Paper No. 129 (Washington: International Monetary Fund).

Schaechter, Andrea, Mark R. Stone, and Mark Zelmer, 2000, *Adopting Inflation Targeting: Practical Issues for Emerging Market Countries,* IMF Occasional Paper No. 202 (Washington: International Monetary Fund).

Sobolev, Yuri V., 2000, "Exchange-Rate-Based Stabilization: A Model of Financial Fragility," IMF Working Paper No. 00/122 (Washington: International Monetary Fund).

Stone, Mark R., 2003, "Inflation Targeting Lite," IMF Working Paper No. 03/12 (Washington: International Monetary Fund).

Truman, E., 2003, *Inflation Targeting and the International Financial System: Challenges and Opportunities* (Washington: Institute for International Economics).

Végh, Carlos, 1992, "Stopping High Inflation," *IMF Staff Papers,* Vol. 39, No. 3 (September), pp. 626–95.

Recent Occasional Papers of the International Monetary Fund

241. The Design of IMF-Supported Programs, by Atish Ghosh, Charis Christofides, Jun Kim, Laura Papi, Uma Ramakrishnan, Alun Thomas, and Juan Zalduendo. 2005.

240. Debt-Related Vulnerabilities and Financial Crises: An Application of the Balance Sheet Approach to Emerging Market Countries, by Christoph Rosenberg, Ioannis Halikias, Brett House, Christian Keller, Jens Nystedt, Alexander Pitt, and Brad Setser. 2005.

239. GEM: A New International Macroeconomic Model, by Tamim Bayoumi, with assistance from Douglas Laxton, Hamid Faruqee, Benjamin Hunt, Philippe Karam, Jaewoo Lee, Alessandro Rebucci, and Ivan Tchakarov. 2004.

238. Stabilization and Reforms in Latin America: A Macroeconomic Perspective on the Experience Since the Early 1990s, by Anoop Singh, Agnès Belaisch, Charles Collyns, Paula De Masi, Reva Krieger, Guy Meredith, and Robert Rennhack. 2005.

237. Sovereign Debt Structure for Crisis Prevention, by Eduardo Borensztein, Marcos Chamon, Olivier Jeanne, Paolo Mauro, and Jeromin Zettelmeyer. 2004.

236. Lessons from the Crisis in Argentina, by Christina Daseking, Atish R. Ghosh, Alun Thomas, and Timothy Lane. 2004.

235. A New Look at Exchange Rate Volatility and Trade Flows, by Peter B. Clark, Natalia Tamirisa, and Shang-Jin Wei, with Azim Sadikov and Li Zeng. 2004.

234. Adopting the Euro in Central Europe: Challenges of the Next Step in European Integration, by Susan M. Schadler, Paulo F. Drummond, Louis Kuijs, Zuzana Murgasova, and Rachel N. van Elkan. 2004.

233. Germany's Three-Pillar Banking System: Cross-Country Perspectives in Europe, by Allan Brunner, Jörg Decressin, Daniel Hardy, and Beata Kudela. 2004.

232. China's Growth and Integration into the World Economy: Prospects and Challenges, edited by Eswar Prasad. 2004.

231. Chile: Policies and Institutions Underpinning Stability and Growth, by Eliot Kalter, Steven Phillips, Marco A. Espinosa-Vega, Rodolfo Luzio, Mauricio Villafuerte, and Manmohan Singh. 2004.

230. Financial Stability in Dollarized Countries, by Anne-Marie Gulde, David Hoelscher, Alain Ize, David Marston, and Gianni De Nicoló. 2004.

229. Evolution and Performance of Exchange Rate Regimes, by Kenneth S. Rogoff, Aasim M. Husain, Ashoka Mody, Robin Brooks, and Nienke Oomes. 2004.

228. Capital Markets and Financial Intermediation in The Baltics, by Alfred Schipke, Christian Beddies, Susan M. George, and Niamh Sheridan. 2004.

227. U.S. Fiscal Policies and Priorities for Long-Run Sustainability, edited by Martin Mühleisen and Christopher Towe. 2004.

226. Hong Kong SAR: Meeting the Challenges of Integration with the Mainland, edited by Eswar Prasad, with contributions from Jorge Chan-Lau, Dora Iakova, William Lee, Hong Liang, Ida Liu, Papa N'Diaye, and Tao Wang. 2004.

225. Rules-Based Fiscal Policy in France, Germany, Italy, and Spain, by Teresa Dában, Enrica Detragiache, Gabriel di Bella, Gian Maria Milesi-Ferretti, and Steven Symansky. 2003.

224. Managing Systemic Banking Crises, by a staff team led by David S. Hoelscher and Marc Quintyn. 2003.

223. Monetary Union Among Member Countries of the Gulf Cooperation Council, by a staff team led by Ugo Fasano. 2003.

222. Informal Funds Transfer Systems: An Analysis of the Informal Hawala System, by Mohammed El Qorchi, Samuel Munzele Maimbo, and John F. Wilson. 2003.

221. Deflation: Determinants, Risks, and Policy Options, by Manmohan S. Kumar. 2003.

220. Effects of Financial Globalization on Developing Countries: Some Empirical Evidence, by Eswar S. Prasad, Kenneth Rogoff, Shang-Jin Wei, and Ayhan Kose. 2003.

219. Economic Policy in a Highly Dollarized Economy: The Case of Cambodia, by Mario de Zamaroczy and Sopanha Sa. 2003.

218. Fiscal Vulnerability and Financial Crises in Emerging Market Economies, by Richard Hemming, Michael Kell, and Axel Schimmelpfennig. 2003.

217. Managing Financial Crises: Recent Experience and Lessons for Latin America, edited by Charles Collyns and G. Russell Kincaid. 2003.

216. Is the PRGF Living Up to Expectations?—An Assessment of Program Design, by Sanjeev Gupta, Mark Plant, Benedict Clements, Thomas Dorsey, Emanuele Baldacci, Gabriela Inchauste, Shamsuddin Tareq, and Nita Thacker. 2002.

215. Improving Large Taxpayers' Compliance: A Review of Country Experience, by Katherine Baer. 2002.

214. Advanced Country Experiences with Capital Account Liberalization, by Age Bakker and Bryan Chapple. 2002.

213. The Baltic Countries: Medium-Term Fiscal Issues Related to EU and NATO Accession, by Johannes Mueller, Christian Beddies, Robert Burgess, Vitali Kramarenko, and Joannes Mongardini. 2002.

212. Financial Soundness Indicators: Analytical Aspects and Country Practices, by V. Sundararajan, Charles Enoch, Armida San José, Paul Hilbers, Russell Krueger, Marina Moretti, and Graham Slack. 2002.

211. Capital Account Liberalization and Financial Sector Stability, by a staff team led by Shogo Ishii and Karl Habermeier. 2002.

210. IMF-Supported Programs in Capital Account Crises, by Atish Ghosh, Timothy Lane, Marianne Schulze-Ghattas, Aleš Bulíř, Javier Hamann, and Alex Mourmouras. 2002.

209. Methodology for Current Account and Exchange Rate Assessments, by Peter Isard, Hamid Faruqee, G. Russell Kincaid, and Martin Fetherston. 2001.

208. Yemen in the 1990s: From Unification to Economic Reform, by Klaus Enders, Sherwyn Williams, Nada Choueiri, Yuri Sobolev, and Jan Walliser. 2001.

207. Malaysia: From Crisis to Recovery, by Kanitta Meesook, Il Houng Lee, Olin Liu, Yougesh Khatri, Natalia Tamirisa, Michael Moore, and Mark H. Krysl. 2001.

206. The Dominican Republic: Stabilization, Structural Reform, and Economic Growth, by a staff team led by Philip Young comprising Alessandro Giustiniani, Werner C. Keller, and Randa E. Sab and others. 2001.

205. Stabilization and Savings Funds for Nonrenewable Resources, by Jeffrey Davis, Rolando Ossowski, James Daniel, and Steven Barnett. 2001.

204. Monetary Union in West Africa (ECOWAS): Is It Desirable and How Could It Be Achieved? by Paul Masson and Catherine Pattillo. 2001.

203. Modern Banking and OTC Derivatives Markets: The Transformation of Global Finance and Its Implications for Systemic Risk, by Garry J. Schinasi, R. Sean Craig, Burkhard Drees, and Charles Kramer. 2000.

202. Adopting Inflation Targeting: Practical Issues for Emerging Market Countries, by Andrea Schaechter, Mark R. Stone, and Mark Zelmer. 2000.

201. Developments and Challenges in the Caribbean Region, by Samuel Itam, Simon Cueva, Erik Lundback, Janet Stotsky, and Stephen Tokarick. 2000.

200. Pension Reform in the Baltics: Issues and Prospects, by Jerald Schiff, Niko Hobdari, Axel Schimmelpfennig, and Roman Zytek. 2000.

199. Ghana: Economic Development in a Democratic Environment, by Sérgio Pereira Leite, Anthony Pellechio, Luisa Zanforlin, Girma Begashaw, Stefania Fabrizio, and Joachim Harnack. 2000.

198. Setting Up Treasuries in the Baltics, Russia, and Other Countries of the Former Soviet Union: An Assessment of IMF Technical Assistance, by Barry H. Potter and Jack Diamond. 2000.

197. Deposit Insurance: Actual and Good Practices, by Gillian G.H. Garcia. 2000.

196. Trade and Trade Policies in Eastern and Southern Africa, by a staff team led by Arvind Subramanian, with Enrique Gelbard, Richard Harmsen, Katrin Elborgh-Woytek, and Piroska Nagy. 2000.

195. The Eastern Caribbean Currency Union—Institutions, Performance, and Policy Issues, by Frits van Beek, José Roberto Rosales, Mayra Zermeño, Ruby Randall, and Jorge Shepherd. 2000.

Note: For information on the titles and availability of Occasional Papers not listed, please consult the IMF's *Publications Catalog* or contact IMF Publication Services.